Routledge Library Editions

PLANNING AND PROFITS IN SOCIALIST ECONOMIES

ECONOMICS

Routledge Library Editions – Economics

ECONOMIC SYSTEMS/ COMPARATIVE ECONOMICS
In 5 Volumes

PLANNING AND PROFITS IN SOCIALIST ECONOMIES

JEAN-CHARLES ASSELAIN

Routledge
Taylor & Francis Group
LONDON AND NEW YORK

First published in 1984
Reprinted in 2003 by
Routledge

711 Third Avenue, New York, NY 10017
2 Park Square, Milton Park, Abingdon, Oxfordshire OX14 4RN

Transferred to Digital Printing 2007

Routledge is an imprint of the Taylor & Francis Group

First issued in paperback 2013

British Library Cataloguing in Publication Data
A CIP catalogue record for this book
is available from the British Library

Planning and Profits in Socialist Economies

ISBN 978-0-415-31308-7 (hbk)
ISBN 978-0-415-86646-0 (pbk)

Miniset: Economic Systems/Comparative Economics

Series: Routledge Library Editions – Economics

Planning and profits in socialist economies

Jean-Charles Asselain

Translated by
Jill Rubery and John Andrew Wilson

Routledge
Taylor & Francis Group
LONDON AND NEW YORK

First published in 1981 as Plan et profit en économie socialiste

This translation first published in 1984
by Routledge
2 Park Square, Milton Park, Abingdon, Oxon, OX14 4RN
270 Madison Ave, New York NY 10016

Set in Press Roman 10 on 12 point
by Hope Services, Abingdon

Library of Congress Cataloging in Publication Data

Asselain, Jean Charles.

Planning and profits in socialist economies.
(International library of economics)
Translation of updated text of: Plan et profit en
économie socialiste.
Bibliography: p.
Includes index.
1. Central planning–Soviet Union. 2. Soviet Union–
Economic policy–1917- 3. Profit–Soviet Union.
4. Central planning–Europe, Eastern. 5. Europe, Eastern
–Economic policy. 6. Profit–Europe, Eastern. I. Title.
II. Series: ILE.
HC335.A82713 1984 338.947 84-6882

British Library CIP data also available

ISBN 0-7102-0257-1 (C)

Contents

Tables and Figures

Tables

Figures

Foreword

The waves of economic reform in the Soviet Union and Eastern Europe over the last thirty years have created a rich and complex body of evidence on the incentives to reform the traditional centrally planned economy, and the inertial forces which frustrate efforts at reform. Many valuable studies have documented in considerable detail particular reform efforts in an individual country during a limited time period. Very few scholars have been willing to undertake the difficult, and very challenging, task of analyzing the Soviet and East European reform experience as a whole, over time. Professor Asselain was willing to face the challenges of the broader analysis, and the result is a welcome addition to the English-language literature on the process of economic reform.

The entire post-Stalin period in Eastern Europe has involved a gradual differentiation in the East European economic system, both among themselves, and relative to what the author calls the centralized model, originated by Stalin, and still intact in its fundamentals in the Soviet Union and some East European countries. It is that differentiation which makes it increasingly difficult and risky to generalize about the Soviet and East European economic systems. Nevertheless, it is striking how these increasingly diverse systems constantly struggle with a common set of problems stemming from the essence of the centralized economic system and its legacies. Hungary's distinctive approach to resource allocation should not obscure the persistence of many elements of the traditional centralized model.

Professor Asselain manages to convey quite skillfully the common elements in the Soviet and East European experience with the traditional centrally planned economy, and in the efforts of each country to reform that model. Yet he does that without in any way losing a sense of the distinctiveness of individual reform efforts, and the particularities of the individual time periods encompassed in the many reform efforts of the post-war period.

One of the more valuable consequences of viewing the post-Stalin period as a whole, and doing that for the Soviet Union and Eastern Europe, is a strong sense of the dynamic and cyclical nature of reform processes. Reform programs and retrenchment from them are both common elements of the post-Stalin reform experience, and this book both highlights those cycles, and analyzes their causes.

In the final chapters the author devotes particular attention to the Soviet, East German, and Hungarian reform experiences, the experience of these three countries having defined the bounds of the reform experience of the last quarter century. Each of these cases is important in its own way. The Soviet experience suggests that – at least in a country with the resource endowments of the Soviet Union – the inability or unwillingness to reform the traditional centralized model is not fatal to economic performance or the stability of the regime. The history of East Germany's economic system suggests that even a relatively small, industrially mature economy can make do with a streamlined version of the traditional centralized model. The Hungarian case clearly shows that, while there are benefits to moving away from the centralized model, the effort required to do so is enormous, and the time required is quite substantial. It is in the Hungarian case that one can most fully appreciate the cyclical nature of reforms, even in a country where the leadership is strongly committed to a fundamental transformation of the economic system.

One of the advantages of an overview of the past is a sense of the future. One comes away from this book with a deep sense of the almost constant and inconclusive struggle between the incentives to reform the traditional centralized model, stemming from poor economic performance in certain areas, and the strong impediments to reform. There is no reason to believe that either of these forces will, in the 1980s, grow considerably stronger than the other. Certainly, the incentives to reform are growing with East Europe's increasing economic difficulties stemming from developments in the world economy. But the impediments to reform are still quite strong and show no signs of abating. As a consequence it is likely that the future (at least this decade) will repeat the past: no major breakthroughs in economic reforms in Eastern Europe, and certainly not in the Soviet Union, but nevertheless continuous efforts to improve the existing systems through partial reforms.

Ed A. Hewett
The Brookings Institution
Washington, D.C.

Introduction

The impact of Liberman's article 'Planning, profits and the bonus system', published in the *Pravda* of 9 September 1962, was almost immediate and unexpected. In this article, Liberman advocated in particular that profits should be adopted as the main 'indicator of success' in any assessment of an enterprise's performance, and also as a criterion for awarding bonuses. As early as November 1962, Khrushchev was already making explicit references to Liberman's arguments before the plenum of the central committee, and the 1965 reform was inspired to a large extent by his arguments.

The 'rehabilitation of profits in the USSR' – despite all the obvious precautionary statements with which it was surrounded – came as a great surprise to Western observers. Identified by Marx with capitalist exploitation, profits were now recognised at least as an instrument for rationalising micro-economic decisions, by means of an economic calculation in monetary terms. This was only one step away from complete defeat of the 'ideology'. Marx is quite unambiguous on this point: not only profits, but all 'commodity and money relationships' were to disappear 'from the beginning of the first phase of communism' (i.e. as soon as socialism was established through the collective appropriation of the means of production). It is true that for a long time the continued existence of money in the USSR – involving monetary payments even among state enterprises – had been a problem for Marxist theoreticians. But at least the direction of development had not been in question. Soviet leaders could conceive of planning only as the absolute antithesis of adjustment to market forces, which was a synonym for capitalist 'spontaneity' and 'anarchy'; and an author like Strumlin was able to state that, even during the period of the NEP, the aim had always been 'to limit the anarchy of the market until it was totally supplanted by central planning'. However, the intention, announced about 1965, of increasing the decision-making autonomy of enterprises and the role of profitability seemed very much like a break with the past. Frightened by the very term profit, certain French translators preferred to render the Russian term *'pribyl'* with the more discreet word 'yield', as if this euphemism was necessary to lessen the shock . . .

Liberman, an eminent practising economist, was in fact quite the opposite of a radical innovator. Western observers of the Soviet Union, who were virtually unanimous in recognising this to be the fact, were also able of one accord to recognise that he had contributed – well before his 1962 article – to the formulation of the crucial problems facing the Soviet economy. Material incentive has in fact coexisted with planning since the beginning of the Soviet system of economic planning, and it is identified largely with the bonus system, which is considered indispensable in mobilising the initiative of enterprises and their personnel in a society where the danger of 'bureaucratisation' had been spoken of for a long time. The aim of the reform was to establish a 'rational co-ordination of planning and bonuses, the two fundamental principles in the construction of a socialist society', according to Nemchinov (*Pravda*, 21 September 1962). It is precisely here that the reference to the profits of enterprises arises. The reform should not be seen either as a ready-made solution to these problems or as a sudden resurrection of a notion which in actual fact had never been totally eliminated. Instead, we have to consider under what conditions, during the Stalinist period, the profits made by enterprises came to lose practically all their significance, and under what economic and political conditions they could regain a leading role in economic decision-making in a Soviet-type economy.

It is always a daunting exercise to assess the innovatory character of developments that are still in progress. In December 1965, Professor A. Birman, in the journal *Novy Mir*, presented the economic reform agreed by the central committee several months earlier as an historic turning point, comparable in importance to the establishment of the NEP in 1921 or the introduction of centralised planning at the end of the 1920s. Fifteen years have elapsed since this judgement, and it is easy, with hindsight, to regard it as an example of obvious exaggeration. In July 1979, the Soviet government announced a new series of economic measures, presented rather unconvincingly as an 'improvement' or continuation of the reform of 1965, thus implicitly confirming that none of the chronic problems of the Soviet economy had been solved in the interim. Just as the 1965 reform gave rise at the time to serious divergences of interpretation, so also has the decree of 1979, despite ever-increasing scepticism about the possibilities for effective reform within Soviet-type systems. The aim of this book is to interpret the long series of reforms that has taken place in the last twenty years in the USSR and in other East European countries, and to assess their significance by putting them into an historical perspective.

The historical approach encourages us not to consider as a 'new fact' any official statement which recognises a long-identified negative effect of the system. The poor quality of many consumer goods and their unsuitability for meeting consumer demand, the constraints upon innovation and administrative encroachments upon the rights of enterprises are the subject of almost ritual denunciations, which have often been wrongly interpreted by Western observers as indicative of a new approach. The transition to a new, 'intensive' phase of development, where technical progress and the improvement of labour productivity would take precedence over the quantitative growth of the factors of production, has been announced several times, without it being possible to see in it anything other than the reaffirmation of an objective that has existed since the time of the second Five-Year Plan (FYP) (1933-7). It is even more confusing that the statement made during the reforms of the 1960s that henceforth 'the interest of enterprises will be made to coincide with that of the national economy' could have been considered innovatory, as if the incentive system in a socialist economy could have any other aim, and as if material incentive had not existed throughout the whole Stalinist period.

A retrospective study of Soviet-type economies also reveals some striking consistencies. Concessions to the peasants, and measures aimed at increasing the share of consumption, at moderating the increase in basic industrial investment and at strengthening the housing programme, alternate with phases of greater severity. In Poland, plans for a massive increase in the price of meat in 1970, 1976 and 1980 brought about on all three occasions an extremely serious social and political crisis. Concessions to the populace are generally made in order to get out of a difficult political situation, and great care must be taken not to confuse these almost cyclical reversals of economic policy with genuine changes of direction. In some countries at least, institutional development also seems to follow a certain pendulum movement: 'centralising' and 'decentralising' tendencies dominate alternately. The most severe jolts endanger the stability of communist regimes: the first major turning point in 1953, just after the death of Stalin, was followed three years later by the Hungarian uprising of 1956; twelve years later, in Czechoslovakia, the hopes aroused by the 'change of direction' of 1965, exasperation caused by three years of half-measures and the ever-present threat of a retreat by the authorities had, by 1968, created an explosive situation, with the same three-year time-lag, and, shortly afterwards, a new 'normalisation'. The similarity with the recent events in Poland is obvious.

However, in the long term, despite the reversals in economic policy, the period from the beginning of the first FYPs (1928-9 in the USSR, and 1948-9 in the people's democracies) until the mid-1960s was characterised by the exceptional stability of the economic organisation. From the 1930s onwards, the Soviet economy underwent a sort of 'crystallisation': the type of planned economy which emerged from the improvisations of the first FYP, and which strongly reflected the priorities of that period, survived in broad outline through the successive stages of industrialisation. In the post-war period, all the people's democracies conformed to the Soviet model, which is why the period in which the planned economy was established is of such crucial importance for an understanding of present realities: thus we must go back to the first Soviet FYP in order to explain the genesis of the basic institutions and the origin of the present-day problems. As far as the six other countries considered here – Czechoslovakia, East Germany, Hungary, Poland, Bulgaria and Rumania – are concerned, the starting point for the period studied will be about 1948, when their general alignment with Stalinist Russia was confirmed.

It should be clear from the above that the choice of an historical approach will not lead to a detailed description of events or of the variations in the administrative structure which have no influence on the principles by which the economy functions. On the contrary, our task will be to highlight the dominant trends and thus to present a survey of the long-term evolution. Our very simple periodisation will take as its fundamental turning points the introduction in the USSR in 1928 (twenty years later in the people's democracies) of command planning in the interests of accelerated industrialisation, the death of Stalin in 1953, the repercussions of which were felt almost immediately throughout the Soviet bloc, and the large wave of economic reforms from 1963–1968.

As far as the reforms are concerned, the historical approach does not mean that we shall seek to interpret them mechanically as a simple corollary of the 'transition to a new stage of development', while excluding, *a priori*, the possibility that they may also represent the rediscovery, in a particular context, of certain general requirements for economic efficiency. From 1956 onwards, the debates of Polish economists thus gave a certain topicality to theoretical studies, like those of Oskar Lange twenty years earlier which defined an abstract model of a decentralised socialist economy (Lange, in Lippincott (ed.), 1970); none the less, actual experience of the problems of the planned economy made the discussion more concrete. It is obvious that the reforms cannot be discussed without taking into account this temporal dimension. The central problem of the reforms is not only the coherence of their overall conception, but also their introduction into economies whose administrative and economic structures had been determined by the application of the traditional Soviet model over a long period.[1]

The historical approach to the seven Soviet-type European economies leads logically to the application, as far as possible, of a comparative methodology. Various attempts have been made, for example, to compare the overall efficiency of Soviet-type economies to that of Western 'market economies' (generally over a period of time arbitrarily defined according to the data available, without any attempt at precise periodisation, which limits the significance of the conclusions, not to mention the more fundamental difficulties raised by the very principle of such a process). But systematic comparisons of Soviet-type economies with each other were still the exception until at least the end of the 1960s (but see Marczewski, 1955 and 1956). This delay is easily explained. During the Stalinist period, it was as if the Soviet model could be transposed as it stood, without regard to the size and level of development of the economy concerned; it was applied to industrialised countries (Czechoslovakia and East Germany) in the same way as to purely agricultural economies (Bulgaria and Rumania) and to those at an intermediate stage of development (Hungary and Poland). What is the point of comparing these economies which have been cast in the same mould, and whose differences seem destined gradually to diminish?

Nevertheless, a more detailed analysis can lead us to qualify – from the Stalinist period onwards – the initial impression of uniformity. For example, the emphasis on the levelling of incomes in most of the people's democracies (Hungary and Czechoslovakia in particular) contrasts with the maintenance of marked inequalities in the USSR. In other respects, the differences tended to become more pronounced and to multiply towards the end of the 1950s. Only Poland kept a private agricultural sector after 1956, whereas collectivisation was practically concluded within the following few years in the whole of Eastern Europe. Inflationary pressures were under much better control in the East German economy than in the other countries. Bulgaria was the first country to give almost as high a priority to the development of agriculture as to industrialisation; and so on . . .

All these differences contain important lessons. Oversimplistic explanations can be cast aside or qualified (how, for example, are we to attribute the failure of agriculture to the inefficiency of 'collectivism' as such, when we consider the persistent difficulties of Polish agriculture and the recovery of Hungarian agriculture?). They also enable us, indirectly, to define more precisely the fundamental characteristics which link all these economies to the Soviet model and which are the origin of their common problems (thus the survival for a long time in East Germany of a private and mixed industrial sector is in no way sufficient to make the East German economy a 'market economy', any more than Rumania's increasing trade with the West from the beginning of the 1960s had any decisive influence on the organisation of the Rumanian economy). But these 'negative' lessons are not the only ones. The gradual diversification of the Soviet-type economies, although within certain limits, is one of the marked characteristics of the post-Stalinist development, and it helps to explain the variations in the respective reforms of the years 1963–8. As far as the economic reforms themselves are concerned, comparative analysis takes on a new significance: to speak of 'economic reform in the whole of Eastern Europe' would obviously be wrong; it is the actual scope of the reforms as applied in each country that must be assessed.

Our comparative analysis will be based on a fundamental distinction between three constituent elements of the economic system of the socialist countries:[2] the model, economic policy and planning techniques.

The model, in the sense given to the term by the Polish economist W. Brus,[3] denotes the economic institutions, the principles by which they function and the nature of the relationships which are established between them within the national economy. The model thus includes not only the system of planned management (the co-ordinated package of directives, regulators and incentives), but also the interdependent relationships between the economic units and the self-regulating mechanisms which may perhaps coexist with a planned management system. This use of the term 'model' is not incompatible with current usage (when it is used, for example, to describe the alignment of the people's democracies with the Soviet model), but it is, of course, perfectly neutral (not every model is worthy of imitation!); on the other hand, it implies no particular reference to any attempt at mathematical formalisation.

By economic policy, we shall understand the hierarchy of priorities defined by the central authorities. These priorities concern the broad direction of all economic and social development; they are concerned not only with the share of the final product according to broad categories of final uses (consumption, investment etc.), but also the strategy of development, i.e. not only the ends, but also the means; they are expressed basically in the form of sectoral priorities. A quantitative readjustment of economic policy as thus defined must be carefully distinguished in principle from a reform of the model (which changes the way in which the economic institutions function), even if this distinction is not always easily applied.

Planning techniques are concerned more specifically with the drawing-up or revision of the national economic plan. It seems over-restrictive to identify, as is often the case, the study of the way in which socialist economies function with the study of 'socialist planning': the realisation (or non-realisation) of the plan is at least as important as the planning process proper, and the elimination of all spontaneous processes must be considered simply as one extreme to which no existing economy seems to come close. However, certain planning techniques – the use of input-output tables, for example – are in no way exclusive to socialist economies, and their improvement can to a certain extent be considered as an 'independent variable'. On the other hand, the type of planning in use (the extent of the area covered by planning, the nature of the relationships between the central planning agencies, the planning administration and the production units, and the relationships among the production units themselves) is an integral part of the definition of the 'model'.

Only the combined effects of a certain model of economic policies and of the planning techniques associated with it can be observed directly, and the very notion of a 'Soviet-type economy', which implies similarity of economic policies, of institutions and of planning methods in a broad sense – with the assumption that these three elements, considered to be of equal importance, form a 'stable mixture' – tends to conceal the fundamental distinction that we are suggesting. But this distinction becomes all important with the increasing diversification of the socialist economies in the course of the period under consideration. It is justified by the fact that each of the component parts evolves at a rate and according to methods specific to it. Planning techniques, partly under the influence of Western studies, have been gradually improved, which has made it possible to tackle ever more complex tasks, with the result that the pessimistic forecasts which predicted that the system would seize up before long, have been regularly contradicted. Since the end of the Stalinist period, the hierarchy of priorities has undergone appreciable readjustments, the extent of which varies considerably from country to country; there is no *a priori* reason why the same model, used to attain new objectives, should not give very different results.

But the relative autonomy of economic policy and planning techniques in relation to the model certainly does not mean that their mutual interactions can be ignored. For example, while the field of planning covers all micro-economic decisions (detailed decisions about the day-to-day activity of each firm), experience shows that recourse to approximations, short cuts and relatively crude techniques – all things being equal in other respects – is necessary in order to complete such an enormous task. The traditional Soviet model no longer seems compatible with all economic policy orientations: for example, any freedom that the leaders have had to decide on immediate concessions to the welfare of the people (1953–4) has been offset, as a study of long-term development makes clear, by certain constant requirements, which seem to prevent any lasting large-scale readjustments in favour of consumption, whatever the promises made by the leaders, and whatever the political risks that may arise if these promises are not kept.

The very nature of the relationships between the model and economic policy has undergone real historical change: devised initially as an instrument in a revolutionary development strategy, the centralised model has increasingly become a factor blocking such development.

Indeed, the origin of the Soviet model is the great turning point in economic policy represented by the first FYP; it arose directly from a strategy of accelerated industrialisation, based on absolute priority for heavy industry. Essential resources were taken from the non-priority sectors which served as 'shock absorbers' in the event of a shortage of energy or raw materials.

However, the very first signs of the return to a less unbalanced hierarchy of priorities, or at least of the first declaration of intent in that direction, were seen as early as the 1930s in the USSR. Then, after the war, reconstruction and the spread of the 'Stalinist' economy to the whole of Eastern Europe, this development tended, from 1953 onwards, to be maintained to different extents, according to the country; the measures in favour of agriculture and the increased housing programme are particular evidence of this. The readjustment of economic policies seemed in some way to take the place of fundamental reform, which would call into question the model itself.[4] But the multiplication of priority aims had a much more serious effect than anticipated on the functioning of the Soviet-type economies: how could the economy be protected from unforeseen difficulties, if all sectors became priority sectors at the same time? Growth not only slowed down, but suffered serious hiccups. And yet, at most, the traditional priorities were only moderated. Soviet-type planning remained, to a large extent, a prisoner of its initial orientation, crystallised in certain institutions and in certain types of indicators of success. Because of inadequate technical progress and the low efficiency of investment, the priority development of the capital goods sector, which was in the beginning a fundamental strategy decision, became increasingly a constraint linked to the model, with the result that growth was restricted. Thus the contradiction between the rigidity of the model and the need for a new economic policy of 'intensive growth', manifested itself more and more clearly.

It was just at this stage that the notion of the model appeared almost simultaneously in Poland and in Hungary,[5] in about 1956-7. Overshadowed for a long time by the assumption that the Soviet path had necessarily to be followed by all, the notion of the model led in fact to that of a choice between different models of the socialist economy. Thus, in 1961, W. Brus contrasted the traditional 'centralised' model ('centralist' model would no doubt be closer to the author's thinking, since it clearly emphasises that the concentration of all the control levers in the hands of the central authorities was not enough to ensure them complete control of the economic processes) with a 'decentralised model' based on close association between a system of planned management and market mechanisms. Even if this contrast remained too schematic, it is clear that it was not the result of simple *a priori* deductions, but of a very concrete analysis of the problems affecting the functioning of all the socialist economies. Brus's words are echoed by those of I. Friss, one of the main originators of the Hungarian reform of 1968, writing on the eve of that reform: 'The fundamental problem for all the socialist economies is the degree of centralisation: what can be and what must be decided, determined, controlled and stipulated centrally, that is, put into the national economic plan?'

The similarity between these analyses is significant. The decade after 1956 was particularly rich in lessons for the economists of the socialist countries. The successive readjustments of economic policy did not solve the permanent difficulties of any of the countries, despite the fact that they became ever more clearly identified. Only a minority of mathematical economists put their hopes in increased centralisation: the majority were of the opinion that modernisation of planning methods and the increased use of computers would not be sufficient to ensure that the 'production network' would adapt to a 'higher level of development of the forces of production', without an economic reform that would establish a new type of relationship between the centre and the periphery. Finally, the failure of a whole series of half-hearted reforms had already clearly proved that it was impossible to put right the 'excesses' of over-centralisation without bringing into question the model itself, while at the same time demonstrating the power of the recentralising mechanisms whenever partial reforms were attempted. All these observations seemed to be suggesting a 'radical' reform, consisting of a redefinition of the very notion of command planning and the removal of all compulsory indicators at the level of the firm, and not just some of them. In 1971, three years after the Hungarian reform described by those responsible as a 'model of the regulated socialist market', R. Nyers, the politician principally responsible for implementing the reform, once again put forward this idea of a major discontinuity: 'We have crossed the invisible Rubicon which separates an economic system based on quantitative regulation from a system based on profitability'.

The notion of a model as a consistent whole will be the keystone of our analyses. We shall attempt to define which of the principal problems of the socialist countries are linked directly or indirectly to the fundamental principles of the centralised model. Our interpretation of each reform will attempt to answer this question: is the reform a limited adjustment of the model that has been in use since the Stalinist period, or is it a move towards the establishment of a new model[6] of the socialist economy, which relies for its consistency on principles of organisation and functioning distinct from those of the centralised model? What has been the result of these attempts in the various countries? What has been the viability of the intermediate forms of the model? How can we explain the different decisions of the various communist governments, and the differing fates of the reforms which started out with a common inspiration?

Part I
The centralised model and the Stalinist hierarchy of priorities

1 The fundamental elements of the centralised model

Although the theoretical concept of a centralised model was late in emerging (it is in fact as recent as the notion that there is more than one possible model of a socialist economy), the high degree of centralisation has been one of the most striking characteristics of the Soviet economy ever since the 1917 Revolution. Despite the interlude of the NEP, the identification of a socialist economy with a centralised economy became so complete that in 1940 Schumpeter was able to write in *Capitalism, Socialism and Democracy*: 'The type that can be called "centralised socialism" seems to me to prevail so clearly that it would be a waste of time to analyse other formulae' (Schumpeter, 1950, p. 272).

In the USSR, centralisation existed before and even determined the setting up of the planning structures. The development of the centrally planned economic system is inseparable from the historical circumstances of the birth of the Soviet regime and the conditions in which it had to struggle for survival from 1917 until the 1940s. The institutions of the Soviet economy were not inspired by any general structural plan that can be seen as an abstract prefiguration of the model. They were set up primarily in response to the requirements of the industrialisation policy that was implemented after the first FYP (1928-33), in accordance with the constraints characteristic of this stage of the development of the Soviet economy, but which helped to shape its basic features for several decades. Thus the overriding desire to concentrate maximum resources on a few key objectives had a direct and lasting influence on the choice of means – the institutions and the principles by which the centralised model permanently functions.

The very idea that within the framework of the objectives determined by the central authorities there can exist an area of politically neutral decision-making which has its sole origin in economic calculation is foreign to the logic of Soviet-type economies. For example, social policy (such as, overcoming the resistance of the peasants, and making living conditions in the town and in the country more equal), regional policy (giving priority to the development of a particular region for strategic reasons), and international policy (giving greater importance to trade with a particular partner) are not used in retrospect to adjust the results of prior economic calculations; they are from the outset at the heart of the decision-making process. At any given moment, the fate of the populace depends in the most direct and immediate way – even down to supplies in the shops for the Christmas and New Year holidays – on the decisions taken by the central authorities.

Such are the basic realities underlying the notion of the 'centralised model' on which the whole of our analysis relies.

Nevertheless, there is no question of assuming that the 'central authorities' constitute a homogeneous group, exempt from any conflict of interest. Nor can it be assumed that the 'centre' is in fact capable of gaining complete mastery over the economic processes by making all 'peripheral' activities subject to its decisions within the framework of the national plan: the history of Soviet-type economies since the first FYP shows the contrary to be the case.

We shall now examine the crucial problem of the relationships between the economic administration and the units of production: how can the central authorities' claim that they make virtually all economic decisions be reconciled with their very real dependence on the units of production, which must supply most of the information necessary to draw up the plan and also carry out the planned objectives?

The system of directives

The concentration of economic power in the hands of the central authorities

1 Potentially at least, the scope of centralised decision-making covers the whole of economic life.

The central authorities must, of course, fix the rate of growth, the basic macro-economic proportions (the division of GNP between investment and collective and individual consumption; the sharing out of investment funds according to sector), and the broad outlines of income distribution. It is not here that the originality of the model lies, since all planning, even indicative planning, includes the fixing of such objectives. Nevertheless, even in this respect, there is one fundamental difference: in Soviet-type economies, the aim of central decision-making is not to influence spontaneous development, but to replace all decentralised decision-making.

This is why the plan makes no distinction between final objectives (consumption and investment) and intermediate goods (production of steel or electricity). It involves the detailed fixing of production targets according to product and enterprise. The national plan undergoes a process of 'vertical disaggregation', from ministry level to the management of the various sectors, to the regions, to groups of enterprises and finally to individual enterprises; at the end of this process, the firm receives from its supervisory authority its own plan, which lays down, point by point, the volume and structure of its production.

An even more typical characteristic of the centralised model is that the various means of production are allocated to the enterprise by its superiors in the hierarchy. Energy, raw materials and plant are allocated and in each case the sources of supply are specified (in the same way, the enterprise must deliver its production to purchasers specified by name). The number of workers with different qualifications that the enterprise is authorised to employ, the amount of wages that it can pay out, with a breakdown by category, are also laid down; likewise, the enterprise has no right to alter the assigned utilisation of the means of production allocated to it.

2 The combination of management by directive and the centralised determination of objectives is doubtless not a necessary attribute of all socialist planning. But the fact that they exist side by side within the framework of the centralised model is in no way fortuitous.

It can be explained first of all by a deep ideological mistrust of all 'spontaneous' economic processes, which are identified with capitalist 'anarchy' and all the wastage and antagonisms between private interests and social interest which are supposed to result from it. It also reflects a refusal on principle to allow the main objectives of the central plan to be brought into question should a planning error arise. The non-priority sectors must be deprived of any chance to 'divert' the production factors necessary for the realisation of these objectives. In this respect, any system of indirect orientation contains very real risks, because it requires planning methods that are much more complex and precise than those required for planning by directive. This latter system at least allows the central authorities, by making corrections in individual cases where necessary, to make the non-priority sectors suffer the consequences of planning errors.

Under these conditions, the proliferation of directives, far from being a mere manifestation of 'bureaucratic tendencies', must be regarded as a constraint arising from the internal logic of the model. It is absolutely essential for each enterprise to be allocated sufficient production resources for it to be able to meet its planned obligations. Nor can the economic administration impose production targets without accepting responsibility for the sale and distribution of what is produced. The planning authorities must therefore organise directly all inter-firm deliveries. In order to establish some sort of equilibrium, the authorities are forced to formulate all production targets in an extremely rigid and detailed way, even if they themselves have no specific preferences. This means in particular that consumers have no direct influence at all on the structure of production, not even in the area of trivial choices between similar products, where the political authorities could not possibly have any preferences of their own to set against those of consumers.

3 The system of planned management, which involves the adjustment of all micro-economic flows, is an enormous administrative task. Such a complex machine can function only if the tasks are divided up, both on a functional level (involving the setting up of specialised institutions to allocate the labour force, to share out production goods and to deal with foreign trade) and on a sectoral level (according to the type of activity: the Soviet 'industrial ministries').

However, any difficulty requiring arbitration between the different institutions must be resolved at a high level, because of the very nature of the hierarchical organisation and the vertical compartmentalisation that it involves. The government or the central planning office may intervene at any time in order to ensure that priority targets are met. Such corrective interventions, which take place on an individual basis, are part of the logic of the model, since no spontaneous adjustment mechanism exists.

On the other hand, there is an administrative hierarchy between the industrial ministries and the enterprises answerable to them, both on a sectoral level (the ministerial agencies in charge of each sector) and on a regional level: the number of intermediate levels depends on the size of the enterprise (whether it operates on a national, regional or local basis). Transmitting economic information and directives down through an administrative hierarchy poses a whole series of problems, which can be schematised by examining the intervention of a single intermediary that we shall call the 'supervisory body'.

The hierarchical subordination of the enterprise to its supervisory body may be compared to that of a factory within a Western firm; its decision-making autonomy is often in fact even more restricted.

The managers of each enterprise are appointed by the administration, and can be dismissed in the same way. The enterprise has no property rights over the means of production allocated to it, nor over the results of its activity. Its role is basically that of a technical institution whose task it is to determine the most efficient way of using the resources allocated to it, bearing in mind that its production structure is imposed from above. The supervisory body must not in theory interfere in this area. But it can redistribute existing production capacities among its enterprises, if it considers it necessary for the realisation of the plan; it can adjust the targets it has set, even as the enterprise is attempting to fulfil them, particularly to offset the delays of the weaker enterprises against the results of the more dynamic ones. It is responsible for its own errors to the central authorities, but not to the enterprises under its control.

The organisation of deliveries between enterprises is inseparable from the system of hierarchical planning by directive. The essential precondition for an enterprise wishing to obtain necessary means of production is possession of a delivery slip (*nariad* in the USSR, *Kontingente* in East Germany) issued by the competent authority. We have so far deliberately avoided any mention of the role of money, since it is in no way fundamental to the supply system.

This system, in fact, goes even further than the rationing by coupon used in wartime in Western economies, since the holder of a delivery slip has no choice of supplier. The designated partners are invited to conclude together a 'planned contract' whose sole purpose is to clarify the details of the transaction (delivery dates, etc.). In fact, any failure on the part of one manufacturer inevitably has a chain reaction on all the enterprises in the system.

The passive role of money

Despite persistent ideological hostility to 'commodity and money relationships', money and prices have survived even in relationships within the state sector. Apart from the investment allocations, which are free of charge, any financial allowances and any real flows give rise in return to flows of money. However, despite certain superficial similarities, money by no means fulfils the same functions as in the 'market economy'.

It is clear from what has been said above that economic management by directive does not allow enterprises the freedom to adjust their activity by carrying out an economic calculation based on prices. The enterprise is isolated from the consumer goods market and from the evolution of retail prices. But production prices themselves play a subordinate role. Rationing of the means of production prevents enterprises from deviating from their plan in order to make substitutions which appear to have a relative price advantage. In order to obtain any resource necessary to production, monetary payment is indeed a necessary but not a sufficient condition. In the words of W. Brus (Brus, 1970, p. 100):

> Money is not an active instrument, influencing the movement of real factors in the production process. . . . The enterprise makes its calculations not before, but after having taken (or rather received) its decisions. . . . The planned financial result (profit or loss) is thus a passive reflection of the price structure and the compulsory indices.

To suggest that 'the passive role of money' is a fundamental principle of the centralised model does not mean that this is always the case in reality – on the contrary – nor that prices can be ignored. Nevertheless, 'when the allocation of resources is dominated by monetary considerations, and not by the actual plans, it is no longer being carried out according to the principles of the system, but in violation of them' (Wellisz, 1968, p. 165). The way in which prices are determined by the authorities, which leads to great rigidity, makes them fundamentally unsuitable to play a leading role in economic decisions. The *raison d'être* of the rationing of the means of production is precisely that, faced with an unexpected deficit in a raw material, it is infinitely quicker to modify some of the quotas than to revise the whole relative price structure in such a way as to achieve indirectly a new equilibrium which conforms to the targets being pursued. However, on the other hand, the existence of rationing encourages price rigidity by making it possible to hide imbalances without removing the cause of them.

In this model, money remains principally an instrument of aggregation and control.

Money is used, of course, as a unit of account in the calculation of aggregates. The concern with making comparisons over time easier is an added incentive to maintain price stability.

Money is also used as a unit of account in the transmission of directives. The burden of the planning authorities would be enormously lightened if an overall target in monetary terms were fixed for each enterprise, but this would open up the possibility for enterprises to make substitutions incompatible with the principles of the centralised model. Directives expressed in monetary form thus merely transcribe and recapitulate the directives detailed in kind; they are added to them, without the enterprise being able to take advantage of them in order to escape from any of its specified obligations.

The use of money as an instrument of control is much more characteristic of the centralised model. All payments from one state enterprise to another must be made by credit transfer from their accounts with the state bank. This creates a practically autonomous monetary system, which could in theory be quite distinct from the system used to express retail prices: the only points of contact are, in fact, the withdrawal of notes by enterprises in order to pay their employees, and receipts from retail trade (or savings banks deposits). Enterprises are authorised to hold only very limited reserves of bank notes, and they must not grant each other credit.

Quite apart from any economic and financial control over the management of firms, the bank's right to examine is used first of all as an instrument of detailed administrative control. There is 'a separate budgetary constraint for each type of expenditure' (Grossman (ed.), 1968, p.6) (purchase of raw materials, repairs, wages, etc.). The compartmentalisation of money flows goes even further: in order to make a payment, the bank requires justificatory documents (a copy of the delivery slip, for example) and checks that the transaction conforms with the plan for the enterprise.

Thus 'everything has been done to rid money of its versatility, which is a source of dangerous freedom, and to transform it into an efficient instrument of control' (Marczewski, 1955 and 1956, p.417). The necessity for detailed control arises precisely from the fact that money does not have the same value in all its uses. The compartmentalisation of expenditure of various kinds is merely the counterpart of rationing. For the central authorities, a reduction in costs and an increase in production by exactly the same amount have a very different meaning according to the product in question. It would be just as irrational to assess the performance of an enterprise in terms of an overall financial result as to allow it to determine its own activity on the basis of current prices. In all respects, therefore, money has lost its role as a homogeneous source of information.

Under these circumstances, how are we to interpret the maintenance of the principle of balanced accounting (*khozraschët*) inherited from the NEP?

This official Soviet definition of *khozraschët* provides a basic interpretation: 'A method of planned management for socialist enterprises . . . which requires the carrying out of tasks determined by the state, with the greatest possible economy of resources . . . in order to ensure the profitability of enterprises.'[1]

The enterprise thus retains accounting autonomy. However, *khozraschët* is applied only within the very narrow limits fixed by the central planners. There is no question of enterprises being allowed to increase their profitability by contravening the directives! Besides, in this respect, better adjustment to demand would have no effect. Profitability is of significance only in purely accounting terms, and depends basically on decisions taken outside of the enterprise. The planner may very well decide that the enterprise should undertake activities that are unprofitable on the basis of the prices in force. He has the power in this case to raise the price applicable to any product of any enterprise or group of enterprises, in such a way as to make appear profitable in retrospect a decision already taken on the basis of criteria other than monetary ones. But he can also allow certain enterprises to function with a permanent 'planned deficit'.

The planner's freedom of action is thus in no way limited by the principle of *khozraschët*. On the other hand, it imposes an additional obligation on enterprises: they must achieve the 'greatest possible economy of resources'. They must seize every opportunity of exceeding the planned level of profit – or of reducing the planned loss – by 'mobilising their internal resources'. In contrast to the detailed directives, such an obligation formulated in very general terms implicitly reflects the uncertainty of the planner as to the real potential of each enterprise: if he had precise knowledge, he would have to insist that the compulsory indices be adhered to in order to guarantee maximum efficiency in production. That, however, is not the case.

The introduction of this element of uncertainty again calls into question the idea of the omniscient planner, on which the whole system of management by directive is based. The concern with mobilising decentralised initiatives, which is absolutely essential if the planned targets are to be achieved and exceeded, explains the existence of an incentive system for enterprises which runs parallel to the system of directives. In this way, the enterprise acquires interests of its own: its role can no longer be reduced to simply carrying out directives, since it must at the same time, at the express wish of the planner, pursue its own target, which is expressed in terms of the variable indicators of success, but which, more often than not, involves prices. The problem of prices must, therefore, be put back into the more general context of the incentive system for enterprises.

We started from the idea that the centralised model follows a logic of its own, based on the concentration of all decisions at the highest level, and not on a system of prices that is supposed to reflect the interaction of all the participants in economic activity. Now, however, it appears that, in reality, no centralised economy can follow this logic to its conclusion. As a result, and to an extent that will have to be determined, money regains an active role in the decisions taken by enterprises.

The incentive system

The central authorities' task is to take account of their dependence on enterprises – both when drawing up the national plan and also when putting it into practice – without surrendering any of their economic sovereignty whatsoever. The problem is very clearly stated by J. Berliner:

> If we assume that the correct decision is the one that the state would itself make if it were practically possible for it to make every decision for each enterprise and each workshop, two conditions must be fulfilled if the correct decision is to be made. The first is that the management of the firm should be motivated . . . ; the second is that there should be some means for the management to know what the correct decision is. (J. Berliner, 1957, pp. 200–1)

The coexistence of directives, indicators of success and incentives is a fundamental characteristic of the centralised model: the *de facto* impossibility of making a perfect centralised calculation means that the state can neither control everything by direct command, nor rely entirely on the decentralised decisions made by suitably motivated enterprises to reach a fully predetermined set of results ('perfect indirect centralisation' in Novojilov's sense of the term). A rough and ready solution must therefore be sought in a combination of direct commands and indicators of success. These latter are used not only as incentives for enterprises; their primary function is to allow the planner to restrict greatly the number of directives and to enable the enterprise to 'decipher' the wishes of the central authorities in the absence of detailed commands.

The 'management formula for enterprises', as we shall call it,[2] is made up of the following elements:

(a) the directives as such (e.g. enterprise *A* must take delivery from enterprise *B* of a given quantity of a given raw material at a given price);
(b) the constraints expressed in the form of maxima or minima: they relate to the total consumption of various inputs, to the intermediate consumption norms per unit produced, to the volume of production (the principal constraint being that the enterprise must at the very least meet the 'planned production targets' for each product), and to the structure of production and its quality (there must be no more than *x* per cent rejects in the total production . . .);
(c) the indicators of success, which for the enterprise are targets which are subject to variation. They are normally fewer in number than the constraints, and there is no strict correspondence between the two (the enterprise may not, for example, be encouraged to exceed the imposed production targets for all products). It is the task of the economic administration to lay down appropriate indicators of success for each group of enterprises; the authorities have absolute freedom to choose either very specific indicators expressed in physical units, or synthetic indicators expressed in monetary terms, or even a combination of the two;
(d) the rules governing incentives. The first of these rules, which is implicit in the very definition of the centralised model, is the absolute primacy of the system of directives: adherence to all the commands and constraints (which leads to what is called the '100 per cent fetish') must be the first condition that the enterprise must fulfil in order to have the right to any reward. Next in line are the assessments of the performance of the enterprise according to each of the indicators of success (for each percentage point by which a particular target is exceeded, the enterprise receives so much). Setting aside the sanctions and the non-material incentives, it is the amount of bonuses paid into its incentive fund that enables the enterprise to weight the various indicators of success and thus to decide between competing targets. This is the reason for very precise rules: even quality can be assessed only by means of a small number of simple, predetermined, measurable criteria.

There is no reason to be surprised at such complexity. The 'management formula' must cover all aspects of the activity of an enterprise: maximum volume of production, with a structure in accordance with the needs of society, quality standards, the best possible use of labour, raw materials and capital goods, and the maintenance and optimal renewal of this last factor with a view to future growth in production. In the absence of a general mechanism of adjustment which expresses spontaneously the interaction of these different criteria, as the price mechanism is supposed to in the model of the competitive economy, the central authorities must determine separately each element of an enterprise's activity with a battery of commands and appropriate incentives. They need complete freedom of action in order to adjust, as the need arises, both their directives and any element of the incentive system whenever the behaviour of certain enterprises does not meet their expectations. As far as prices are concerned, they are used as one element among others in the calculation of bonuses. Let us assume, for example, that a group of enterprises operates with the total value of their production as the only indicator of success. If the supervisory authorities want to encourage enterprises to exceed their planned targets for a given product, they can obtain the same result either by recalculating the whole system (and fixing a whole set of new production targets) or by fixing an increased purchasing price for quantities delivered over and above the planned minimum, or by introducing a specific bonus. The first solution is the only one that preserves the coherence of the price system, but it is unlikely to be adopted because of its complexity. It could almost be suggested that the notion of a correct price has in itself no meaning, since the only question is whether in each particular case the prices applied to a given enterprise, in conjunction with the other elements of the incentive system, bring about the consequences desired by the central authorities. This process inevitably leads to a breakdown in the unity of the price system: thus, the price of the same product may vary from one producer to another, or even for the same producer according to whether delivery has been made within the planned minimum targets or in excess of them; moreover, the sum received by the seller does not necessarily correspond to the price paid by the purchaser.

From the point of view of the managers of an enterprise, the role of the incentive rules is very similar to that of prices. An enterprise which has no freedom in the choice of its inputs or in the structure of its output can nevertheless regard an excess of x per cent over its production target and an improvement of n points in one of its indices of quality as 'substitutable outputs', and compare them according to the amount of the relevant bonuses. The particular economic calculation made by the managers of an enterprise in a Soviet-type economy lends itself quite well to a formalisation modelled closely on that of the theoretical behaviour of a firm in a market economy: to assume that their aim is to maximise the annual incentive fund is perhaps less unrealistic than to explain the decisions of a Western firm by using the maximisation of profits as a criterion. It must be recognised that the essential characteristic of the incentive system in Soviet-type economies is that it is based on the short-term development of a small number of measurable indicators.

The imagination that has always been shown by Soviet managers in 'massaging' their performance figures has often been remarked on – even in the USSR – and there is a whole literature on the sometimes very ingenious frauds perpetrated by Soviet firms in order to obtain extra bonuses. As A. Nove has written, 'there are a hundred ways of expressing production targets, and each one gives rise to a particular type of distortion'. The traditional gross production indicator was a very simple device: it encouraged enterprises to concentrate on producing the articles most advantageous to themselves, i.e. those using costly raw materials, and the result was obvious wastage. But the gradual introduction of more sophisticated indicators led only to the development of increasingly sophisticated frauds.

It is impossible to give details here of all these distortions. But it must be stressed that the fundamental distortions appear even in the most simple and favourable cases. So let us suppose that an enterprise manufactures one single, homogeneous product, the quality of which is perfectly controllable, and that the total amount of production resources allocated to the enterprise is a constant factor. In this case, the authorities can make the physical volume of production the sole indicator of success. By maximising the quantity produced, the enterprise automatically achieves both maximum economy of resources per unit of production, or, in monetary terms, maximum reduction in costs and maximum profits.

But in order to define the incentive formula, a term of reference is still needed by which to assess the performance of the enterprise. Two basic formulae can be considered within the framework of the centralised model. The first is a comparison between the results achieved by the enterprise and a prior estimation by the authorities of its production capabilities; if I is the total bonus, x_0 the minimum planned target laid down for the enterprise, and x_t the performance of the enterprise during the planning period, then:

$$I = f\left(\frac{x_t - x_0}{x_0}\right)$$

The second formula is a comparison between the performance of the enterprise and its total production during the preceding period, x_{t-1}:

$$I = f\left(\frac{x_t - x_{t-1}}{x_{t-1}}\right)$$

1 Incentive based on an a priori *assessment by the authorities*

If the formula is of the type $I = f((x_t - x_0)/x_0)$, it will be just as important for the enterprise to bargain for an 'easy' plan with an unambitious target x_0 as to produce efficiently and maximise x_t.

The enterprise does not, of course, fix its own target. But it is not without influence, since it plays an essential role in the gathering of the information used in drawing up the plan. It is in the interests of the enterprise to underestimate its production capacity, and particularly (since it is especially difficult to carry out checks in this respect) to conceal any opportunities for innovation or reorganisation which would increase production but not the amount of resources used. A bonus system that is designed solely to encourage enterprises to achieve their planned targets will, therefore, have very serious repercussions on the quality of the micro-economic information which is the basis of the plan.

The supervisory authorities, for their part, will react by trying to take this systematic underassessment into account in advance, with the result that the distortions become cumulative: the enterprise which would be prepared, *a priori*, to make an honest declaration of its production potential must also conserve for itself a 'safety margin', or risk having an unrealistic production target imposed, which it could neither exceed nor even fulfil. The only winner, at least in the short term, will be the enterprise which succeeds in concealing more than the average and in escaping checks, or an enterprise which the authorities deliberately favour, for one reason or another, by granting it 'easy' targets.

Finally, a balance must be found within the framework of a genuine bargaining relationship between the supervisory authorities and their enterprises. Within a relatively large margin, which depends on the experience of the participants and the exactness of the checks, the final outcome is indeterminate. This is both a source of arbitrariness, which weakens the effect of the incentive and becomes a demoralising factor, and an extra element of uncertainty, which discourages the enterprise from any attempts at forecasting.

Enterprises are encouraged to retain 'safety margins' by the threat of having overambitious targets imposed on them. But the logic of the centralised model leads the authorities to seek to counter this with stricter controls, both external and internal (the chief accountant is answerable directly to the supervisory authorities, and not to the director of the enterprise), and by requiring the enterprise to fill in a great number of detailed forms, the 'standardised presentation' and cross-checking of which are designed to leave no loopholes. But the proliferation of controls is not only very costly in terms of hours of work, both in the administration and the enterprises, but also has the effect of worsening the climate of relations between these reluctant 'partners' in the centralised economy. While the system is certainly effective in preventing fraud, it is of little use in getting from the enterprise the unroutinised information that it alone possesses.

In short, the bargaining relationship affects not only the way in which the plan is drawn up, but also the way in which it is implemented. Indeed, for an enterprise to exceed by a large amount a production target that was too low is the same as revealing in retrospect to the authorities that the enterprise has succeeded in deceiving them by underestimating its capacity. By putting itself in this situation, it risks having much more ambitious targets imposed for the next period, as well as a doubling of controls.

However, the threat of a brake on production is even more serious with the second variant.

2 *Incentive based on comparison with the previous year's performance*

The second formula, $I = f((x_t - x_{t-1})/x_{t-1})$ is, on the surface, more objective: x_t and x_{t-1} are measured values (unlike x_0, which is the result of an *a priori* estimate). Nevertheless, it is in fact combined with an administrative decision which fixes the planned production target for each enterprise, in the form of a minimum imposed growth rate $\bar{r}$.

The incentive system can, therefore, be schematised in the following way (r is the rate of growth achieved in the period t):

$I = O$ if $r < \bar{r}$
$I = A$ if $r = \bar{r}$ (A bonus for fulfilment of plan)
$I = A + k(r - \bar{r})$ if $r > \bar{r}$ (k bonus for exceeding plan).

This incentive formula brings into play the 'ratchet effect', in two different ways. On the one hand, any increase in production, once achieved, is considered to be irreversible, and is incorporated into the minima imposed for the following year: this is clearly understood, and should not really cause any major difficulties for a dynamic enterprise. On the other hand, and this clearly has far greater consequences, an enterprise which has a very rapid growth rate for one or several years ($r \gg \bar{r}$) runs the risk of having its minimum imposed growth rate increased in subsequent plans, and will not be able to obtain a downward adjustment until much later, after repeated failures to fulfil its targets.

We shall assume that this danger basically concerns enterprises that attract the attention of their superiors in the hierarchy because of an acceleration in their growth rate, and we shall formulate this hypothesis about the behaviour of the authorities in the following way:

$$r_t = r_{t-1} \qquad \text{if } r_{t-1} \leqslant r_{t-2}$$
$$r_t = r_{t-1} + a(t_{t-1} - r_{t-2}) \quad \text{if } r_{t-1} > r_{t-2} \text{ (with } O < a < 1)$$

Contrary to what is sometimes assumed to be self-evident, such a formula, despite the ratchet effect, does not necessarily prevent enterprises from aiming at as rapid a growth rate as possible, any more than continually raised norms, provided they remain realistic, act as a disincentive to workers regularly to increase their efforts.

But this incentive formula fails in three important cases:

(a) when the enterprise takes into account the uncertainties hanging over its future activity;

(b) when it is contemplating major innovations introducted in several stages;

(c) when no growth can be achieved without a prior reorganisation, resulting in a temporary fall in production.

(a) Taking uncertainties into account encourages the enterprise never to exceed its target by very much, so as to keep a 'safety margin' for the future. This risk of a 'braking' effect is even greater since the bonus A, paid for fulfilling planned targets, is relatively greater than bonus k, paid for exceeding the target; the risk increases even further if the enterprise has to fear sanctions should it not achieve its target.

In order to prevent enterprises from retaining safety margins, the supervisory authorities can act in two opposite directions.

They can raise the value of the bonuses paid for exceeding the planned targets, or even, in an extreme case, reward the enterprise for any increase in production, independently of the planned target. This solution would have great advantages (it would eliminate the '100 per cent fetish', and, at the same time, the lack of incentive for certain enterprises which know that, whatever happens, their target will never be reached, and thus give up trying . . .), but it is hardly compatible with the fundamental principles of command planning and the centralised model. In particular, how could all deliveries between enterprises be organised directly, if the production of each enterprise is not known in advance?

Another, quite different solution is for planning to be systematically tight. The authorities would confiscate all surplus stocks of means of production, would impose on each enterprise a growth target $\bar{r}$, which would be as close as possible to the maximum rate $\hat{r}$ (which is unknown to the planner), and would punish any failure to meet the target, at least by withholding bonuses. This second solution, which is the counterpart on the level of the enterprise of tight macro-economic planning, is more frequently used. It carries the permanent risk of imposing on certain enterprises an unachievable rate of growth ($> \hat{r}$), which can only disrupt the functioning of the national economy. These enterprises are justified in resisting it, and in that case the bargaining relationship already mentioned is again encountered.

(b) The incentive system also breaks down in the event of discontinuous waves of innovations: the enterprise has no incentive to make immediate use of all its opportunities for increasing its productivity, for the simple reason that it can foresee that growth will inevitably slow down later.

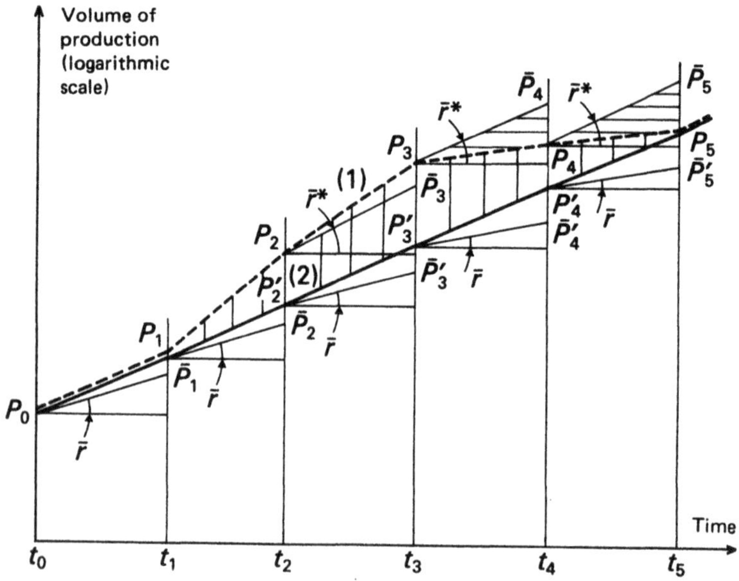

Figure 1.1: Built-in disincentives to innovation

Figure 1.1 illustrates this type of distortion. If the enterprise permanently makes maximum use of its potential for innovation, we shall assume that it can achieve the growth profile (1) $P_0P_1P_2P_3P_4P_5$: our hypothesis is that this is the most favourable eventuality for the national economy. But the enterprise gets nothing out of this, since, from the period t_3 onwards, the target fixed in terms of growth rate will be increased ($\bar{r}^*$ instead of $\bar{r}$) and, from the period t_4 onwards, the enterprise will no longer be able to fulfil its target (the deficit in t_4 is represented by the horizontally shaded area $P_3P_4\bar{P}_4$, and in t_5 by $P_4P_5\bar{P}_5$).

Let us assume, on the other hand, that the enterprise practises a wise policy of spreading out its productivity gains arising from innovation, and achieves regular growth according to the profile (2) $P_0P_1P'_2P'_3P'_4P_5$. In this case, the target $\bar{r}$ is not increased and the enterprise never fails to meet its own target. But for several periods the national economy has to carry a deficit (represented by the area between profiles (1) and (2), shaded vertically on the graph) in relation to the maximum production potential.

There is, therefore, an obvious discrepancy between the interests of the enterprise and those of the national economy. Rather paradoxically, it is to the extent that managers take only a short-term view and allow themselves to be guided during the periods t_3 and t_4 by their immediate interests that the growth profile chosen by the enterprise will be closer to profile (1) than to profile (2).

(c) On the other hand, however, this short-term outlook on the part of the managers of an enterprise has a negative effect whenever a reorganisation of the enterprise is a precondition for introducing an innovation, with a resultant short-term fall in production: the managers are reluctant to take risks in the interests of an uncertain future result, from which the enterprise will at best gain a temporary advantage (since its target will soon be increased), while they themselves, judged on their poor short-term results, will perhaps have been transferred in the meantime.

This is an even more serious danger than the previous one, since it is no longer just a question of staggering increases in productivity. In fact, many minor innovations, which are the responsibility of the enterprise and which can take place only at the instigation of the enterprise, will never be implemented at all, for all the reasons already mentioned: the ratchet effect, the high degree of uncertainty, and the predominance of managers' short-term preoccupations. It is practically impossible for the central authorities to discover individually each of these 'failures to innovate' (or wasted opportunities), but the result is felt at the macro-economic level: the consequence is extensive growth, based essentially on an increase in the volume of inputs (labour and capital stock), while the overall productivity of the factors hardly grows at all.

Thus, in the words of W. Brus, the indicators of success appear to be a 'Trojan horse' introduced into the centralised model. The problem is not that material incentive through the payment of bonuses is insufficient, but that it is a double-edged weapon. In many cases, the incentive system, which was conceived simply as a complement to the system of directives, has the opposite effect. It is the cause of conflicts of interest between producers and users, the latter having no direct means of making their preferences felt. It is the central authorities' task, and theirs alone, to win acceptance for their own concept of the general interest. However, if all the elements that have to be taken into account are considered, the problem of an optimal weighting of the different types of bonuses is an insoluble problem: in order to tackle it with success the economic authorities would have to have the means not only to make a 'perfect centralised forecast', but also to predict all the reactions of the managers of enterprises to the incentive system, which seems wholly unrealistic. Under these circumstances, the only solution for the supervisory authorities will often be to interfere more and more in the working of enterprises. However, their efforts in this direction also have their limits, and are not successful in preventing the development of 'uncontrolled processes' which ought in theory to have no place in the centralised model.

2 From the requirements of the model to the realities of socialist countries

The actual functioning of Soviet-type economies never seems to conform fully to the fundamental principles of the centralised model, i.e. the concentration of all decision-making powers in the hands of the political authorities, the use of directives as the guiding principle for the activities of enterprises and the elimination of the active role of prices in the allocation of resources. The frequency of 'deviations' and the permanent and systematic nature of most of them mean that they cannot be interpreted as accidental or individual failures. It is clear that they originate in the contradictions of the centralised model, the logic of which demands, in effect, that the planner: (a) limits the number of directives and constraints (taking into account his true capacity for collecting and processing micro-economic information); (b) insists, however, on strict adherence to his directives and constraints (which is the only way of preventing the very notion of directive becoming meaningless in the long term); (c) and never allows the influence of the incentive system to be felt outside of the framework established in the plan. However, indicators of success that are too simple and one-sided inevitably create conflicts between the interests of the national economy – identified with the implementation of the plan – and the interests of the enterprises which receive the incentives and are thus ready to take risks. The only answer is then to develop more and more complex incentive systems, accompanied by a proliferation of directives and more and more extensive interference by the economic authorities in the activities of enterprises (contrary to the first of the three requirements outlined above). This is the crux of the problem.

In these circumstances, the actual functioning of Soviet-type economies depends primarily on the shifting balance between the system of planned central management and the influence of the peripheral decision-making centres.

The freedom of the enterprise and the aims of the intermediate supervisory bodies

The limits of the command economy

Several factors combine to maintain an irreducible margin of autonomy for enterprises: the gaps in the system of planned management, the efforts of the enterprise to alter the orientation of their activity as planned by the authorities and the occasional or even systematic disregarding of some of their directives.

1 The gaps in the system of planned management are caused in various ways.

The system of direct centralised allocation never includes all producer goods. There are different categories of products, the definition and importance of which have varied greatly, but even at the height of Stalinist centralisation there have always existed 'products subject to a decentralised purchasing system' (raw materials of secondary importance), which are sold locally to enterprises.

In the same way, enterprises have some freedom to determine the structure of their production within the framework of the planned range of goods. It is often the case, for example, that the list of targets fixed in volume terms for the main products does not equal the total production target expressed in value; to make up the difference, the enterprise can choose the solution most advantageous to itself, without infringing its obligations. At the very least, it can almost always risk lowering the quality and degree of finish of its goods.

The practice of exceeding production targets is also a factor in the autonomy of the enterprise. As we have seen, the aim of the system of planned management in Soviet-type economies is not, paradoxically, to fulfil targets but systematically to exceed them. The enterprise which, by the '25th of the month' has already succeeded in reaching its planned target, can work more or less 'on its own account' for the last few days of the month. Unless specific instructions to the contrary are received, the enterprise will alter the nature and flow of its additional production to suit its own interests. Moreover, exceeding targets often gives the enterprise a minimum of financial autonomy. 'Profit-sharing', far from being a creation of recent reforms, is almost as old as the FYPs. In the USSR, the 'director's fund' set up in 1936 (which has since become the 'enterprise fund') was originally to receive 4 per cent of planned profits and 50 per cent of any profits in excess of the planned level. Even if the sums in question are modest in relation to total sales, they play a not insignificant role in enabling the director to strengthen his position in the labour market, to keep his workers for longer (notably by building accommodation and financing holidays), to make additional investments to those planned, and also to seize every possible opportunity to increase his stocks of raw materials over and above the official norms.

More unexpectedly, enterprises sometimes 'profit' from the delays which occur regularly in the drawing up of the plan. Indeed, little respect is paid to the planning timetable: the national economic plan for a given year has, for example, been published between February and April, whereas enterprises have operated until April or May without having received their own 'technico-economic plan'. This situation is, however, far from being advantageous for those enterprises which are then at risk of having their supplies cut off, since they are not able to escape the checks by the supervisory authorities. Nevertheless, in certain cases, it does allow them to present a *fait accompli* to the supervisory authorities.

2 There are also various courses of action open to the enterprise.

Their resistance to the fixing of overambitious targets has already been assessed; they bring into play a whole range of defence mechanisms in order to attempt to exert a braking effect: in particular, enterprises 'protest against the "excessive difficulty" of production targets they then prepare quite happily to exceed' (Kornai, 1959, p. 133).

However, when it is a question of influencing the allocation of investment, the managers of an enterprise play a much more active role. Since it is very much in their interest to increase the production capacity of their enterprise, they have no hesitation in presenting deliberately undervalued estimates of investment, or even in forcing the hand of the supervisory authorities by starting work without waiting for official authorisation: once work has started, it will have to be finished sooner or later, unless all the funds invested are to be lost. 'Free capital' for those enterprises not paying interest on their fixed capital was for a long time a factor contributing to the worsening of the problems of overinvestment, but the reintroduction of interest during the 1960s – even before the economic reform in certain countries, such as Hungary – was by no means sufficient to put an end to such practices, which arise from the very logic of the centralised model.

Before thinking about increasing their production potential, managers concern themselves with the deficiencies of the supply system and try to restrict the risks of a sudden interruption in production. At the very least, enterprises tend to accumulate 'emergency reserves' in the form of stocks over and above their immediate production needs. But, in order to reduce their dependence on outside agencies, many enterprises develop their own repair shops and spend considerable sums of money on prolonging the life of old, worn-out equipment which it would be more economical to replace. Some large enterprises go even further and start to manufacture their own spare parts (which are always very difficult to get hold of from external suppliers), semi-finished goods and most of the specific equipment that they use.

The unreliable supply system and the resultant problems go a long way towards explaining the general tendency of enterprises to 'hoard their labour force', since it is vital for them to have the necessary personnel available at peak periods. As long as the basic problem remains unsolved, any directives imposing a reduction in the work force may well not be enforced.

3 Generally speaking, a not insignificant proportion of the directives to enterprises are not adhered to. The frequency of these violations, attested to by many accounts published in the press of East European countries, may be surprising in an economy based theoretically on subordination to the hierarchy.

Three types of infringement can be distinguished. Firstly, there are individual criminal acts (embezzlement and corruption). Their proliferation reveals profound social demoralisation, but the causes largely extend beyond the particular characteristics of the 'economic mechanism' that we are attempting to analyse. Secondly, there are the minor falsifications designed to make the results of the enterprise look better, in order to obtain bonuses or avoid sanctions. The imagination shown by some managers of enterprises has long been a source of delight to students of the Soviet system, but it is usually just a question of anticipating the results of the next period, or of concealing a temporary drop in performance. It is quite understandable that controls are not particularly strict, provided that these practices remain within reasonable limits. Thirdly, certain kinds of directives are almost systematically ignored, even by the leading enterprises which succeed in winning the maximum amount of material and honorific awards.

It is the third type of violation that is the real problem. The most serious and the most common ones are the excessive inflation of cost prices, and, more particularly, overspending on the planned wage bills (due both to over-recruitment of workers and concealed wage increases), the non-enforcement of directives on technical progress and the introduction of new products, and failure to produce the planned range of goods. The fact that the authorities draw up 'an index of adherence' to the prescribed range of goods is revealing in that the authorities are implicitly recognising that the index is only one variable among others used in assessing the performance of enterprises (and not one of the main ones, since there is no specific reward attached to it), whereas, according to the logic of the centralised model, absolute adherence to all constraints ought to be an essential condition for the allocation of bonuses.

In fact, it is often the case that deviations are all the more pronounced the more successful a firm is according to the criterion of quantitative increase in production. These deviations are the cause of disruptions that have incalculable consequences for industrial users, the final consumer and the national economy, where growth is thrown into a state of imbalance by inflationary pressures, and, eventually, retarded.

In one sense, therefore, all the main failures in the functioning of Soviet-type economies can be attributed to the violation of the fundamental principle of the centralised model: the absolute primacy of centralised directives. Nevertheless, we still have to explain why this simple rule is so constantly broken.

There is certainly no lack of controls. Apart from the control carried out within the enterprise by party members, who constitute a parallel hierarchy, the enterprise is subject to the control of its supervisory authority (which has an unrestricted right to examine all aspects of its activity), to the control of the services answerable to the ministry of finance, and, finally, to control by the banks. This last form of control alone ought to guarantee that the working of Soviet-type economies is particularly transparent, since all deliveries, all delays in delivery, difficulties in distributing surpluses and the costs and financial situation of each enterprise are all reflected in changes in bank accounts.

There is one inevitable conclusion: if the controls prove to be ineffective in putting an end to certain almost permanent distortions, the consequences of which are easily observable, it is because the authorities do not wish to act.

The simplest explanation, in many cases, is that it would be impossible to enforce all the directives, even if enterprises tried wholeheartedly to do so, even against their own interests. The supervisory authorities are persuaded to recognise tacitly that their own instructions are unrealistic and contradictory. The enormous number of directives is enough to explain the lack of co-ordination and the contradictions which arise as a result. For example, the overall production target expressed in value, the amount of resources allocated and the prescribed range of goods are mutually irreconcilable. So in ignoring the last term, e.g. by stopping production of a particular article for which the raw materials have suddenly become unavailable, the enterprise is in no way trying to gain for itself an advantage, legal or otherwise, but is attempting to adhere as closely as possible to its plan. The supervisory authorities recognise this and make allowances for it.

The incessant revising of targets during the planning period worsens the situation. Even if the plan is initially balanced and consistent, it has little chance of remaining so. As we have seen, in the absence of any spontaneous adjusting mechanisms, it is inevitable that any corrective decision will be made at the same level as the initial decision. In practice, however, the central authorities do not have the time to calculate all the planned balances, so that approximate and incomplete revisions are often the cause of additional contradictions. For the enterprise, the problem becomes 'overdefined', and can be solved only by getting rid of some of the constraints.

Thus, paradoxically, the proliferation of directives and excessive centralism lead in the end to a certain freedom of action for enterprises. This is particularly so for those answerable to several superiors in the hierarchy, which can therefore take advantage of the lack of harmonisation between the directives received from their various superiors in order to oppose each of them all the more effectively. More generally, it is no longer a question for the enterprise of maximising its advantages within the framework of the directives handed down to it, but of deciding which of the directives absolutely must be adhered to, and which it is possible to infringe. However, while their room for manoeuvre and their responsibilities are thus considerably increased, success depends on their playing a particularly tight game. The enterprise is constantly negotiating a path between two dangers: it must try not to step outside the framework laid down by the indicators, nor finish up in an impasse; it is never sure that it has not underestimated the risks of incurring sanctions if a particular directive is infringed. Usually, however, it will quickly learn to recognise the cases where it can rely on a sort of 'complicity' on the part of its supervisory authorities.

The ambiguities of the system of planned management

The schematisation of the relationships between the 'centre' and the 'periphery' provides a convenient framework of analysis for a study of

the fundamental problems of Soviet-type economies. In reality, however, the 'centre' denotes the complex whole made up of:
(1) the *central political authorities* (the government and the central committee of the communist party);
(2) the *technical planning organisation* (the central planning office) and the other national 'functional' organisations (material and technical supply office, the manpower department, the prices office, etc.);
(3) the central agencies of the *economic administration* whose task it is to carry out the planning and day-to-day management of a particular sector ('industrial ministries' and their subdivisions, and the management organisations for the individual sectors).

These agencies play a pivotal role in the functioning of Soviet-type economies. Their operations are not limited to passively transmitting the impetus of the national economic plan, or to clarifying it in order to make it operational. They must be considered not as mere 'relay stations' for the central authorities, but as intermediate decision-making bodies, comparable to a large extent to the regional agencies which existed in the USSR under the name of *sovnarkhoz* during the brief period from 1957 to 1965, when the system of planned management was organised on a regional rather than a sectoral basis. These intermediate agencies, whatever form they take, have interests of their own; they pursue aims which are not entirely the same as those contained in the plan. This explains the complexity of their relationships both with the enterprises under their supervision and with the central authorities.

1 The relationship of the intermediate agencies to their enterprises is dominated by the fact that they themselves are judged by their superiors according to criteria that are less clearly defined, but in which the quantitative increase in production plays an important part.

Accustomed always to mistrust their enterprises (which is understandable, in view of the faults in the incentive system), the supervisory authorities have to resort to interfering in even the most technical aspects of the operations of their enterprises. This is, for example, the case in agriculture, where the local authorities, in addition to fixing production and delivery targets, plan in detail the sowing patterns of each co-operative. Very often, the proliferation of directives concerning the same target (e.g. intermediate consumption norms, the ceiling for the overall allocation of scarce raw materials, and the index of production cost per rouble of goods sold) is the cause of ambiguity, which may well cause inconsistency if there is any error of calculation or any attempt at partial revision of the plan, with the consequences noted above. The outright encroachments by the economic administration on areas that normally fall within the jurisdiction of the enterprise, attributable to a sort of 'contagious bureaucracy' (hypercentralisation in the strict sense of the word), must not, however, hide the fact that most of the directives are, in fact, essential to the normal functioning of these economies, given the co-ordinating role of the supervisory authorities. Nevertheless, these encroachments are a great source of additional friction and complication.

On the other hand, an enterprise which regularly exceeds its production targets is guaranteed lenient treatment from the supervisory authorities. Its supervisors will be prepared to ratify and 'cover up' any increases in manpower and in wages bills over and above the planned levels. All the attempts to tighten financial controls during the 1950s and 1960s, and the repeated protests by the banking authorities against excessive laxness have had only limited results, particularly in the USSR and Poland.

2 Moreover, the intermediate agencies of the economic administration often behave in a similar way.

The uncertainty of depending for supplies on outside agencies encourages them to seek to increase their own self-sufficiency, but on a much larger scale than the enterprises. The tendency of the *sovnarkhozy* to give excessively preferential treatment to intra-regional connections, thus leaving themselves open to accusations of 'localism' ('*mestnichestvo*'), significantly influenced the decision to terminate the regionalisation experiment. But the Soviet ministries also (until 1957, and since 1965) have tried to limit their own dependence on outside agencies by starting to produce as much of the equipment and intermediate goods necessary to their activity as possible. A given factory supplies all the enterprises answerable to the same ministry, scattered all over the USSR, even though suppliers answerable to other ministries are available in each region. Under a system of management by sector, this autarchic behaviour, taken to extremes, may result in much to-ing and fro-ing of goods across the whole country. At the same time, the correspondence between the sectors and the boundaries of each ministry's sphere of influence becomes more and more blurred. However, whether it be a question of excessive vertical integration, of diversification or one of regional integration, the principal negative effects arising from it are fairly similar: the development of rational specialisation[1] is hindered, there are diseconomies of small scale and duplication in research and development, etc. These distortions are also caused by rational attempts, from the point of view of those concerned, to limit the uncertainties which hang over their activity, and it is in practice very difficult to prevent them from investing in those activities which help to increase their level of self-sufficiency.

The planning of large-scale investment is an area which, in theory, lies very much within the jurisdiction of the central authorities. However, the number of investment projects examined each year in the USSR is in the tens of thousands. The central planning office (Gosplan) is inundated with project plans, and is unable to examine directly anything other than the largest projects. The choice of investment thus becomes principally the responsibility of the intermediate levels between the enterprises and Gosplan, i.e. of the sector management organisations and the ministries. These latter have the same aim as the enterprises, which is to 'push' their investment projects as much as possible. They succeed to a large extent, although in theory their own responsibilities extend only to the sharing out of the total sum allocated to each sector. They achieve this through their policy of committing funds to a large number of building projects, on the one hand, and, on the other, of systematically undervaluing the total amount of the estimates. The sector management organisations and the ministries are then able to bring pressure to bear in order to have supplementary funds allocated to them, by pointing out the enormous waste that would ensue if an unfinished investment project were to be abandoned. As for exceeding the estimates, which generally results from an earlier deliberate underestimation of the cost of the project, an attempt will then be made to justify this in part through a future increase in the originally planned production capacity, which enables two birds to be killed with one stone: the central authorities will resign themselves to financing in retrospect a project both more costly and larger than planned. These practices, which largely explain the tendency to overinvestment in Soviet-type economies (an attempt will be made to measure the overall effect of this), are not always equally effective. It is mainly the most powerful ministries which, by virtue of their place in the hierarchy of priorities at any given moment, apply pressure in order to strengthen their position. This constitutes a dangerous element of rigidity in the system, and was the method adopted by the Soviet coal industry to oppose the development of other energy sources in the 1950s; in the same way, under Khrushchev, the metal industries succeeded in slowing down the shift in investment towards the chemical industry contained in the seven-year plan. The expansion of activities on the boundaries of two sectors (such as the petrochemical industry) may well be hindered by administrative compartmentalisation, unless, on the contrary, it gives rise to competition between ministries anxious to extend their sphere of influence.

3 At first sight, the practices analysed above can easily be interpreted in terms of a 'desire for power', and indeed, the career, prestige and influence of those in charge of the administration of the economy have everything to gain from as rapid a development as possible of their sector, even at the expense of over-recruitment of labour, unbalanced investment and costly 'despecialisation'. But their behaviour stems largely from the 'fetish of production for production's sake' that prevails from the top to the bottom of the hierarchy. The way in which the central authorities themselves tolerate excessive wages bills, recruitment of labour and investment credits shows clearly that balance is deliberately sacrificed, in accordance with the logic of 'tight planning'; quantitative criteria play a decisive role in assessing the performance of the intermediate agencies, as they do for enterprises. This 'fetish' is itself explicable: since there is no real synthetic indicator of success, the Soviet-type centralised economy cannot do without certain points of reference, however imperfect they may be; the increase in production achieved by an enterprise or a sector is a tangible reality, that seems easily measurable, whereas there is no reliable method available to the planner to evaluate the opportunity cost[2] of a given product.

Planning *versus* 'spontaneous processes'

Para-legal relationships, currency and pseudo-markets

1 The existence of the official supply and distribution system ought in theory to enable enterprises to concentrate on the technical aspects of production. In fact, each director recognises that the normal functioning of his enterprise depends on a daily struggle to obtain the supplies to which he is entitled and, should the need arise, to make good the failings of the centralised allocation system. The boundary between legal and illegal activities tends at this point to become blurred:[3] actions range widely in legality, from the most official actions to the use of clandestine intermediaries, the *tolkachi* (those who 'give a little push in the right direction'), who are sometimes paid on a percentage basis from the secret funds of an enterprise according to the 'effectiveness' of their activities – a curious example of a 'liberal profession' created by the faulty working of the centralised model.

Approaches will often be made to those in charge of the supply system, with a view to the trading of favours (*blat*): the managers of enterprises and the party cell put their networks of personal contacts at the disposal of their enterprises, in good faith. However, problems of supply are also often solved by direct approaches to other enterprises, without any hierarchical intervention.

For this latter solution, a 'currency of exchange' is required. Bank controls mean that this cannot really be the official currency. The enterprise will try, for example, to gamble on the amount of rejects that will be allowed by the ministry: if it produces less than the authorised maximum, it will take advantage of this by selling good quality products as rejects, at a price determined by the enterprise itself. But it is above all the surpluses received through the supply system, the stocks built up by making discreet economies in the official levels of intermediate consumption that give the enterprise a relatively abundant and diversified 'currency of exchange'.

These unofficial relationships between state enterprises are, in the words of J. Berliner, an 'embryonic form of the market economy trying to pierce the hard shell of centralised planning' (Berliner, 1957, p. 206). There is a great deal of evidence that there are frequent 'exchanges of friendly services' between enterprises, and that they are a significant corrective to the rigidity of the centralised model. However, the minimum conditions for us to be able to talk of 'market relationships' – some flexibility in prices or exchange relationships and a minimum of openness enabling several potential exchangers to compare what is available and what they are looking for – are fulfilled only to a very variable extent. Transactions are usually only bilateral, involving small quantities, and are carried out on the basis of official prices, either to limit the risk of sanctions, or because the partners in the exchange have no precise point of reference to establish a different price. Many transactions, however, take the form of an exchange, which creates a degree of flexibility: bank control is eliminated, and the exchange relationships can be adjusted more easily. Nor must it be forgotten that one good turn deserves another.

2 These parallel quasi-markets are a tricky problem for the managers of a Soviet-type economy. The services they perform obviously have a high cost. The habit of having constantly to infringe if not the spirit at least the letter of the regulations endangers in the long term a state of mind that may well encourage embezzlement for private ends. Official concessions to the principle of the market would often give better results;[4] making the transactions public would be enough to prevent

certain enterprises in a position of strength from exploiting their partner. But the establishment of a genuine market system within the centralised model is considered ideologically and politically unacceptable (largely because the means of production may well be diverted towards non-priority sectors), and, in any case, would cause insurmountable difficulties.

Conversely, if the black market were effectively suppressed, or attempts made to do so, the result would be the abolition of a whole network of spontaneous exchanges which make a contribution to the implementation of the plan, and which are essential to the centralised economy. Leaving a producer good out of the official allocation of supply quotas, or a shortage of spare parts, not of any great value but unobtainable, is often enough to bring everything to a halt: it is then up to the enterprise to take steps to limit the damage. Without the voluntary exchanges, production would no doubt be more frequently and more seriously interrupted. This is why the legal measures to suppress the 'black market' have never been vigorously applied.

The unofficial agreements between enterprises are, therefore, tolerated, but only within strict limits, and their influence is marginal. They are too uncertain and too restricted to contribute to more rational specialisation by enterprises in defiance of the directives. They are principally a defence mechanism to help each enterprise to function normally, and their aim is rarely to ensure better adjustment to demand (particularly to final consumer demand). In short, the very fact that exchanges are possible further encourages enterprises to stockpile materials for which they have no use: any delivery of any product which could later be used as currency of exchange will automatically be accepted, in the absence of adequate financial disincentives.

It is clear, therefore, that, while the central allocation system has serious faults, the voluntary exchanges play only an inadequate and uncertain corrective role. The centralised fixing of prices, on the other hand, plays an essential *de facto* role in the functioning of the system.

The historical process of price distortion

1 For the various reasons mentioned above, prices in a Soviet-type economy are not only a means of summarising the planned objectives and controlling their realisation by the enterprises, but are also, at least intermittently, an active influence on the allocation of resources and

the orientation of production. It would thus be logical to take them fully into account in the processes of the planned management system and to try to remove any contradiction between the influence of the directives and that of prices. This has certainly been the central problem of economic reforms for fifteen years. However, until the 1960s, both the practice and the general philosophy of the planners were in this respect uncertain and often even contradictory.

Ever since the setting up of the planned economy, price determination has been, in principle, the uncontested prerogative of the central authorities, and a certain amount of 'management by prices' has always coexisted from time to time with the directives.

For example, faced with an acute shortage of a particular raw material, the central authorities, instead of resorting solely to rationing, may also decide to raise the price, in order to slow down consumption while stimulating production, in accordance with a mechanism based on that of the market economy. This is why, in the USSR in 1950, a decision was made to make a massive increase in the price of non-ferrous metals with low impurity levels, in order to stimulate production. Initially, demand went down to the level of production, that was still too low, and equilibrium was restored. In the medium term, however, the producers, as a result of this stimulation, all turned to producing high quality metal, whereas users shifted their demand to less pure and less expensive products. The result was disequilibrium in the opposite direction, and the difference in price between the two grades had after a time to be reduced. This sequence of events is proof of the active role of prices in the Soviet economy, and clearly shows that *ex post* adjustment is not the prerogative of market economies. In this case, a spontaneous adjustment according to market mechanisms would undoubtedly have been both more gradual and quicker, whereas price adjustments by the authorities always mean that reaction will always be somewhat delayed: but the difference is only one of method.

This is at least a consistent use of prices, which is far from being always the case. The most serious inconsistency remains the systematic and long-lasting underpricing of production goods (plant and raw materials).

There are two possible assumptions. The first is that the actual functioning of Soviet-type economies does not deviate fundamentally from the centralised model, i.e. that the allocation of resources and the choice of investments are effectively controlled by the centralised decisions. In this case, the official justifications, presented paradoxically as if the Soviet economy obeyed price mechanisms, are totally without foundation: the underpricing of the means of production is merely ineffectual. The argument that it enables 'the state as investor to save money' (or even that it increases investment, encourages the modernisation of plant and boosts industrial development) then becomes absurd: it springs from the purest money illusion, as if the central authorities had to try to hide from themselves the real cost of their own decisions.

Or it can be acknowledged that, in all areas, the price structure has a limited, but never negligible influence. In this case, the underpricing of the means of production seems not only illogical but dangerous. It tends to discourage producers; certain activities function at a loss, and their financial deficit increases at the same time as the volume of their production. In order to counteract this disincentive, more weight must be given to the 'gross production' indicator, with the negative consequences already noted. At the same time, all enterprises are encouraged to bring pressure to bear in order to obtain as much additional plant as possible, while there is much less incentive to economise on raw materials.

Only an historical explanation, going back to the origins of the centralised model, can fully account for the artificial underpricing of producer goods.

2 The price system of a centralised economy is not created out of nothing, any more than the initial potential for production. The planner inherits an historically determined price system, which is going to be much modified in the course of time, but not dismantled overnight. The prices in force in the USSR towards the end of the NEP were certainly far from forming a consistent system of 'competitive' prices, but they were both an approximate reflection of production costs, and ensured some sort of (static) equilibrium between supply and demand, at least as far as producer goods were concerned. But there could be no question of basing the macro-decisions of the first FYP on them, since the aim was completely to change all the basic economic relationships, and, indirectly, the price structure itself.

The exceptional nature of this task, together with the ideological distrust of monetary calculation, explains the absolute predominance at this stage of planning in terms of physical quantities. The basic task of the central economic authorities was to organise the rationing of production goods and to solve the problem of bottlenecks. The permanent adjustment of several tens of thousands of prices would in any case have been technically impossible for them; but, moreover, the authorities were confronted with the much more immediate problem of inflation in the retail market, caused by the deficit in the production of consumer goods, and by enterprises hiring more labour than laid down in the plan, with a consequent increase in aggregate remuneration. The need to limit the imbalances in the market made a massive increase in consumer prices necessary. The increase in the price of producer goods, however serious the deficits were, appeared less urgent because of rationing; the financial deficits incurred by producers were not considered serious and were automatically made up. It was in these conditions, in the 1930s, that the relative underpricing of producer goods was first established. Large productivity increases in the capital goods sector (which benefited from the bulk of investment) were relied on to absorb the difference. When these proved inadequate, other justifications were put forward after the event. In the post-war period, a similar process occurred in the people's democracies when centralised planning was established.

3 The planner subsequently remains to a large extent a prisoner of the distorted price structure in force. The general rigidity of prices, combined with the occasional revision of a few of them for particular purposes, explains why the price structure tends gradually to become inconsistent.

In theory, prices are based on production costs. But, since increases in costs cannot be reflected as they occur in the price structure (not to mention equilibrium between supply and demand), the authorities limit themselves to occasional modifications. Their actions seem to vary without any clearly defined criterion. The main cause of distortions is the fragmentary nature of their interventions: in general, they affect only a narrow range of products, rarely an entire sector (although even this is a considerable administrative task); at best, the authorities consider the effects on the production costs of direct users, but go no further; if necessary, the granting of a subsidy to those most affected prevents any spread effect. In this way, the price structure and the substitution relationships within the national economy are not called into question. Any subsidy, once granted, tends to last indefinitely.

The contradictions which arise from the elimination of the influence of the market are well illustrated by the problem of new products. The administration can fix their prices only by reference either to the price of the most comparable existing articles, or to the production cost declared by the enterprise. The first solution is difficult to implement and is to a large extent arbitrary. With the second solution, there is the risk of making the new products either excessively or insufficiently profitable for the enterprise. It is profitable to launch new products in a period of inflation, when their price is calculated on the basis of actual production costs,[5] whereas the price of existing products will not have been increased for some time. Enterprises thus have an incentive to introduce minimal changes to their products, with no other justification than an attempt to obtain a new price: the new products serve as a pretext for disguised price rises tolerated by the administration. Conversely, new products are just as frequently less profitable for the enterprise – particularly in the short term – than existing products. Indeed, for existing products, the accumulated gains in productivity gradually create the difference between a rigid price and decreasing production costs, whereas the price of new products generally only includes a minimum 'planned profit' margin. In fact, the low profitability of new products, which discourages real innovation, is a more serious danger than excess profitability. But above all, it must be remembered that these excesses do not balance each other out: they are both proof of the failure of a price system which is unable to reconcile the interest of enterprises and that of the national economy.

4 Over time, therefore, the price structure ceases to reflect a theoretical principle of price determination, whatever it may be, and is no longer anything but the product of a long series of administrative decisions dictated by circumstances.[6] The authorities often implicitly recognise the inconsistency of the system of prices actually in force. Thus, in the USSR until 1950, the 1926-7 prices were used to express the production targets for most enterprises, and were also used as a basis for determining bonuses (it was considered preferable to calculate in the constant prices of a year long past than to use current prices). This was obviously a stop-gap measure, since it was tantamount to ignoring the considerable changes that had taken place since then in the structure of the Soviet economy. Nevertheless, it must be considered a lesser evil than the cases where the planner, giving in to a sort of money illusion, bases his own decisions on current prices which have lost any economic significance.

Attempts to put some order into the price structure have, it is true, been made at long intervals (general reforms of wholesale prices in 1949 in the USSR, and in 1959 in Hungary). The result was to reduce to a certain extent the divergences between the price structure and the structure of production costs, without ever eliminating them totally, or preventing the same distortions from recurring. On the subject of Hungary at the beginning of the 1960s, for example, J. Bognar is quite accurate when he speaks of the 'sclerosis of the economic environment', and at the same time of 'growing irrationality' (Bognar, 1969, p. 37) because of the lack of connection between prices and the general development of the economic processes.

In these conditions, the functioning of Soviet-type economies often leads to an accumulation of distortions of all kinds. Financial preoccupations are not enough of an incentive for enterprises to make savings in producer goods, both because these latter are underpriced, and because their influence is neutralised and defeated by that of the target of maximising gross production. Technical substitutions between production factors under the influence of relative prices are, in any case, very limited because of rationing. On the other hand, the range produced by each enterprise remains very sensitive to the influence of prices: the slightest discontinuities in the list of official prices give enterprises an incentive to deviate from the prescribed range, and, *a fortiori*, from the needs expressed by their customers (industrial enterprises and commercial organisations), to the particular detriment of the final consumer.[7] The weaker the price system grows, the more the methods of economic management must rely on direct instructions, despite the obvious damaging effects of excessive centralisation.

Obvious imbalances and hidden malfunctionings

1 An analysis of the distortions which affect the Soviet-type economies should not lead us to believe that they usually function in a state of chaos.

> A price system that would have created intolerable confusion if enterprises had been free to react to the profit motive has not prevented the [Soviet] economy from functioning. . . . Of course, the Soviet system does not produce vast quantities of useless surpluses. The variety of controls and revisions enables the system to function most of the time in a fairly orderly way. (Nove, 1961, p. 212 and pp. 246-7)

The most obvious imbalances cannot fail to attract attention. Microeconomic planning and the centralised allocation of resources are weaknesses, but it would be an exaggeration to believe that they are totally ineffective.

The influence that the principle of the market still exerts on the periphery of the system – that is, with regard to the choices of workers, on the one hand, and of consumers, on the other – also helps to limit the imbalances.

Although one must be very cautious in talking about a 'labour market' in Soviet-type economies, the fact is that all work gives rise to the payment of a money wage, and that the compulsory allocation of workers became a rarity even before the end of the Stalinist period. The need to provide all the jobs necessary for the implementation of the plan seriously limits the authorities' discretion in the wage determination process.[8] Thus, the authorities still have a basis of reference for the reassessment of production costs when they decide on a general reform of wholesale prices: this limits the deterioration of the price system.

In the same way, everyday consumer goods are not directly allocated,[9] but are sold to consumers. Articles which are absolute rubbish, or which are marketed at a price out of proportion with that of substitutes available on the market, will not be sold, and this will eventually provoke a reaction, despite all the rigidity of the economic administration.

However, the centralised model does not succeed in eliminating a certain number of 'spontaneous processes' (in the negative sense given to this term in the communist countries) which correspond neither to the logic of the plan, nor to that of the market.

2 There are many obvious imbalances. Within the state sector, one of the most notable is the periodic inflation of the total amount of uncompleted investment projects. The cause, already discussed above, lies in the pressure exerted by enterprises, which leads to 'overinvestment', and an excessive number of building sites being started up simultaneously, with the active complicity of the supervisory authorities. This is one of the worst examples in Soviet-type economies of money being squandered. Enormous sums, equivalent to several months of GNP, are immobilised for absolutely nothing; funds are committed to a large number of building projects and construction deadlines extended, which increases the total cost of the investments; and delays in finally bringing the new capacity into service cause incalculable disruptions, since the destination of the production of the still unfinished factories has already been fixed in advance and the authorities are unable to find alternative sources of supply. Although this problem has long been recognised, no progress seems to have been made towards solving it.

Imbalances in the consumer goods market are an even more obvious reality. They have only appeared in their present form – shortage of certain products and, at the same time, an accumulation of unsold stocks of other products – since the end of the serious inflation of the Stalinist period. Until then, the problem was simply one of general shortage. The persistence of specific shortages should not be interpreted as proof of a stagnating standard of living; the direct cause of the shortages is the maintenance of prices at a level that is too low to ensure equilibrium in the market. The price of basic products has increased in a series of discontinuous leaps, separated by long periods of rigidity, during which the fixed price gradually ceased to ensure equilibrium between supply and demand; when it is decided to make an adjustment, the increase is massive[10] and becomes almost an affair of state, as if the authorities were seeking to avoid the political risks inherent in such a situation. But shortages of certain articles are often also only the counterpart of excess stocks of other articles. The rigid method of price determination is enough to explain this double disequilibrium. The seriousness of these imbalances has without doubt decreased over time, but they continue to be a feature of everyday life.

3 However, even if all the imbalances were eliminated from the consumer goods market, there would be no guarantee that the system would respond correctly[11] to the needs of the populace.

Let us assume that consumer goods are produced in quantities out of proportion to consumer demand. This obviously means that, if the goods were put on sale at a price proportional to their production cost, there would be surpluses of some and shortages of others. Faced with such an imbalance, and except for the extreme case of totally aberrant planning (the manufacture of utterly useless articles . . .), the authorities still have the power 'to carry out the consumption plan'[12] – that is, to have the available production 'absorbed' by consumers – by putting an extra tax on the articles of which there is a shortage and subsidising those of which there is a surplus. This then creates a system of 'double prices', which means that the original structure of production can be maintained: the system of 'prices to consumers' designed to achieve equilibrium in the market is entirely divorced from 'production prices' based (in theory) on production costs. It is the positive differences (caused by the state levies under the name of 'turnover tax'[13]) or negative differences (i.e. subsidies) that reflect the degree of divergence between the two systems of valuation.

Some of these differences correspond to clearly defined social preferences – penalising harmful consumption such as that of alcohol, and subsidising cultural goods and services – which are in any case common to most systems. But the originality of the centralised model is that it gives the authorities the means of maintaining generalised divergences. In the extreme case, the more precise the adjustment of retail prices becomes, the more it becomes possible to ignore consumer preferences:

there is then no perceptible symptom of disequilibrium (Brus, 1970, p. 129). For this reason, the double price system, which 'introduces a gap between consumer preferences and what it is technically feasible to produce', has been accused of making money an 'instrument of subservience', since it is used 'not as a means of adapting production to current demand, but as a means of adapting current demand to the product on the market' (Marczewski, 1955 and 1956, p. 400); such a system 'expresses the absolute refusal of the planner to attach equal importance to the preferences of the authorities and those of the individual consumer' (Kende, 1964, p. 476).

One cannot fail to be struck by the degree of divergence between the two price systems. In Hungary, for example, where attempts at 'price rationalisation' began even before the end of the 1950s, the differences shown in Table 2.1 existed on the eve of the 1968 reform.

Table 2.1 *Dispersion of the rate of tax on turnover in Hungary (1967)*

	Minimum	Maximum
Cotton goods	+ 20	+ 71
Woollens	− 47	+ 68
Blankets	− 47	+ 35
Women's clothing	− 28	+ 39
Glassware	+ 2	+ 55
Pottery	− 98	+ 45
Dairy products	−225	− 30
Liqueurs	+ 43	+ 93

Source: B. Csikos-Nagy in Friss (ed.), 1969, p. 144.

However, the main question is whether the unco-ordinated variations in the tax can be explained in terms of conflict between the preferences of consumers and the production structure laid down by the planners. Is it not often rather a case of being unable precisely to adjust production to demand? What specific preferences would the planners have to set against those of consumers, when making detailed choices between similar articles within the same group of products?

In fact, the obvious imbalances in the consumer goods market would be even greater if the planners did not in general try approximately to satisfy demand on the basis of the prices in force. In a Soviet-type economy, it is more expedient to modify the production targets of an enterprise than to revise centrally determined prices (or, with even more reason, to make reciprocal adjustments to prices and quantities). Price rigidity can thus to a certain extent be offset by direct action on quantities, but this still allows the gap between consumption prices and production prices to persist.

At the same time, the rate of turnover tax fails to fulfil its role in consumption policy as a means of expressing social preferences. Indeed, whichever of the two sequences is followed as shown in Figure 2.1, the rate of tax is determined residually in both cases. Sometimes, despite everything, the rate expresses social preferences (typical examples are alcohol and books), but that is not always the case, and at best the correspondence is only approximate.

In the absence of specific and social preferences, a simple *a priori* rule could be devised (i.e. at the very least, for adjustments within the same group of products) which would bring the structure of production closer to consumer preferences: increase the production of the most heavily taxed items, while reducing production of those which can only be sold with a subsidy. Such a rule would in fact amount to allowing the rate of tax – considered as an indicator of the strength of demand – to play, within certain limits, the role of the rate of profit in a market model. In fact, progress in this direction has remained very limited, partly because of administrative inertia, but also because of social resistance to any price increase, because of the multitude of particular cases to be taken into consideration, and because of the uncertainty which hangs over the calculation of production costs.

Thus, even more than the obvious imbalances in supply and demand, the aberrant variations in the rate of turnover tax are evidence of the lack of precision in the system of planned management. And within the state sector, other examples could be found of uncontrolled processes which bear no relation either to consumer preferences or to those of the central authorities.

Thus the reality of Soviet-type economies diverges from the theoretical principles of the functioning of the centralised model. This permanent disparity does not prevent us from clearly recognising the underlying characteristics of the model, but it does explain the apparently contradictory criticisms made of the functioning of these economies: excessive mistrust and actual complicity between enterprises and their supervisory authorities, price rigidity and the unco-ordinated revision of certain prices, waste of investment and excessive prolonging of the life of old equipment, general lack of stocks and the building up of reserves by enterprises, the stifling of decentralised initiative under a deluge of directives and the proliferation of uncontrolled processes.

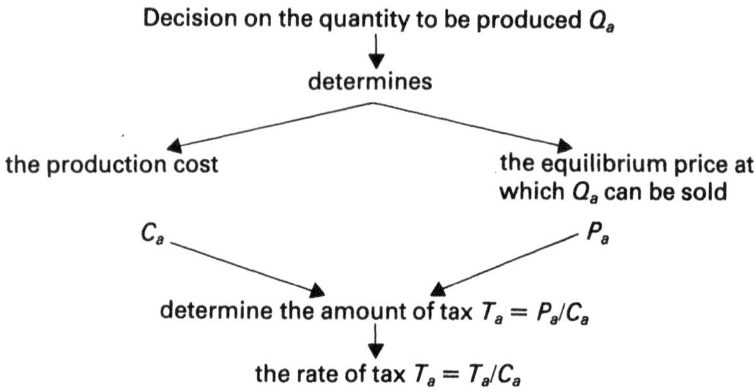

or, as more often in reality, as follows:

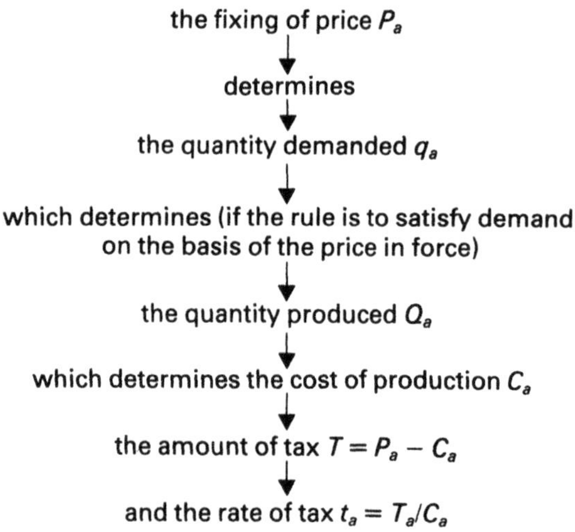

Figure 2.1

These contradictory excesses are in fact the counterpart of each other, and they reveal the approximate nature of centralised adjustment: the task given to the planning and economic management authorities is beyond their real capabilities.

Forty years ago, Schumpeter, in his introduction to his analysis of 'the structure of a centralised socialist economy', said: 'For the moment, I shall assume, not without boldness, that the adequate margin of freedom will have been fixed experimentally and actually allocated to the managers, at a point half-way between the anarchy of individual ambition and an Ubuesque bureaucratism' (*Capitalism, Socialism and Democracy*, p. 279). Despite the qualification ('not without boldness'), Schumpeter, in his generosity towards the enemy, seemed close to admitting that 'almost unlimited freedom of action should be granted to the "men on the job", i.e. the managers of the various sectors or factories' (*ibid.*, p. 273), without questioning the supremacy of the central plan, or the efficiency of centralised control. Our already long experience of the functioning of Soviet-type economies no longer justifies such optimism, which contrasts, for example, with this diagnosis made just before the 1968 reform by a former leading official in the management of the Hungarian economy: 'The lack of relationship between micro- and macro-economic processes is not simply one possible difficulty among others, nor is it, as is often said, a fault which becomes obvious when the plan is put into practice, but a fundamental, functional weakness of the system of management' (Bognar, 1969, p. 31).

Part II
Economic policies in the post-Stalinist period and the origins of the reforms

Introduction to Part II

The distortions analysed in the first part are as old as Soviet-type planning itself, but their significance was largely ignored, as long as the centralised model remained a generally effective instrument for the fulfilment of the priority aims of the leaders.

Stalinist economic policy, implemented in the USSR from 1928 and in the whole of Eastern Europe from 1948, was undeniably consistent. Everything was subordinated to one basic aim: the construction within a few years of a powerful industrial base. The 'voluntarism'* of the planners was reflected in a series of extremely well defined and closely related characteristics, which will serve as a point of reference in an assessment of subsequent developments:

(1) growth targets were hyper-ambitious, fixed at the limit of what could be achieved;

(2) the relative shares of consumption and accumulation deliberately sacrificed the present to the future; record rates of investment were attained within a few years;

(3) the structure of investment is even more revealing: the priority given to basic investment, heavy industry and defence reduced to the minimum the shares of light industry, agriculture and housing;

(4) the levies on agriculture were used to finance accumulation in industry;

(5) the organisation of foreign trade was aimed at developing the autarchy of the countries of the socialist bloc; import policy systematically favoured capital goods, in order to accelerate industrialisation;

(6) the uneven implementation of the plans further strengthened the priority given to accumulation, to the detriment of the sectors producing for consumption, which acted as shock absorbers.

*Translators' note: Voluntarism: the theory that the will rather than the intellect is the ultimate principle of reality. It seems to be used here to describe the return to planning based on a grand design of industrial development rather than current economic conditions.

This policy could not possibly be maintained without a high degree of constraint, exerted both within each country and within the framework of the Soviet bloc.

However, after the death of Stalin in 1953, the people began to demand an improvement in their standard of living commensurate with the progress of industrialisation. And the leaders thought it possible to satisfy them with partial concessions, without tackling the basic problem. An impressive economic transformation had just been achieved within a short space of time. The inherent shortcomings of the centralised model (the lack of innovation and the imbalances between supply and demand for different articles) could still pass relatively unnoticed in the context of general shortages. Particular imbalances were 'concealed' behind the fundamental imbalance that operated to the detriment of consumption. The most urgent task was to redefine the priorities and, at the very least, to reduce the excesses of Stalinist *economic policy*. In that respect, 1953 was a turning point. But only in that respect, since the problem of the *economic model* was only just beginning to be posed.

3 Quasi-cyclical changes

The post-Stalinist period from 1953 to 1965 was characterised by fairly frequent shifts of direction. This applies both to institutional reorganisations and to economic policies proper.

Barely a few months or even weeks separated the death of Stalin in 1953 and the official announcement of a revision of priorities in favour of consumption. Under the pressure of events, leaders in the Soviet bloc engaged in more or less severe self-criticism[1] and made unequivocal undertakings. 'The essence of the new direction,' stated Grotewohl and Ulbricht in East Germany, 'lies in the rapid improvement of the standard of living of the working class and of the populace as a whole. . . . The production of consumer goods must be further developed than hitherto.' In Hungary, where Stalinist economic policy had been applied in a particularly extreme way, Imre Nagy, on his return to government, distanced himself even more clearly from the excesses of the past; he recognised that the far too ambitious targets of the first Hungarian plan 'resulted in the recent drop in our standard of living . . . nothing justifies too rapid industrialisation or a tendency to industrial autarchy'. At the same time, he denounced the attitude of the regime towards individual peasants, the premature development of co-operatives and the policy of forced collectivisation. To a greater or lesser extent, all the people's democracies initiated a similar reorientation. And the Soviet government was not to be outdone. In August 1953, Malenkov announced a massive increase in investment in agriculture and light industry, and promised a much more rapid increase in consumption for the following two or three years.

But it was in 1956, with Khrushchev's report to the XXth Congress, the dramatic return to power of Gomulka in Poland and the Hungarian uprising, that the crisis caused by the uncertainties and the inadequacies of de-Stalinisation reached its height. The unity of the 'Soviet bloc' seemed for a moment to be seriously threatened. New concessions were thus considered essential, both in the relationship between the USSR and the people's democracies and in the orientation of the national economies. In about 1957, in certain countries, this more flexible economic policy was accompanied – which had hardly been the case in 1953 – by detailed discussions of the model, and by an initial series of decentralising reforms which in various respects foreshadowed the reforms of 1963-8.

The years 1953, 1956 and 1965 thus represent the principal milestones in the questioning of the general orientations of the Stalinist period. But this was in no way a linear progression.

Since 1955, all the East European countries had been drawing up a new series of FYPs, the simultaneous launching of which in 1956 was to symbolise the return to normality after the concessions of 1953. The resumption of agricultural collectivisation, explicitly announced in the plans, triggered off the events of 1956 in Hungary and Poland.

The political and economic consolidation, achieved in 1957 in better conditions and more rapidly than expected, was quickly followed by a new change of direction, the significance of which was not immediately apparent. This was because, in 1958, the leaders' declarations more than ever stressed the improvement of the standard of living, and certain measures, such as the abolition in the USSR of the machine tractor stations and compulsory deliveries at low prices, were interpreted at the time as introducing a more liberal agricultural policy. However, there was no doubt about the reaffirmation of economic 'voluntarism'. It was reflected throughout Eastern Europe in a new leap forward in investment (from 1958), followed a little later (1960-1) by a sharp increase in military expenditure. In all the people's democracies, except Poland, agricultural collectivisation resumed at a rapid pace, and was concluded this time without compromise. The slowing down of trade with the West was also evidence of a general hardening of policy, even in Poland, where the 'disciplining' and realignment with the USSR were almost complete by 1959. This was the context in which the reforms of the end of the 1950s were to be made, although any really innovatory element had been removed from the schemes. These first attempts at partial decentralisation, made in a context of severe economic imbalances which allowed them no chance of success, were to be very quickly brought into question.

The swings in economic policies

The 'new direction' of 1953

The leaders' promises were given concrete form first of all in financial measures. On 25 June 1953, the Soviet people learnt that the compulsory annual loan had been fixed at the level of two weeks' wages, instead of three or four as in previous years. In all the Eastern European countries, the price of many popular consumer articles had been cut. However, a corresponding increase in supplies was necessary, and the production of consumer goods had thus to be increased as a matter of urgency.

1 The priority given to the revival of agriculture was necessary for obvious reasons. In the first instance, it took the form of concessions to private agriculture. In the USSR, the taxation of private plots, which were to be increased, was reduced; after several years of continuous reduction, the amount of privately owned livestock immediately started to increase. In the people's democracies, all the governments considered a temporary halt in the collectivisation of agriculture to be inevitable, and there was even partial decollectivisation in Czechoslovakia and Hungary, where tens of thousands of peasants actually exercised the right they had been granted to withdraw from the co-operatives.

The reduction in the compulsory low price deliveries is equally clear proof of the change in agricultural policy. In Hungary, for example, the compulsory deliveries had accounted for 86 per cent of commercial agricultural production in 1952; this proportion was to be reduced to 46 per cent, according to the plan for 1954. At the same time, a whole series of complementary measures was taken in order to raise the level of the peasants' incomes. Taxes were lowered and tax arrears remitted, the selling price of industrial supplies was reduced (and supplies improved) and the various categories of production prices fixed by the state were increased. Thus in the USSR, as a result of the increased revenue of the *kolkhozy*, the money wages per workday unit rose by 160 per cent in four years, and the total real income of each *kolkhoznik* household rose by 60 per cent between 1952 and 1956, thus exceeding for the first time the 1928 level.

The increase in the peasants' incomes really seemed, particularly for the USSR, to be the main new element. However, the much greater priority given to agriculture than in the past was also reflected in about 1954 in all socialist countries in the increase in agricultural investment as a proportion of total investment, and, in real terms, in a marked acceleration in deliveries of agricultural equipment, lorries and fertilisers. The number of qualified specialists (agronomists, etc.), which had been very low in the *kolkhozy* in 1953, increased for several years at a very rapid rate.

2 The readjustment of priorities in favour of consumption also affected industry. Whereas 'the law of priority growth for the sector of the means of production' (sector A) had dominated the whole of the Stalinist period, the growth rate of the consumer goods sector (sector B) in 1954 in every country was, contrary to previous trends, equal to or greater than that for sector A. However, the very sharp reduction (particularly in Hungary and Czechoslovakia) in the growth of sector A only made possible limited and temporary growth in sector B: this is the first example of the redoubtable difficulties inherent in any attempt to restructure an economy shaped by the application of the Stalinist 'model'. The planners have very limited room for manoeuvre, since they are caught between two contradictory demands: on the one hand, to reduce the proportion of investment in national income with the aim of an immediate increase in the share of consumption, and, on the other, to increase investment in the disadvantaged sectors, in order to correct the imbalances of earlier growth. This difficult choice was settled in various ways according to the country (and the period), in accordance primarily with the political context.

In the USSR, the overall increase in investment went down only very slightly in 1953: while the share of private consumption rose slightly until 1955, contrary to the earlier tendency, this increase corresponded basically to the reduction in military expenditure. In the people's democracies, on the other hand, except in Bulgaria, the growth in investment was checked sharply in 1953–4 and, at the same time, the share of consumption rose, in Hungary, for example, from 46 per cent of national income in 1953 to 60 per cent in 1955.

However, the structure of investment developed in almost the same way in all the socialist countries. The same change in favour of those sectors supplying consumption can be observed everywhere: investment in agriculture, light industry and house-building increased in all countries.

This reorientation of priorities was not only a question of political decision: it challenged all the economic balances. The house-building effort, for example, came up against the shortage of building materials and the inadequate capacity of the building industry. Thus sustained growth might well require in the medium term a revival in basic investment

Table 3.1 *Distribution of investment (1951–3 and 1954–5)*

	USSR		GDR		Poland		Hungary	
	1951–3	1954–5	1951–3	1954–5	1951–3	1954–5	1951–3	1954–5
Heavy industry	54.2	49.8	46.6	43.1	45.8	42.2	45.7	35.4
Transport	11.4	10.4	8.5	9.2	13.5	11.7	13.1	7.2
Total A	65.6	60.2	55.1	52.3	59.3	53.9	58.8	42.6
Agriculture	8.7	10.2	8.1	12.1	8.7	13.6	12.8	22.9
Light industry	4.8	7.0	5.9	9.2	8.7	4.6	3.1	5.8
Commerce	0.8	1.0	1.3	1.7	3.7	4.3	2.2	3.5
Total B	14.3	18.2	15.3	23.0	21.1	22.5	18.1	32.2
Housing	13.0	15.2	16.1	14.4	10.8	13.3	5.0	10.1
Administrative and social investment	7.0	6.3	4.7	4.0	8.7	10.3	8.5	11.6
Total C	20.0	21.5	20.8	18.4	19.5	23.6	13.5	21.7

Source: *Etude sur la situation économique de l'Europe en 1955*, pp. 268–76. The distribution is not always exhaustive (% total is sometimes less than 100).

(independently even of any new change in the hierarchy of priorities). The question was more acute in the people's democracies where the restructuring of investment had gone hand in hand with a sudden drop in the total volume of investment. In Hungary, particularly, the halting of several prestige projects (such as the Budapest underground) was not enough to avoid the proliferation of bottlenecks. In several sectors, the reorganisation of production was reflected in 1954 in a temporary drop in production and productivity. More balanced growth was subsequently established, but at a price: 'Our present difficulties,' wrote a former president of the central planning commission in 1954,[2] 'are partly the price that we have to pay for having pursued a great power policy: Hungary, "country of iron and steel". . . . This excessive industrialisation and our neglect of agriculture have cost our national economy its natural equilibrium, which it will now be difficult to re-establish.'

3 The new direction of economic policy could not fail to increase the importance of foreign trade. The exaggeratedly autarchic character of earlier development had been the subject of criticism even in the USSR. Foreign trade was to make an immediate and active contribution to the revival of agriculture, to the development of light industry and, even more directly, to the improvement of the standard of living, through increased imports of capital goods, of raw materials and other means of production (e.g. fertilisers), as well as consumer goods (e.g. tropical foodstuffs). Although the 'programme' thus outlined was only partially put into practice, for various reasons, the 'new direction' of 1953 was immediately reflected in the development of foreign trade.

In the first instance, the terms of trade between the USSR and its partners were readjusted in favour of the people's democracies. The East German economy was the main, but not the only, beneficiary; from August 1953, an agreement with the USSR put an end to war reparations, which enabled East Germany sharply to increase its 'commercial' exports (by more than 60 per cent in 1954) and, as a result, its imports.

On the other hand, the USSR accepted a certain renewal of the traditional trade links between East and West Europe, although she herself had more reservations than most of the people's democracies about following this path. At that time, Poland and, particularly, Hungary were the two countries which went furthest in re-establishing trade with the capitalist countries; in 1955, the USSR's share in the total of Hungarian foreign trade had fallen to 22 per cent, compared with 39 per cent for trade with the West. The increase in hard currency trade was generally accompanied by a trade deficit and a worsening of the terms of trade with the West.

The 'new direction' of 1953 contained several lessons. It confirmed the very strong influence of the central authorities in the short term on the standard of living of the population; the fact that the various 'trend indicators' tally is revealing in this respect. However, government decisions are themselves taken in a political context: the more vulnerable the regimes feel, the more substantial are the concessions. But it soon appeared that any lasting readjustment in favour of consumption had a much higher cost (e.g. in terms of the reduction in military expenditure or the temporary slowing down of growth) than had first been thought. The new FYPs drawn up for 1956–60 bore witness to the governments' reluctance to go any further in this direction.

The upheaval of 1956

1 There is a characteristic dissymmetry in the economic policy cycles of the socialist countries: the swings in favour of consumption are publicly orchestrated and thus easily spotted; swings in the opposite direction are much more discreet and often less clear. This was the case in 1955.

It is true that the plans for 1956–60 did not mark a return pure and simple to the options of the Stalinist period. The movement towards less tight planning, for example, tended to be strengthened: growth targets were less ambitious than those of previous plans, and were even lower than the results announced for the five-year period from 1951 to 1955; a great effort was to be made to build up stocks.

But in two areas, the hardening of the line in comparison with the 'new direction' of 1953 was very marked.

Firstly, in Czechoslovakia, East Germany and Rumania, the level of investment once again began to rise more quickly than national income – which meant a fresh increase in its share in the total of final uses; there was the same trend in the USSR (where the relative weight of investment had, however, tended to increase after 1953). The setting up of the Warsaw Pact in 1955 gave rise, at the same time, to plans for military budgets to begin growing again. The structure of planned investment hardly confirmed the reorientation of 1953: in the USSR, for example, the share of heavy industry in total investment was to rise still further in comparison with the average for the years 1951–5 (and, *a fortiori*, with 1954–5); while the share of agriculture was to continue to increase somewhat, a relative decrease was planned for housing. Two countries, Hungary and Poland, were exceptions to the general trend: their plans provided for moderate growth in investment (lower than that in national income), and in general confirmed the relative priority given to agriculture, light industry and housing since 1953. The Hungarian plan, in particular, was reminiscent in several respects of the initial draft of the first plan (1950–4), which was much less 'voluntarist' than the final version which had been revised under pressure from the USSR.

In another area, however, all the people's democracies announced comparable intentions almost simultaneously: the process of agricultural collectivisation was shortly to be relaunched. Under the Hungarian plan, for example, the area farmed by the co-operatives was to be doubled, and in Poland it was to be tripled. This programme had already begun in the early months of 1956, and this obviously helps to explain the events of October in Poland and Hungary.

2 The Polish and Hungarian uprisings were not the result of a further short-term worsening of material living conditions, but must both be seen in the context of the incomplete and precarious process of de-Stalinisation. The political elements of the problem were in any case different in the two countries, as also was the outcome. Nevertheless, there were also strong similarities.

Less industrialised than Czechoslovakia and East Germany, but less exclusively agricultural than Bulgaria and Rumania, the Hungarian and Polish economies accumulated all the characteristic imbalances of the Stalinist period. Their first plans, particularly in the case of Hungary, were to bring them close to the leading group, taking all the short cuts necessary. At the beginning of the 1950s, both countries were confronted by a series of new problems linked to their rapid industrialisation. These included overcrowding in the large urban centres, a worsening of the food balance and the need to export a growing proportion of the production of their engineering industries. However, the problems of rural over-population and the shortage of skilled labour – due to the lack of traditional industries – improved only slowly. The effects of the giant investment programmes on the standard of living were particularly harsh.

It was in Hungary from 1953–4 onwards that the political will to break with the Stalinist-type economy was most forcibly asserted. The drive to restructure caused additional very acute short-term difficulties in certain sectors, while it was proving a long and difficult task to reduce the disproportions inherited from the past. And both Hungary and Poland, while limiting their investment, felt more than any other country the need to turn towards Western Europe and to balance their foreign trade again. The concerns of the Soviet government faced with this 'centrifugal' development can be easily imagined.

But it was particularly the imminence of agricultural collectivisation that precipitated the events. In Poland, the peasants' attachment to individual farming had already, in the post-war period, made it necessary to share out the large estates, and put a more effective brake than anywhere else on the development of co-operatives. In Hungary, the partial decollectivisation of 1953, accompanied by incentives for small-scale private agriculture, had given rise to hopes which were then brutally challenged. It is true that in the autumn of 1956 the spread of co-operatives was very limited in Poland, whereas in Hungary the collective sector had returned to the level of 1953: in both countries, the peasant uprising occurred at the very moment that a decisive threshold was about to be crossed.

3 Despite the contrast between the Soviet repression in Budapest and the almost unanimous support enjoyed by Gomulka in Poland, the development of the two countries after 1956 was in many respects parallel. While co-operatives were almost totally split up in Poland, Hungary immediately undertook a process of decollectivisation that was even wider in scope than in 1953 (at the beginning of 1957, only 2,089 co-operatives were left of the 5,191 there had been in the autumn of 1956); it was only two years later, in 1958, that the two agricultural systems began to develop in different directions. The contrast in foreign relations was more marked: the Polish government agreed to accept American credit, and continued to develop trade with the West (its share in total Polish trade rose from 37 per cent in 1955 to 45 per cent in 1958, a proportion which had not been equalled in a communist country since the war); the Hungarian government, on the other hand, immediately had to apply the brake (the share of trade with the West went down from 39 per cent in 1955 to 33 per cent in 1958). However, both Poland and Hungary also received in 1957 considerable Soviet credit, which enabled them to recover from the shock of 1956 much quicker than expected (after two months of almost total paralysis in Hungary). The other people's democracies also received considerable benefits from the USSR at the same time (debts were written off, prices readjusted and, in particular, fresh credit granted): whereas in 1955 most of them had a trade surplus with the USSR (which could be interpreted as a draining off of goods), in 1957, the USSR massively increased its exports to the people's democracies, particularly of basic foodstuffs.

The upheaval of 1956 had an effect on economic policies comparable to that of the death of Stalin in 1953. Hungary abandoned its FYP and cut back its investment programmes still further. In 1956-7, the Polish government publicly laid the blame on the excessive burden of arms expenditure for the persistently low standard of living. The Polish medium-term plan was thoroughly restructured: the new version laid emphasis in all respects on accentuating the priorities introduced in 1953. The events of 1956 also had indirect repercussions on East Germany and Czechoslovakia: agricultural collectivisation was halted for a time; the short- and medium-term plans were modified, although to a lesser extent, in order to increase the housing programme. It is impossible not to bring out the symbolic contrast with the fate of the first FYPs, which were revised at the time of the Korean War with the aim of strengthening still further the priority given to heavy industry.

4 The period 1953-8, taken as a whole, can be contrasted with the Stalinist period in terms of the general increase in the standard of living and the rapid, if not always regular increase in the overall level of real wages and of peasants' incomes. All the socialist economies – even, relatively speaking, the USSR – became more 'open'; for two countries, Poland and the USSR, trade with the West in 1958 reached or exceeded the volume of trade in 1938. Within each national economy, most of the fundamental imbalances stopped growing more acute.

The recovery of agriculture in the USSR appears impressive, at least in quantitative terms: if the average for 1955-7 is compared with that for 1951-3 (even without taking into account the record harvest of 1958), the index of Soviet agricultural production increased by 35 per cent, which is comparable to that of French agricultural production between 1905-13 and 1955-8 (+ 37 per cent in half a century). It is true that the increase in grain production was partly illusory, to the extent that it was the result of the opening up of the 'virgin lands' (which were to be exhausted rapidly after a few years). However, the regeneration of livestock, the improved yields and the general effects of greater incentives for the peasants also contributed greatly to the progress achieved. In the people's democracies, on the other hand, agricultural results remained at best mediocre: in Czechoslovakia and East Germany, the average grain harvest (1955-7) was less than the average for 1934-8; and in four countries (Hungary, Bulgaria, Czechoslovakia and East Germany), the number of cattle decreased between 1953 and 1957, which, of course, was not unconnected with the prospect of collectivisation.

In about 1958, the socialist countries found themselves faced with a series of important decisions. A solution was required for three problems, among others: the problem of the structure of agriculture (which after all had hardly changed since the end of the Stalinist period, either in the USSR or in the people's democracies), the problem of basic investment (in the energy sector, building materials and the chemical industry), essential for maintaining or re-establishing steady growth, and – already – the problem of reforms likely to ensure that the system of planned management functioned more efficiently, and with it, the socialist economy as a whole.

The reaffirmation of economic 'voluntarism' (1958-64)

Although the hardening of policy which began in 1958 did not explicitly call into question the policy of raising the standard of living, it was very obvious – sometimes even brutally obvious – in all areas (agricultural and investment policy and foreign relations). It reflected, to a variable degree, both the undamaged confidence of the leaders in the traditional development strategy, and also the weight of structural constraints: the limits of readjustment in favour of consumption that were possible within the framework of the plan in force had been reached in about 1957 (for several years, the increase in real wages had exceeded that in production); without a new expansion in investment, bottlenecks and imbalances of all sorts were bound to multiply. The return to the systematic fixing of very ambitious targets in the plans drawn up in about 1958 (beginning with the Soviet seven-year plan for 1959-65) was symptomatic: it enabled the foreseeable implications of the fundamental decisions of 1958 for the subsequent development of the standard of living to be avoided, at least on paper.

1 Firstly, the years 1957-8 marked a crucial turning point in agricultural policies.

The policy of gradual collectivisation (which had the effect of discouraging private investment in agriculture, and led to an awkward coexistence between individual and collective farmers) without doubt created the most unfavourable possible conditions for agricultural production. Thus the governments decided almost simultaneously to give a decisive push to the process. At the beginning of 1957, the private agricultural sector was the larger one in all the people's democracies, except Bulgaria; barely four years later, at the end of 1960, 90 per cent of the agriculture sector in every country had been collectivised (with the exception of Poland, of course), an achievement clearly in advance of the 'programme' decided on in 1955, despite the interruption caused by the events of 1956. The mode of enforcement was different from country to country, being relatively flexible in East Germany and Rumania, and markedly more rigid in Bulgaria, Hungary and Czechoslovakia. Nowhere, however, did collectivisation lead to violence comparable with that seen in the Soviet countryside. It was accompanied by a rapid increase in agricultural investment (partly to meet the demands of collectivisation – the building of collective stables, for example – and consequently without any direct effect on production), and an increase in the materials and equipment (tractors, fertilisers) available to agriculture. On the other hand, the increase in the peasants' incomes was on the whole very mediocre throughout this critical phase, particularly in Hungary and Czechoslovakia until the beginning of the 1960s.

This is in striking contrast to Poland, where the peasants succeeded in retaining a largely dominant private agricultural sector. The evolution in the first few years after 1956 was favourable: the peasants built up their livestock and increased their investment; they enjoyed a certain improvement in the terms of trade, and their incomes increased. But the situation worsened gradually at the beginning of the 1960s. The government intended to put a brake on the rise in agricultural prices and incomes. On the other hand, they were encouraging the development of agricultural organisations designed to provide a stock of materials for collective use, and which were generally thought to be the 'vanguards' of a new socialist transformation of the countryside. But this attempt at 'gradual socialism by the tractor' came up against the general mistrust of the peasants. By about 1965 it had obviously failed. The splitting up of farms (average size 6.7 ha.) was an insurmountable handicap. Polish agriculture was outstripped by all the other socialist countries – even Rumania, despite its initial delay – in the degree of mechanisation: the retention of two to three million draught horses was both an anachronism and a heavy burden for a country with a serious grain deficit.

The problems of Soviet agriculture were radically different.

On the basis of results obtained in previous years, Khrushchev estimated that 'it will not be long before (Soviet agriculture) is producing large surpluses' (*Izvestia*, 28 March 1958). Anticipating future progress, and stressing that from then on considerations of efficiency would be paramount, he had adopted in the spring of 1958 an agricultural reform of unprecedented significance. At first sight, it simply involved the abolition of the two key institutions of the Stalinist period: the Machine Tractor Stations (MTS) and the system of compulsory deliveries. The *kolkhozy* were to buy back the equipment held by the MTS and to take charge of the management (and financing) of the equipment. The abolition of the compulsory low price deliveries was part of a complete recasting of production prices and the collection system. The reform in no way implied that deliveries would cease to be planned by directive, but only that purchase prices would be standardised by the state, at an intermediate level between the prices applied respectively to compulsory deliveries and sales over and above the quota. Moreover, the agricultural price structure was modified in order to reflect more accurately the structure of production costs: one of the aims of the reform was to encourage, on the basis of the new prices, more rational specialisation on the part of the *kolkhozy*: however, the differences in profitability between products were still far from being eliminated (despite the growing strength of the needs to be satisfied, milk and meat paradoxically remained the least profitable products), and it was consequently out of the question, at least immediately, to let the *kolkhozy* themselves decide on the orientation of their production. The final stipulation was that agricultural prices would henceforth be both stable (in the medium term) and flexible (in the short term: higher in years of bad harvest than in years of good harvest), in such a way as to regulate the peasants' incomes.

The true significance of the 1959 reform was not immediately clear, but it soon turned out to be rather different from what had been thought. In June 1958, Khrushchev made an unequivocal announcement of his intention to limit the increase in the overall cost of purchasing agricultural products for the state; the new prices were then fixed at a very moderate average level, taking into account that the harvest promised to be excellent. The additional revenue was to be used in part to finance, in addition to the initial purchasing of the MTS stock, a rapid growth of agricultural investment, of which more than two thirds was now to be the responsibility of the *kolkhozy*: it really seemed, moreover, that this transfer of burdens, which meant large savings for the state, was in fact one of the main aims of the reform. Given these conditions, the peasants made less personal profit from the record harvest of 1958 than if there had been no reform. From 1957 to 1958, the average payment per workday rose by only 6.5 per cent, and the overall amount of payments to the *kolkhozniks* by 19 per cent (compared with an increase of 45 per cent for the production expenses of the *kolkhozy*, and 70 per cent in the payments to their investment funds). However modest this increase might have been, the authorities concluded from it that it was no longer advisable to 'favour' the peasants: from now on, the increases in their income were to be in line with the rest of the population. And, above all, it was calculated that the peasants would be increasingly able to do without the additional income from their individual plots: 1958 saw the beginning of a new offensive to reduce the amount of private livestock and the area of the private plots.

In fact, the average income of the *kolkhozniks* stagnated in absolute terms for several years, until 1961 (it even went down in certain regions), while the government continued to put pressure on the *kolkhozy* to increase their investment to the maximum. This period is, therefore, one of the clearest examples of the action of the 'law of inverse correlation': any agricultural recovery rebounds, in the medium term, against the interests of the peasants! The consequent damage to the national economy is, in the final analysis, considerable. The inadequacy of the *kolkhozniks*' income, despite all the pressures, had an effect from 1960 onwards, on the level of investment,[3] and it was the state which, little by little, had to take over: in 1961, it once again assumed responsibility for more than half of agricultural investment, contrary to the initial target. Transforming the poorest *kolkhozy* into *sovkhozy*, in order to give those concerned a guaranteed wage, was an even heavier burden for the state. On the other hand, no increase in the prices fixed in 1958 was granted for several years, which meant that it was impossible to restore adequate incentives for many products. The government did not decide to do this until 1962 onwards (for meat, in particular), especially after the catastrophic harvest of 1963 (conforming once again to the 'law of inverse correlation', which this time acted in favour of the peasants). But this turnabout was too late to prevent the agricultural situation from worsening throughout this period, and in 1965 a new series of much more substantial concessions was to become necessary.

2 The evolution of investment policy as a whole also went through contrasting stages.

The plans for 1956-60 generally had to be abandoned prematurely, and replaced by a new series of seven-year (in the USSR and East Germany) and five-year plans, providing for the simultaneous launching of several large investment projects, as if the slowing down of the previous phase had to be urgently compensated for. The three years 1958, 1959 and 1960 were thus marked by a new leap forward in investment almost comparable to that of the first FYPs (the annual growth rates range from 11 per cent for Poland, and 27 per cent for Bulgaria). The burden of this investment was to be all the heavier since military expenditure had also begun to increase very rapidly once again at the beginning of the 1960s.

In the USSR, the investment drive was maintained, with some hiccups (the overexpansion of 1961), and despite a certain deceleration at the end of the period, throughout the whole duration of the plan. The overall target fixed for the level of investment was almost reached, but at the price of considerable divergences from the planned structure. Compared with the 1956-60 plan, the priorities of the seven-year plan were fairly clearly investment in agriculture (21.4 per cent of the total instead of 18.3 per cent) and in housing (16.4 per cent instead of 14.7 per cent). The evolution was very different, and particularly uneven.

Table 3.2 *Distribution of investment (1955-65)*

	1955	1958	1959–61	1962–4	1965
Industry	41.5	37.4	38.8	39.8	39.6
Sector A	37.0	32.5	33.8	35.3	35.0
Sector B	4.5	4.9	5.0	4.5	4.6
Transport	7.8	7.5	8.4	9.3	10.0
Agriculture	19.1	15.8	14.6	17.1	18.2
Housing	19.1	25.1	21.5	17.8	16.7
Services; social and administrative investment	12.5	14.2	16.7	16.0	15.5

Sources: JEC, 1970, p. 54; JEC, 1964, pp. 41-2; *Etude sur la situation économique de l'Europe en 1966*, ch. 2, p. 35.

The most significant evolution was that of housing. Initial progress was rapid: in 1959, for the first time, the construction of new houses passed the three million per year mark, and the targets of the seven-year plan seemed on the way to being exceeded. In fact, there was a sudden break about 1960-1. Time after time, the construction targets in successive annual plans, despite being adjusted downwards, could not be met (there was a 16 per cent deficit in 1961 and 1962), and there was an absolute decrease in the number of units finished up until 1964. Although it was not a deliberate decision, it became necessary, as soon as it was obvious that the plan as a whole could not be realised, to sacrifice 'unproductive' investment to the needs of basic industries on which the sustaining of growth depended (as did military potential). A more detailed analysis of the investment in industry confirms this impression of rigidity. Three sectors alone – energy, iron and steel, and engineering – still absorbed more than half of total industrial investment (88 per cent for all heavy industry). The priority given to the chemical industry, which was a long way behind other heavy industry in its development, took many years to take shape, it did so, however, about 1963, while the modest progress in food and light industries towards the end of the 1950s gave way within a few years, as for housing, to another relative decline.

Yet the results obtained in the USSR, however unfavourable they might be for those sectors supplying consumption, were nothing in comparison with the dreadful crisis which was then hitting the Czechoslovakian economy, and to a lesser extent, that of East Germany. After several years of rapidly increasing immobilisation of resources, the chronic problems caused by committing funds to a large number of building projects and the lengthening of construction deadlines, the mechanisms of which have already been analysed, became more acute. In fact, from 1959 onwards, the reappearance of frequent shortages of the means of production (cement, energy), and the general shortage of manpower[4] (particularly in the construction industry), clearly indicated that a decisive threshold was about to be crossed. Instead of taking measures in time, the governments reacted with a sort of headlong flight. The East German plan for 1962 did not provide for any slowing down in the rate of new building sites being started and still reserved 30 per cent of the investment fund for new projects to be started within the year. In Czechoslovakia, the government at first merely put a brake on the decentralised investment that had resulted from the reforms of 1959, whereas it was large-scale centralised investment that was largely responsible for the imbalances. When the reasonable decision to concentrate efforts on completing the most urgent projects had at last been taken, it ran into a whole series of problems – the rapid transfer of available resources, the precise co-ordination of building work and deliveries of equipment – that the centralised economy was particularly ill-equipped to solve. From 1962 onwards, it was obvious that the then current plans could not be realised: in 1963, the Czech national income fell in absolute terms. A period of restructuring, spread over several years, then started for the East German and Czech economies. Thus it was not by chance that East Germany introduced the series of economic reforms of the 1960s; partly for this reason, it succeeded in recovering from the crisis quicker than Czechoslovakia.

Apart from a few small differences, the other less industrialised socialist countries experienced similar problems, although to varying degrees. Except right at the beginning of the period, the policy of the Polish government was in no way more favourable towards the standard of living.

3 The change of direction in comparison with the 1953–8 period can also be seen in the evolution of foreign trade.

All the countries, except Hungary and Rumania, planned to check the increase in their foreign trade in comparison with the trend of previous years. Three countries, the USSR, Czechoslovakia and Poland, even had a growth target for their foreign trade that was lower than that for NMP, which implied a reduction in the openness of their economies. No doubt the caution of the people's democracies can be explained by their difficulties with their balance of payments and by their concern to limit their indebtedness towards the West. But there was also a political desire to increase the degree of self-sufficiency of the socialist economies.

The four countries which provide indications of the geo-political structure of their foreign trade, Poland included, all planned for a fresh increase in the share of the socialist market.

Table 3.3 *Composition of total foreign trade (1958–65)*

	1958		1965 (planned targets)	
	Eastern market	Western market	Eastern market	Western market
Czechoslovakia	71	29	75	25
GDR	72	28	76	24
Hungary	68	32	75	25
Poland	55	45	65	35

The breakdown of trade by product confirms the traditional orientations. The share of consumer goods was to fall once again: despite its low relative weight, this non-priority item was the first to suffer the reductions necessary to bring out the balance of payments into equality again.

There were many divergences between the actual and the planned evolution. The sudden interruption of trade with China (although as late as 1959 it was still planned to expand greatly) seriously affected East Germany and, particularly, Czechoslovakia, by depriving them of an important outlet and an essential source of supply. The general deterioration in agriculture at the beginning of the 1960s – including

Table 3.4 *Share of consumer goods in total imports (1958-65)*

	Czechoslovakia		Hungary		Poland		GDR	
	1958	1965	1958	1965	1958	1965	1958	1965
Foodstuffs	25	16	9	5	12	12		
Manufactured							31	23
consumer goods	4	1	5	5	8	5		

Source: *Etude sur la situation économique de l'Europe en 1959*, p. 52, with additional information for Hungary and GDR from *Bulletin économique pour l'Europe*, 1, 1962, p. 59. Percentages for Czechoslovakia refer only to imports from socialist countries.

in the USSR – was reflected in the balance of trade in food for each country and for Eastern Europe as a whole. Trade with the West, which became more and more necessary for all the countries of the group, including Bulgaria, began to increase quite quickly towards the end of the period. Overall, the volume of foreign trade increased more quickly than had been forecast, and the openness of the various socialist economies increased without exception between 1958 and 1965.

However, despite these divergences, there is a striking determination about the attempts of the communist governments, in more difficult circumstances than anticipated, to stick to the broad policy orientations outlined at the beginning of the period. The brake on trade with the capitalist countries, announced in the plans, was indeed put into effect. For East Germany this was a fundamental political decision (1961 was the year of the construction of the Berlin Wall) that the government was prepared to put into operation at all costs. Developments in Poland were less abrupt, but also resulted in a loosening of links with the West.

The general adherence to the traditional priorities and the primacy given to the mechanical engineering industries within the Comecon framework[5] were reflected in the development of trade in capital goods. In 1965, this heading accounted for 38 per cent of the reciprocal trade of the Comecon countries; the most recently industrialised countries, such as Bulgaria, became in their turn considerable exporters of machinery, while the traditional exporters, such as Czechoslovakia, had to look for distant outlets in the Third World.

Faced with the consequences of the agricultural deficit, all the governments tried to balance the inevitable increase in imports of basic products (on top of the vital imports of raw materials) with restrictions on 'less necessary' products, such as butter and meat, for which East Germany, for example, reintroduced rationing. At the same time, certain agricultural exports to Western Europe were maintained as far as possible, in order to finance the purchase of the means of production most essential for technical modernisation.

Foreign trade policy thus became more 'voluntarist' in nature in comparison with the 1953-7 period. Its general orientation was compatible with the other aspects of economic policy.

4 However, economic 'voluntarism' in no way implied that all the planned objectives were 'defended' with the same energy. The contrast with the preceding period, already foreshadowed in the plans, becomes even clearer if the *ex post* development is considered. The best aggregate indicator of this was the sudden slowing down in the increase in real wages, that the statistics do not even attempt to hide. The development of peasant income was no more favourable.

Table 3.5 *Evolution of the average annual growth rate of real wages (1952-64)*

	1952-7	1957-61	1961-4
USSR	5	3	1.5
Czechoslovakia	5	4.5	0.5
GDR	9.5	6.5	1.5
Poland	7	1.5	1.5
Hungary	11.5	2.5	3
Rumania	8	5	4
Bulgaria	11	3	1

Source: *Les revenus dans l'Europe d'après-guerre*, United Nations, Economic Commission for Europe, Geneva, 1969.

It would no doubt be absurd to see in this a deliberate decision – but it was a consequence of the basic economic policy options. These options were initially hidden to a certain extent by the systematic fixing of overambitious targets: while each individual target could be achieved, the overall target was unrealistic. It was as if it had been decided to meet needs of all kinds at the same time (consumption, housing, productive investment, defence), even if it meant putting intolerable pressure on available resources. Decisions on competing targets had been put off as long as possible. When they became inescapable, the government had to make some extremely difficult decisions, which help to reveal even more clearly than the text of the plans the true hierarchy of priorities (except in the case of general economic disorganisation, such as in Hungary in 1956 or in Czechoslovakia in 1963). The development of the Soviet economy is both representative and particularly clear.

The major fact is not the drop in the overall growth rate, which was

Table 3.6 *Evolution of the growth rate of principal final uses of Soviet GNP (1950–64)*

	1950–8	1958–64
Private consumption	7.2	3.8
Public (civil) consumption	5.2	6.2
National defence	−2.8	6.3
Fixed productive investment	12.0	9.4
Housing	18.0	−0.3
GNP	7.1	5.3

Source: S. H. Cohn, 'Soviet growth retardation: trends in resource availability and efficiency', in JEC, 1966, p. 99.

the main preoccupation of the leaders, but the much more marked drop in private consumption and house-building after a fairly brief period of recovery. And it is impossible not to wonder about the long-term significance of growth which does not lead to final needs being better satisfied.

This persistent discrepancy can be partly explained by circumstances particular to each period. The short-term repercussions of collectivisation in rural areas and the mistakes in agricultural policy, which resulted everywhere in an unprecedented failure to meet planned targets, no doubt played an important role, but the main explanation lies in the permanent elements of inefficiency that are inherent in the centralised model and that have already been identified.

Decentralising reforms and the process of recentralisation

Two very different types of reforms were introduced in about 1957–8. In the USSR, the 1957 reform created an intermediate decision-making level of administration: these were the *sovnarkhozy*,[6] or regional planning authorities. The Polish, Hungarian and Czechoslovakian reforms, on the other hand, set out to increase the enterprises' freedom of action, while at the same time guiding them by the use of 'economic levers' (incentive rules, prices and financial methods).

The two types of reforms are grouped together here, despite their different inspiration, because they have their origin in the same fundamental problems, which follow directly from the application of the same model: all the Soviet-type economies suffer both from the overloading of the central agencies of economic management, and from the stifling of local initiative. None of these reforms, however, called into question the centralised model. But despite their limited scope, they met with growing resistance on all sides. They are thus an excellent area in which to study the processes of recentralisation that inevitably follow any attempt at partial decentralisation in a Soviet-type economy.

Regional administrative decentralisation: the sovnarkhozy *reform (1957-65)*

1 The *sovnarkhozy* reform, accomplished in a few months in 1957 without any prior discussion, bears the hallmark of one of Khrushchev's improvisations. The prime motive was undoubtedly political. Faced with adversaries (Malenkov, Kaganovich) who relied for support on the staff of the central administrative agencies, Khrushchev planned to obtain the support of the party officials in the regions. The industrial ministries, which until then had been the mainstay of the system of economic management, were abolished. A planning system based on regional planning replaced a system based on the functional principle. The boundaries of the *sovnarkhozy* were drawn in a way that coincided approximately with the regional political organisation at the level of the '*oblast*'. This is why there were so many of them (104), and why they were restricted in size.[7]

However, there was no lack of technical justification for the reform. The old system took little account of the spatial dimension of planning problems. The setting up of transport programmes had been rejected at the final stage of the drawing up of the plan, as if transport costs were a minor variable in an economy of the size of the USSR. The transport networks, overloaded by the to-ing and fro-ing of goods across the USSR, had been functioning at the limits of their capacities, with frequent bottlenecks. Moreover, the gradual exhaustion of the reserves of labour required more precise co-ordination of the establishment of new factories according to the natural and human resources available on the spot. In particular, however, it was the 'autarchic tendencies' of the ministries, the abuses of power by the most powerful among them, and the obstacles to specialisation that were justifiably called into question.

The *sovnarkhoz* reform in no way changed the basic mechanisms of economic management. But it did imply, at least in its initial version, real decentralisation – although limited and quickly called into question – of certain decision-making powers, to the benefit of the regional political authorities.

From the point of view of the enterprise the transfer of supervision from the ministry to the *sovnarkhoz* made it subject to even greater constraints. Although the management methods were the same, the physical proximity of the supervisory authority made controls and direct interventions easier. Despite the complaints of those concerned, there was an increase in the number of changes made to targets even as the enterprise was attempting to fulfil them. The result was greater flexibility, but to the detriment of incentive.

However, the fact that centralisation (within each *sovnarkhoz*) took place within a limited framework alleviated some of the disadvantages of Soviet-type planning. The regional planner was able to carry out direct comparisons between enterprises, instead of being forced always to work at a high level of aggregation and to fix *a priori* targets for each sector as a whole. Some *sovnarkhozy* tried in particular to encourage better utilisation of available resources to the benefit of the region, and to bring production more into line with local demand.

But the success of the reform depended above all on establishing a balance between national and regional planning, and it was the problem of inter-regional trade that constituted the stumbling block.

2 By about 1957–8, there is no doubt that decentralisation had gone further than planned. The creation of the *sovnarkhozy* and the abolition of the industrial ministries had the immediate effect of weakening the centralised management system. The *sovnarkhozy* were officially given the right to redistribute capital goods and investment funds within their region. The result can be judged by the criticisms that were immediately levelled at the *sovnarkhozy*: they cared only about the interests of their own regions and diverted the resources put under their control for the satisfaction of local needs, to the detriment of deliveries to other *sovnarkhozy*. The common accusation of '*mestnichevsto*' (particularism or localism) vividly sums up this criticism.

In response, however, the rights of the *sovnarkhozy* began immediately to be eroded. A decree of April 1958 ordered them to give priority to extra-regional deliveries. This apparently had no effect, since the injunction had to be repeated a year later, in May 1959. At the same time, fourteen central agencies, attached to Gosplan, were created, in order to administer inter-republic deliveries.

Since it proved impossible to eliminate completely the autarchic tendencies of the *sovnarkhozy*, attempts were also made to correct the initial error of making them too small. The initial aim was to strengthen the intermediate decision-making levels between the *sovnarkhozy* and the central planning authorities.

In 1960, *sovnarkhozy* were created at the republic level in Russia, the Ukraine and Kazakhstan, in order to co-ordinate the activities of the *sovnarkhozy* within their jurisdiction. In May 1961, seventeen 'major economic regions' were added to the existing organisations, in order to serve as a framework for long-term planning and for large-scale regional development projects. A much more logical decision was the reduction, at last, of the number of *sovnarkhozy* from 104 to 47 in November 1962.

The final period of the *sovnarkhozy* was characterised above all by the gradual re-establishment of the system of central organisation by sector. Little by little, but particularly from 1963 onwards, a certain number of state committees regained part of the powers of the old ministries. These included co-ordination (particularly of technological development) and, increasingly, planning and even the day-to-day management of certain enterprises which were directly attached to them. Gosstroj (the state building committee), for example, behaved both like a 'functional' agency, responsible for investment in all sectors, and as a 'sectoral' agency, with building firms directly answerable to it.

The multiplication of sectoral or functional co-ordinating agencies required, in its turn, a new co-ordination effort at the top. The *sovnarkhoz* in the USSR, which had been created in the 1962 reorganisation, had inherited the tasks of the day-to-day management and control of the centralised supply system, but planning proper (the responsibility of Gosplan) and construction (the responsibility of Gosstroj) remained outside its jurisdiction. The creation of the Supreme National Economic Council (VSNKh) in March 1963 marked the completion of the upper part of the pyramid.

At this stage, it was no longer only the excessively strict supervision carried out by the *sovnarkhoz* which was paralysing enterprises, but more particularly the inconsistent instructions emanating from all the authorities to which it was simultaneously answerable. A manager of a telephone enterprise complained of receiving orders at the same time from the regional sector management, from the *sovnarkhoz*, from the *sovnarkhoz* of the Republic of Russia and from the Gosplan of the USSR, 'without counting five state committees, two federal ministries, and so on and so on. Each one thinks that the enterprise must function according to their own plan'.[8]

It did not take long for this situation to be judged untenable: the abolition of the *sovnarkhozy* and the complete re-establishment of sectoral organisation by ministries introduced the economic reform of September 1965. The only lasting legacy of the *sovnarkhoz* reform was the concern to integrate transport and regional planning (with the division into eighteen major economic regions) more closely into the drawing up of the national plan. The interlude of failed regional decentralisation thus led, at the very moment when the reform of the enterprise was starting, to renewed development of centralised planning. In retrospect, the main lesson of the *sovnarkhoz* experiment was to show that the autarchic behaviour of which the ministries had been accused in about 1957, as were the *sovnarkhozy* several years later, is in fact inherent in any intermediate agency in a Soviet-type economy: any attack on the primacy of the central plan thus contains serious risks, which might often cause the reforms to be challenged.

Economic decentralisation: the Polish, Hungarian and Czechoslovakian reforms

The reforms of the end of the 1950s fit into the political history of each country in different ways. Those in Hungary and Czechoslovakia passed almost unnoticed by Western observers, while the 'liberalisation' of the Polish regime, on the other hand, was largely overestimated. Nevertheless, the content of the economic reforms was really very similar in all three countries; their limits were the same, and their fate was very similar, although there were slight differences which helped to determine developments in the 1960s.

1 At the outset, of course, the historical context was radically different in the three countries. Whereas the Czechoslovakian leaders maintained their positions, the new Polish regime enjoyed the general support of the population and seemed synonymous with national renaissance, radical criticism of the Stalinist past and the opening up of the country to the West. Hungary was occupied by Soviet troops and underwent an almost immediate process of 'normalisation'; the efforts of the Kadar government to limit the repression could not prevent the execution of Imre Nagy, in violation of official promises.

However, with the passing years (or even months), the difference became less marked. The fate of the workers' councils, which appeared spontaneously in the large enterprises in Poland and Hungary in the autumn of 1956, illustrates this paradoxical convergence. They survived in Hungary for a short time, and helped to organise a sort of passive resistance[9] until the end of 1956; their elimination at the beginning of

1957 marked the consolidation of the regime. In Poland, a law of November 1956 gave the workers' councils legal status, which helped them to spread. But the deliberate ambiguity of the status given to them made it possible gradually to take back their rights in the months that followed. In the spring of 1958, when the workers' councils were integrated into the 'conferences for worker self-management', which were dominated by the party apparatus, the nature of the institution was completely changed and the experiment sank among general indifference. Thus the only basic original feature in Poland remained the reprieve granted *sine die* to private agriculture, which did not prevent, as we have seen, a gradual hardening of the policies towards the peasants.

2 In Poland, the ground was prepared for the reform by a phase of intense discussions among economists, to which the government gave an official framework by calling together the 'economic model commission' (autumn 1956-spring 1957). The debate was very free: references to the Yugoslavian model were made without any problems,[10] whereas they were to be in general tacitly excluded in subsequent discussions in the countries of the Soviet bloc.

A whole economic movement, centred around S. Kurowski and J. Popkiewicz, took as its starting point a radical condemnation of the economic policy of the Stalinist period. In an article entitled 'The model and the ends',[11] Kurowski attempted to show that the deterioration of the prices system, hypercentralisation and political repression were a direct result of the desire to impose a production structure contrary to the preferences of consumers: it was the ends (the priority given to the development of armaments and heavy industry) that dictated the means. Thus any reversal of economic policy, to be oriented in the future towards satisfying consumer demand, had to go hand in hand with the setting up of a new model based almost exclusively on the free play of market mechanisms.

This determination to eliminate or to minimise the role of central planning did not gain the support of the majority of Polish economists, starting with the most influential, Lange, Kalecki and Brus. The analyses of Brus, which clearly heralded the notion of the decentralised model, can be considered the most representative. For him, it was only the need to relieve central planning of the impossible task of taking all micro-economic decisions and having them carried out by directives that made it essential to recast the model. The aim was to put the plan into practice by means of decentralised decisions taken by enterprises. The market was thus no longer to be considered as the antithesis of planning, but as a normal means (*the* normal means) of making the interests of the enterprise and those of the national economy compatible with each other, by automatically punishing all production not in accordance with final demand (of the state and of consumers) or with demand from other firms. The market was also to make it possible to check, *a posteriori*, the planner's decisions and, when necessary, to measure their cost in terms of the satisfaction of consumer preferences, without, however, directly bringing about a change in economic policy.

In contrast, the discussions of the Czechoslovakian economists appeared dull, at least until the revival of theoretical debate at the beginning of the 1960s. The reform was a decision from above, taken a little more than a year later than in Poland.

In Hungary, the debate of 1957 certainly did not benefit from the same climate of freedom as in Poland. However, this debate, as Hungarian writers later stressed, directly foreshadowed the 'Liberman discussion' which took place in the USSR from 1962 onwards, as much in its central theme – profit – as in the positions adopted; just as in Poland, the contradictions of the incentive system then in force were subject to radical criticism. Some influential economists close to the government took part in it, such as O. Gado and G. Peter. The latter stressed, like J. Kornai, the notion of 'economic mechanism', closely related to the Polish notion of a 'model' forming a consistent whole, and of which it is not only useless but dangerous to alter a few isolated elements.

3 The content of the reforms, however, fell far short of an overall transformation of the model then in use. The Polish example illustrates perfectly the process of successive compromises, from the theoretical debate to the official declarations of principle, from the declarations to the texts announcing the reform, and from the texts to their implementation, as a result of which almost nothing remained of the initial 'project'.

The 'Theses', adopted in Poland in the spring of 1957, already contained serious ambiguities. The basic principles were admittedly clear: the system of centralised management was to be maintained with regard to the basic decisions, and, at the same time, the autonomy of enterprises was to be increased; the enterprise was itself to draw up its own plan, to determine its own production on the basis of contracts entered into with clients and suppliers, and to retain part of its profits for investment purposes. But the complexity of the problem of reconciling these two requirements was obviously underestimated. If direct instructions were abolished, what guiding principle would take their place? A simple reference to profits was not enough, as several participants in the debate had recognised. The very meaning of profits depends on the way in which prices are determined: although it was anticipated that prices would be revised in order to reflect production costs more closely (the debate crystallised around the technical problem of the price 'formula'), the very principle of price determination by the authorities – with the ensuing rigidity – was not called into question. It was thus inevitable that provisions should be made to maintain the system of rationing by the authorities 'in exceptional cases' for products in short supply, and also to retain the correctives for the system of incentive by profits, in order to take into account the 'factors particular to the enterprise': the real question was how far these exceptions and adjustments would go in each individual case.

The reform was implemented by means of a series of disparate measures, spread out over about two years. Initially, the processes of centralised management were vigorously cut back. The staff of the planning commission was reduced by half and its powers limited to planning proper, to the exclusion of any direct intervention in day-to-day management. In June 1957, 'associations of enterprises' replaced the sector management departments in the ministries: the importance given to this 'intermediate level' was to be one of the distinctive characteristics of the institutional development in the 1960s in Eastern Europe; the Polish 'associations' were in principle formed on the basis of voluntary support from enterprises.

There was also for the time being a general relaxing of constraints: the number of compulsory indicators assigned to enterprises and the number of production targets and intermediate consumption norms fixed by the central authorities had been reduced in 1957; the regulation of wages was made more flexible (and, for once, even more so in practice than in the texts).

However, the positive measures to increase the autonomy of enterprises remained hesitant. The persistence of rationing for 1,150 intermediate goods and raw materials was usually enough to prevent enterprises from redirecting their own activity on their own initiative. Paradoxically, there was greater decentralisation with regard to investment than to day-to-day decision-making. A significant proportion of profits was, indeed, paid into the enterprise's own funds. But this reassessment of the role of profits soon came up against its own limits: how, in the absence of a real reform of prices, could profits be considered an accurate reflection of the efficiency of an enterprise? This is why, from 1958 onwards, attempts were made to palliate the problem by giving enterprises a share in the annual increase in profits (rather than in the total amount of profit), and by separating the development fund (which was used to finance decentralised investment) from the incentive fund (used particularly for the payment of bonuses).

The broad outlines of the Czechoslovakian reform of 1958–9 were closely comparable to the Polish reform. Its aim also was to encourage enterprises to take initiatives, by reducing the level of supervision by the economic administration. It encouraged decentralised investment by enterprises, financed by the proportion of profits left to them or by bank credit. It had the same limits as the Polish reform: the maintenance of price determination by the authorities (prices had been revised in 1958, but had to remain rigid for five years at least) and the continued rationing of capital goods in short supply. Moreover, one of the original features of the Czechoslovakian reform was the attempt to increase the operational role of the medium-term plan (as opposed to the primacy of the annual plan), in such a way as to provide a stable framework for decision-making by enterprises. Guarantees were given that targets (particularly for labour productivity, which became the principal indicator of success used to determine the increase in the average wage) would no longer be arbitrarily revised upwards whenever they were exceeded. Enterprises were invited, in these conditions, to participate actively in the planning process by putting forward 'counterplans' that were more ambitious than the basic targets assigned to them: the reward for fulfilling these targets would be greater than for exceeding the imposed minimum. The incentive system was thus recast in an ingenious way, in order to put an end to the two main vices of the traditional system: the ratchet effect, and the encouragement to 'bargain' in order to obtain an easy plan.

The Hungarian reform was the most cautious of the three. Nevertheless, from 1957 onwards, attempts were made to reduce hypercentralisation and to strengthen the role of contracts between enterprises in deciding the orientation of production. There was a general reorganisation of the prices system in 1959, which – without eliminating completely unjustified differences in profitability – did nevertheless create a relatively favourable context for developing profit-sharing schemes. The Hungarian reform was also characterised by the establishment of a new system of wage regulation, that was both simpler and more efficient: the central authorities fixed a mandatory and uniform maximum rate of growth for the average wage; they also fixed a minimum and maximum wage for each job category; within these limits, however, the distribution of the wages fund was decided freely by the management of the enterprise. On the other hand, the Hungarian reform did not lead to any significant development of decentralised investment: this was without doubt the main difference with Poland and Czechoslovakia.

4 It is easy, after the event, to see the reforms of the end of the 1950s as characteristic examples of half measures which only made the problem worse. However, the few writers who, at the time, studied these reforms stressed their innovatory aspects.[12] And it would be impossible simply to refer to the 'sabotage of the reforms by the bureaucracy' in order to avoid careful analysis of the processes of recentralisation which put an end to the experiment.

Circumstances were initially favourable to the introduction of the reforms. The substantial wage increases of 1957 in Poland and Hungary had been absorbed without too many problems, thanks in part to foreign credit which had at the same time facilitated a rapid economic recovery. But it was particularly the completion and coming into service of the large investment projects launched at the beginning of the 1950s which in all three countries gave a great boost to growth for several years, at the very moment when the share of accumulation was temporarily reduced in favour of consumption; in Hungary, for example, the number of incomplete investment projects reached a minimum at the end of 1958.

These favourable short-term results indirectly very much influenced the fate of the reforms, by fostering the illusion that the correction of earlier imbalances could go on and that growth could continue to forge ahead, without any fundamental change, provided there was a new investment programme. It was sufficient to invest more in the sectors that had been sacrificed until then, while at the same time launching new large-scale centralised programmes in heavy industry and the infrastructure. . . .

The imbalances linked to this new leap forward in accumulation first became evident in Poland. A policy of extreme monetary laxness, together with the relaxing of the ministries' supervision, enabled enterprises to push their decentralised investment to the maximum (35 per cent of total investment in 1959), while at the same time giving way to wage claims. Inflation then caused imbalance on three levels: a foreign trade deficit, a shortage of capital goods, and a shortage of consumer goods. Breaking point was reached in the autumn of 1959, when the difficulties in agriculture worsened (particularly where the meat supply was concerned), bringing about a sudden hardening of policy which marked a turning point in the evolution of the Polish regime: purchasing power was drastically reduced by a massive increase in the price of meat, there was a return to detailed administrative control of each element in an enterprise's wages fund, decentralised investment was halted immediately, and the planning commission regained most of the powers that it had had before 1956.

The Czechoslovakian reform came to an end a little later (1962-3) in similar, but even more brutal circumstances. In 1960, on the eve of the third FYP, enterprises had been encouraged to draw up 'counterplans' that were as ambitious as possible. In return, the enterprises had demanded a corresponding increase in their production capacities (rather than mobilising, and at the same time disclosing, their unused 'internal resources'). In general, the planning commission ratified their proposals, opting once more for the most rapid growth to the detriment of equilibrium. The result, until the end of 1961, was a parallel, and equally disproportionate increase in centralised and decentralised investment. But the authorities did not react until 1962, and even then only under the pressure of an acute balance of payments crisis. This crisis had been brewing for a long time (the fundamental cause of it was the very disadvantageous specialisation of the Czechoslovakian economy since the Stalinist period in export industries without prospect of success), but was finally precipitated by circumstantial causes (such as the collapse of trade with China in 1961). In 1962, the shortage of raw materials forced many factories just to tick over. The partial decentralisation of 1959 was then blamed entirely for a crisis which had in fact many other causes, and was completely dismantled: by 1963, the autonomy of the enterprise was 'more restricted than ever before in the decade (since 1953)' (Montias, in Bornstein (ed.), 1969, p. 508).

5 It was thus the macro-economic imbalances which caused the reforms in Poland and Czechoslovakia[13] to be officially abandoned; but they had begun to be eroded much earlier, and it is necessary to analyse at the micro-economic level the processes of 'creeping recentralisation'.

The resistance of the 'bureaucracy', which saw its prerogatives threatened, but which had not been eliminated, certainly helped to thwart the application of the reform. But this factor alone cannot explain the reversal which gradually occurred. During the initial phase, the staff of the central administrative authorities had been subject to strong pressure from the political authorities, and, while biding their time before regaining the ground they had lost, had even in certain cases shown themselves to be too discreet, which had brought unexpected criticism. Certain management departments in the ministries were accused of 'conniving weakness' towards their enterprises because, under the pretext of obeying the spirit of the reforms, they stopped using the requirements of the national plan to override the initiatives of the producers in their sector. Managers of enterprises themselves sometimes turned to their supervisory authorities to ask for the detailed directives to which they had become accustomed.

In fact, the problems of day-to-day adjustment that arose from the application of the reforms could not remain unsolved; and experience very quickly demonstrated that, in the absence of a market, the return to centralised co-ordination was necessary, not just in exceptional cases, but as the general rule. All the hopes that day-to-day management might be made less cumbersome rested on the development of 'direct links' between enterprises. But the enterprises, having long since ceased to be responsible for moving their own production, knew very little about demand. In order to correct the distortions inherent in administrative planning, the 'direct links' ought to have brought about a complete restructuring of trade flows among enterprises, which was, of course, completely out of the question. Basically, therefore, the reform only amounted to a recognition of the relationships that already existed between partners nominated by the authorities. Any element of competition continued to be missing in the majority of cases; if the interests of an enterprise were damaged, its only recourse was an appeal to its superiors in the hierarchy. The conflicts at the lowest level of the system thus turned out to be one of the most powerful centralising factors. They triggered off a very general process that can be divided schematically into two phases: the first phase of interventions in individual cases led very soon to renewed overloading of the central apparatus (although the aim had been to lighten its load), since each conflict had to be settled at the highest level; the second phase saw the re-establishment of precise and constraining norms (particularly as regards selection and quality), in order to avoid conflicts and to reduce arbitrariness.

The persistence of the centralised supply system thus appears to be the key to the problem. At the outset, the planned allocation had been maintained, as a necessary evil, for a limited number of products in short supply (of which there were many more in Poland – more than 1,100 – than in Hungary – 350 – because of the much more pronounced inflationary disequilibrium in the former); it was assumed that in the long term these shortages would resolve themselves of their own accord as production increased. Not only did no such thing happen (even in

Hungary, the number of products whose distribution was fixed by the central plan had risen to 400 by the beginning of the 1960s), but it was necessary, for the time being, to reintroduce more detailed and more extensive rationing, carried out at the level of the selling organisations answerable to the ministries. As a result, the rights granted in principle to enterprises as regards the orientation of their production were doubly challenged: on the one hand, the activity of an enterprise depended directly on the supplies allocated to it; on the other hand, the interventions of the supervisory ministries, even in day-to-day management, were justified to the extent that the co-ordination of micro-economic flows was their responsibility. In Poland, from the middle of 1959 onwards, the number of mandatory directives to enterprises had increased from 8 to 19 (36 in certain sectors). The role of the 'associations' was changed completely: they increasingly became administrative agencies, whose function was to transmit directives, to disaggregate the mandatory production targets and to ensure that they were fulfilled.

Alterations to the annual plan as it was being carried out remained as frequent as in the past, with any unexpected event – such as decentralised investment running out of control – requiring correction by the central authorities. The initial intention, announced particularly in Czechoslovakia, of providing a stable framework for decision-making by enterprises for the duration of the FYP, and of putting an end to an incentive system based exclusively on exceeding short-term targets, had sunk without trace. Enterprises continued to be rewarded above all for meeting targets fixed and arbitrarily revised by the authorities. The system as a whole could be described as 'a system for protecting delays' which, 'by taking from those who work well to give to those who work badly . . . permanently ruins the effectiveness of economic policy' (Action Programme of the Czechoslovakian Communist Party, adopted on 5 April 1968[14]).

The persistence of fundamental distortions did not exclude some progress being made towards better regulated incentive formulas. In accordance with an old tendency, a solution to the problems of the centralised economy was sought in the diversification of bonuses and in an ever more complex system of calculating them. At the beginning of the 1960s, the reduction of costs and the annual increase of profits still played an important role in determining bonuses, especially in Hungary. But nowhere did profits really become the basis of the incentive system. The reason is obvious. The supervisory authorities made little distinction, among enterprises failing to meet their targets, between those whose financial losses were due simply to the inconsistent price system, or, on the other hand, to bad management, or even to other factors outside their control (the non-renewal of equipment). Thus, at the beginning of the 1960s, the simpler and less ambiguous gross production indicator regained almost all of its traditional importance, at least in Poland and Czechoslovakia. Liberman's illusion that all distortions could be corrected simply by adopting profits as the only indicator of success had disappeared for good in the countries which had already made an initial attempt at reform.

It would be an exaggeration to claim that nothing was ever learnt from the reforms. For example, the segmentation of the wages fund into several items, each subject to separate control, was never reintroduced in Hungary after 1957. This new system of regulation was much more successful in restricting unplanned wage increases than the attempts made in Poland and Czechoslovakia to restore detailed control. Similarly, the banking system was more or less relieved of the task of checking each transaction and request for credit for conformity to the plan, and at the beginning of the 1960s, in Hungary and in East Germany, in a clearly less inflationary context than in Poland or Czechoslovakia, it gradually regained greater freedom of assessment and a more active role in the granting of credit. Thus, in the most favourable case, the possibility of more balanced economic management could be detected, linked to a limited adjustment of the centralised model. The importance of the aggregate financial indicators was thus re-assessed, in accordance with the principle of '*khozraschët*', with a corresponding reduction in controls by the authorities. On the other hand, the centralised allocation of production resources and detailed directives concerning range of goods, quality and innovation remained an absolute necessity; whatever the division of responsibilities among the central authorities, it fell to them to establish and permanently maintain the adjustment of supply to demand in a non-market economy.

The institutional evolution up until the middle of the 1960s is thus markedly cyclical in character: the decentralising reforms were followed by a phase of gradual recentralisation, until the resurgence of the same problems made a new reform necessary. Nevertheless, the lessons drawn from the failure of the first reforms became in certain countries, as we shall see, a new and decisive factor, which broke this cyclical evolution. The most obvious of these lessons was that any decentralising measure taken in the framework of the model in force could not necessarily, *ipso facto*, be considered to be a step in the right direction: hypercentralisation was not the accidental result of a bureaucratic aberration, but was inherent in the very logic of the model.

The experiments of this period also enabled economic policy decisions and the problem of the reforms to be better situated with respect to each other. In the short term, the fate of the populace was much more directly affected by the changes of course in economic policy than by the reforms, which went largely unnoticed. But, in the absence of a reform of the model, the immediate concessions of 1953-7 in themselves brought about only a temporary improvement in the standard of living; the relative delay in investment had to be compensated for urgently a few years later. Conversely, the fate of the decentralising reforms (irrespective of their lack of internal coherence) was jeopardised immediately by the corresponding hardening of economic policy, the return to tight planning and the imbalances which ensued.

Towards the middle of the 1960s the leaders of the socialist countries perceived more clearly the complementarity that exists between institutional reforms and a general redefinition of the priorities of economic policy. But the time that had elapsed since 1953 did not make the problems easier to solve, to the extent that most of the fundamental imbalances had continued to worsen in the meantime.

4 The basic trends

The short-term reversals analysed in the preceding pages must not be allowed to obscure the fundamental underlying trends. Indeed, in several respects, an irreversible development had taken place since the end of the Stalinist period: most of the leaders were careful not to identify growth too closely with coal and steel production, but tended in all their declarations to put forward a less one-sided concept of the aims of development. But the proliferation of priority targets was itself a source of increasing rigidities, which helps to explain the bottlenecks that occurred in the more advanced economies and the general worsening of operational problems. Certain specific imbalances inherited from the Stalinist period – delays in oil production, the weakness of the chemical industries – were being resolved, but the overall disproportions continued to get worse until 1965.

The proliferation of priorities and increasing rigidities

1 Throughout the whole period 1953-65, the leaders of the socialist countries never missed an opportunity to repeat that the improvement of living conditions, on the one hand, and technological modernisation, on the other, would henceforth be in the forefront of their preoccupations. The insistence on these broad, permanent aims was largely independent of short-term fluctuations in economic policy.

From the Stalinist period onwards, there were, of course, many ritual references to the growing satisfaction of the needs of the people. But the tone was no longer the same. The competition with capitalism was increasingly conceived of in terms of levels of *per capita* consumption, rather than of steel, cement or energy production: for this reason, the renewed challenges launched by Khrushchev from 1958-61 against the United States sounded a genuinely new note. For example, the aim of the Soviet seven-year plan, adopted in 1959, was to reach, by about

1970, 'first place among all the countries in the world, both in terms of absolute production figures and *per capita* production, which will give the Soviet Union the highest standard of living in the world'. A little later, the twenty-year programme 'For the construction of a communist society', adopted in October 1961 by the XXIInd Congress of the Communist Party of the Soviet Union, renewed the promise of 'a higher standard of living than that of any capitalist country', with, for the first time, a host of details about the structure of consumption in 1980. The leaders of the people's democracies which were most open to comparisons with the standard of living in the West made similar declarations:

> The development of the economy of the German Democratic Republic must within a few years clearly show the superiority of the social system in the Democratic Republic over the imperialist government in Bonn, with the *per capita* consumption of the workers of our country reaching and exceeding the West German average for all the main consumer goods, food products and other goods.[1]

It was certainly no accident that these promises multiplied at the very moment when measures were being taken to increase still further the proportion of investment in GNP. Must it be concluded from this that the only aim of the official presentation of the plans was to hide the true orientations? This interpretation, although tempting, is hardly tenable. As far as propaganda itself is concerned, how can it be assumed that the governments so underestimated the effect of the inevitable disappointments? Why would they have taken the risk of making relatively precise promises and of bringing competition with the West explicitly into the argument, if they had not thought that they had a serious chance of success?

As they reacted against the cult of 'production for production's sake', the communist leaders became increasingly aware of the urgency of a new technological revolution. Besides, it was obvious before the 1960s that 'extensive growth' was leading to a dead end. The gradual replacement of coal by oil, the importance of investment in agricultural modernisation, first of all for mechanisation, then for the improvement of the soil and the production of fertilisers, and the utmost priority given to developing the extremely backward chemical industry in the USSR are proof of the restructuring effort undertaken from 1953 onwards.

All these new priorities did not replace, but were added to those of the Stalinist period. As we have seen, it was necessary to invest at the same time in the basic industries (in order to sustain growth), in road transport (neglected for a long time), in the railways (which were chronically overburdened), and in various sectors of the engineering industry (for the modernisation of the other sectors and for military purposes). It is true that the growth in 'standard' military expenditure slowed down somewhat until the end of the 1950s, only to take off even more rapidly a little later; it was then bracketed together with research for military purposes, particularly with expenditure on space research from which the USSR had been gaining great prestige since 1958.

Three urgent requirements – the strengthening of economic and military potential, technological modernisation and the improvement of the standard of living – thus combined to lead to a veritable proliferation of 'priority' targets (which, taken to extremes, would be the very negation of all priorities). The planning agencies thus faced much more complex decisions than in the past.

2 Thus the movement towards a more balanced hierarchy of priorities had the paradoxical effect in the short term of aggravating (if not of causing) the macro-economic imbalances already analysed. The important point here is not that the final decisions were made to the detriment of consumption, just as at the height of the Stalinist period. The fact is that these decisions were made too late, and were therefore all the harsher. The sudden jolts disrupted growth in some sectors (Hungary was the first to experience them in 1954-5). The more advanced economies, Czechoslovakia and also East Germany, were the most seriously affected, particularly because of the disparity between the amount of labour, energy and raw materials they required and the resources available. There was every incentive, therefore, to restore absolute priority to the basic industries, no longer because of a 'fetish' for steel or cement, but in order to maintain the possibility of more regular growth in the future.

Even within the capital goods sector, the new priorities were not as effective as at earlier stages of growth. The clearest example is that of the chemical industries in the USSR: in order to make up for their backwardness, a quintupling of total investment in the sector (in comparison with the previous seven years) had been provided for in the seven-year plan. At the end of the fifth year of the plan (the end of 1963), only half of the planned amount had been invested, and there was an even greater delay in the rate at which new plant was being brought into service. Consequently, production in the chemical industries had continued to increase less quickly than that in engineering industries, although, according to the plan, it was supposed to increase much more rapidly. This discrepancy can be explained partly by the strength of established positions (the traditionally most powerful sectoral interests remained the best defended, even within the *sovnarkhozy*), and also partly because the engineering industries had to respond to intense demand from a number of sectors. But the pressure of unsatisfied demand was just as strong for the chemical industries; their failure to meet planned targets particularly affected products for light industries (plastics and artificial and synthetic fibres) and, even more seriously, the production of fertilisers.

3 This growing rigidity affected not only inter-sectoral balances, but also micro-economic management processes. The failure to meet often unrealistic targets inevitably led to a redoubling of interventions by the authorities. This was the case, for example, in Soviet agriculture throughout the final years of the Khrushchev era (from 1958). Despite the early disappointments, the twenty-year programme adopted in 1961 increased the growth rate of 7.8 per cent fixed by the seven-year plan for the index of gross agricultural production, by laying down a target of 9.6 per cent per annum for the ten years from 1960 to 1970. In an attempt to force the pace, the authorities were reduced to making widespread and hasty use, through uniform directives, of experimental results achieved in unrepresentative conditions. Since the increase in production was too low, attempts were made to increase the proportion deducted by the state collection system. Khrushchev incessantly criticised the authorities responsible for their passivity ('The administrative agencies do not intervene enough in the day-to-day organisation of production . . . The relationships between the co-operatives and the government cannot be based on the principle of non-intervention'[2]), and increased the number of reorganisations. At the end of this process, the application of the new centralised model had become as rigorous in agriculture (for which it was, however, badly suited) as in industry.

Yet the trend towards tighter constraints was a general one. The statistical apparatus was expanded. The sources of supply of local raw materials were increasingly integrated into the planning of supplies. The growing attention given to problems of quality and the reduction of costs, the concern to adjust supply more closely to demand and the drive towards technological modernisation were also reflected in the increasing interference in the running of enterprises. The list of conditions that an enterprise had to fulfil (at least on paper) in order to be entitled to its bonuses was lengthened: at this level also, the distinction between priority and less important targets was more or less obliterated. For this very same reason, the task of economic administration became more difficult. Innovation, in particular, depends in a Soviet-type economy on detailed instructions sent to enterprises, or, if the authorities have recourse to a system of incentives (a fund for the assimilation of new techniques was set up in Hungary as early as 1959, and in the USSR in 1961), any payment is dependent on an administrative decision in each individual case. Far from solving themselves of their own accord, these problems became all the more important as the economy became more complex and more diversified; they were more acute in the more advanced countries, Czechoslovakia and East Germany. In the USSR, the indefinite increase in the costs of economic administration was becoming, by the beginning of the 1960s, a real cause for concern: an article published in April 1962 pointed out that 'the size of the planning and control apparatus' had increased by about 50 per cent 'in the last seven years',[3] and some writers made some disturbing extrapolations.

4 The evolution of the respective shares of the components of GNP for the whole period from 1953–65 fully confirms this impression of rigidity.

Table 4.1 can be interpreted in various ways. It reflects the alternation of very contrasting phases of economic policy, as well as a fairly considerable diversity in the evolution of the different countries. But above all it shows how close the broad outlines of the structure of final uses in 1965 were to those of 1953. The share of collective consumption remained almost stable; that of investment in the consumer goods sector (by virtue of a special effort in agriculture), of house-building and of other social investment were generally higher, but the increase was far from spectacular. Military expenditure (included under item *V*) represented, in about 1965, a proportionally less heavy burden than in 1953, according to Western estimates, but this reduction was more or less offset (or even exceeded, in the case of Poland, for example) by an increase in the relative weight of basic investment. The result was that everywhere, except in Hungary, the share of private consumption was even lower at the end of the period than at the beginning of the 1950s: the shift in the structure of investment was obviously insufficient to put the Soviet-type economies back on the road to more balanced growth.

Table 4.1 *Percentage distribution of GNP by broad categories of final use (1950–65)*

	I Private consumption	II Collective consumption	III Investment in the consumer goods sector	IV Housebuilding and social investment	V State consumption, basic investment
USSR					
1950	48	10	5.5	6	30.5
1955	51.5	8.5	6.5	7	26.5
1958	50	9	6.5	10.5	24
1960	49	9	6.5	10.5	25
1965	47.5	9.5	7.5	9	26.5
Czechoslovakia					
1952	50	8	6	8	28
1955	48	9	8	11	24
1960	44	7.5	11	11	26.5
1965	44	8	10	10	28
Poland					
1952	56	6	6	6	26
1955	55	5	7	7.5	25.5
1960	55.5	5	7.5	11.5	20.5
1965	51.5	5	9.5	9.5	29.5
Hungary					
1952	49	3.5	8	6	33.5
1955	51.5	4.5	11	8	25
1960	56.5	4.5	10.5	8.5	20
1965	54.5	4.5	10.5	7.5	23

The principal sources are: for the USSR, JEC, 1966, pp. 102–29 and JEC, 1970, pp. 52, 171 and 184; for the other countries, JEC, 1972, supplemented for the breakdown of public expenditure by Pryor, 1968, pp. 318–74.

The increase in the fundamental imbalances

The widening consumption gap

As we have seen, the leaders of the communist countries were more and more resolute in putting the improvement of the standard of living at the top of their list of declared aims: thus to assess the long-term efficiency of the socialist countries by this criterion cannot be said to be doing them an injustice. The results of such an assessment for the period around 1965 are, to say the least, disappointing.

In terms of quantity, dietary requirements, expressed in calorie consumption *per capita*, were adequately satisfied. But the structure of food consumption was still characteristic of countries with a low standard of living: a high proportion of basic foodstuffs (cereals and potatoes), a low share of animal products (even in the exporting countries) and of vegetables and fresh fruit. Tropical products were still considered a luxury. The relative gap in consumption levels was particularly significant in the cases of Czechoslovakia or East Germany,[4] where the pre-war standard of living had been close to that of Austria or West Germany.

However, expenditure on food, despite the relative cheapness of most widely consumed products (which were free of tax or even subsidised), accounted on average for about 50 per cent of total household expenditure on consumption – which provides another similarity with poor countries. And there was hardly any tendency for its share to diminish in most of the socialist countries at the beginning of the 1960s.

Consumption levels for manufactured goods lagged even further behind those in Western Europe, particularly for consumer durables; as the gap narrowed for the 'traditional' articles, such as radios, it widened again for 'new' articles such as TV sets.

Any comparison of aggregate levels of consumption in the East and the West comes up against formidable difficulties. Nevertheless, various estimates by Czech, Hungarian and Polish economists fully confirm the order of magnitude of Western comparisons, and indeed their results are often even more pessimistic.[5] The gravest cause for concern, however, was the general tendency for the gap to widen throughout the whole of this period (to the disadvantage of the socialist countries, of course). Austria, for example, which could serve as an acceptable basis of comparison for the more advanced people's democracies, increasingly outstripped them.

Comparisons among socialist countries – of which there are a certain

Table 4.2 *Relative consumption levels (taking* per capita *consumption in Austria as a base = 100), pre-war to 1965*

	Pre-war	1950	1955	1960	1965
GDR	117	66	86	87	76
Czechoslovakia	117	122	90	81	72
Hungary	107	84	66	63	61
Poland	56	73	61	54	51

Calculated from Ernst in JEC, 1966, p. 90.

number, particularly of Soviet origin – almost invariably result in the following classification (in decreasing order of consumption levels): East Germany and Czechoslovakia, Hungary and Poland, the USSR, Bulgaria and Rumania. The countries in the group which enjoyed a relatively high standard of living were those which had been more highly developed before the war. Despite the very rapid industrialisation of the less advanced economies, the disparity in consumption levels remained very marked for all manufactured goods, which seems to confirm that industrialisation does not necessarily lead to a higher standard of living.

Housing conditions were another problem. In comparison with West Germany, which also suffered heavy war damage, the available living space per inhabitant in 1965 was 10 to 15 per cent less in East Germany, 25 per cent less in Czechoslovakia, 33 per cent less in Poland, and 50 per cent less in the USSR and Hungary (Joint Economic Committee, Congress of the United States (JEC), 1972, pp. 311–12 and 592). The direct competition between housing and productive investment for the limited capacities of the construction industry largely explains this gap. However, there were equally marked disparities in the amenities of the housing stock. In East Germany, where the population was static, the housing stock was ageing (at the beginning of the 1960s only 10.5 per cent of the housing stock in East Germany was of post-war construction, compared with 34 per cent in West Germany); there was hardly any improvement in the comfort and modernisation of existing housing: less than 3 per cent of dwellings had central heating in 1967, compared with 20.4 per cent in West Germany in 1965, and only 26 per cent had a bathroom (half of the level in West Germany) (JEC, 1972, p. 593).

The evolution of public consumption – mainly the health and education services – was much more satisfactory from the 1950s onwards, even in the countries like Bulgaria and Rumania which lagged furthest behind; but it appears remarkable largely because of the contrast with the low level of private consumption. None of the socialist countries succeeded during this period in winning acceptance for a consistent set of social priorities. In this respect, there was a blatant contradiction between the principle of virtually free housing – a symbol of the change to a method of distribution 'according to needs' – and the actual inability to improve the situation in that area. Nor was the retail prices structure a means of achieving a real consumption policy. The motor car is often cited as a kind of private consumption good that was strongly discouraged during this period, and yet the relative price of a small car in about 1965 was no higher, in comparison with Western prices, than those of other 'luxury' products such as oranges, coffee or chocolate, or clothes made of man-made fibres; the price of a litre of petrol relative to the cost of public transport (except for air travel) was decidedly lower in the USSR than in France. Tobacco and alcohol were no more heavily taxed than in the West. Admittedly the preoccupation with directing consumption was never absent, but its influence on the prices structure was outweighed by other very heterogeneous factors (general taxation of imported products, 'accidental' over-production in certain industries, the rigidity of the production system which maintained the chronic shortage of new products).

Thus the unsuccessful efforts to catch up with Western consumption levels pushed an even more basic aim into the background, that of confronting capitalist societies with a more rational, attractive and original socialist 'consumption model'.

During the initial phase, the consumption gap could be explained as a transitory phenomenon, arising from the need to build up an industrial base with a view to more rapid subsequent development. But as time passed, it became more difficult to interpret the ever-widening gap as a temporary sacrifice.

The solipsistic growth of the capital goods sector[6]

What is the explanation for this permanent disparity between the success of the industrialisation effort and the very slow increase in consumption levels?

In all the socialist countries the growth rate in light industry (B) was lower than that of heavy industry (A) (Table 4.3).

There was a striking continuity with the Stalinist period: sector A was still increasing its lead over sector B. The actual gap between the respective rates of growth of sector A industries and those in sector B was often much bigger than planned (particularly at the beginning of the 1960s in the USSR, Rumania, Poland and East Germany). Moreover, a comparison of the periods from 1952 to 1958 and from 1958 to 1964 shows that the gap widened in all the countries except Hungary.

Table 4.3 *Comparative growth of heavy and light industry (1952–64)*

	1952–8 average annual growth rate (%)		1958–64 average annual growth rate (%)		ratio of growth rates A/B	
	A	B	A	B	1952–8	1958–64
USSR	12	10	10.5	6.5	1.2	1.6
Bulgaria	14	12.5	16.5	10	1.1	1.7
Rumania	11.5	9.5	16	10	1.2	1.6
Poland	12	11	11	6.5	1.1	1.7
Hungary	7.5	5	11	8.5	1.5	1.3
Czechoslovakia	10	8.5	7.5	5.5	1.2	1.4
GDR	9-11.5	7.5	7-10	4.5	1.2-1.6	1.6-2.2

Calculated from *Etude sur la situation économique de l'Europe en 1965*, p. 291. For sector A in East Germany, the first figure refers to 'basic industries', the second to 'metal processing'.

Yet this evolution coincided with an increasingly widespread questioning by economists in the socialist countries of the so-called 'law of priority growth for the capital goods sector'. If there is no 'objective law' that dictates that priority should be given to the capital goods sector, must it not be assumed that it is rather a matter of economic policy decision that can be retained or revised by the leaders in accordance with their priorities? However, this approach to the problem may well be misleading.

The policy of giving absolute priority to heavy industry was certainly identified at the outset with the choice of a very specific growth strategy, which was the subject of very vigorous discussions until the end of the 1920s, before becoming established in the USSR and then in the people's democracies.

But the permanent gap between the growth rates for sectors A and B is not enough to prove that this had been, ever since 1953, the result of a deliberate decision, since there were constant reaffirmations of the desire to use the potential of the basic industries in order to develop the consumer sector more rapidly.[7] When it became clear at the beginning of the 1960s that the new rapid expansion in investment would have much more severe repercussions on consumption than had been anticipated, the governments tried to react. In January 1961, for example, Khrushchev attacked the 'routine-minded' officials of the economic administration for simplistically identifying growth with the production of steel:

> We must always remember that a country's prosperity is measured not only by the quantity of metal that it produces; it depends, for example, on the quantity of products that the people receive and consume, on the production of clothes and shoes, and in general to the extent that all the needs of human life are satisfied. Let us not be like the flatfish which can only look in one direction! (*Pravda*, 25 January 1961)

This was no mere statement of principle since, by the end of 1961, the central committee was concerned to accelerate the rate of deliveries of capital goods to the consumer goods sector as a whole 'in order to give impetus to the decision of the XXIInd Party Congress on the narrowing of the gap between the rate of growth of sector A and that of sector B'. Similarly, in Poland, the annual plan for 1962 provided for an increase in the growth rate of sector B in order to bring it to almost the same level as that for sector A. In both cases, however, there was absolutely no result, even in the short term: throughout this period, the actual evolution always contradicted the declared intention.

Rather than assuming a total lack of sincerity on the part of the leaders, or explaining everything by the power of the ministries for heavy industry, we must consider the factors which seem to prevent any lasting readjustment in favour of consumption. What is the meaning of this 'spontaneous' tendency for heavy industry to be strengthened? Why are the Soviet-type economies prisoners of the consequences of the development strategy adopted at the time of their first FYPs? Why was it so difficult, even when there appeared to have been profound changes in the hierarchy of long-term objectives, to bring about a transfer of resources towards light industry (agriculture, service industries and housing) equal to the initial transfer in favour of heavy industry?

The post-Stalinist evolution clearly shows that, in any case, it is not enough to decide on a revision of priorities in order to be in a position to make more efficient use of the potential built up during the preceding phase in order to improve the standard of living.

The transition to a 'new growth path' in itself poses serious problems, which are considerably aggravated by the particular fundamental characteristics of the centralised model. It is, of course, inevitable that bringing basic investment to an abrupt halt, as happened in 1953, jeopardises the growth process, which in turn makes a new investment drive urgently necessary, as in 1958. The maintenance of a given ratio in the distribution of investment between the capital goods sector and the consumer goods sector is, in general, a condition for balanced growth. However, in Soviet-type economies, the critical threshold below which basic investment must never fall in order for a given growth rate to be achieved is much higher than in Western economies. This is not a matter of deliberate choice, but a constraint arising from earlier decisions. Concentrating half of industrial investment in three sectors (energy, iron and steel, and building materials) was still hardly sufficient in the USSR in 1960 to eliminate the most serious bottlenecks. This characteristic is due partly to the structure of final production: although the share of arms expenditure in the total of final uses had been reduced somewhat, it nevertheless accounted indirectly for a large percentage of the investment needs of heavy industry. However, the important fact is that industry as a whole was operating with abnormally high coefficients of intermediate consumption: in the mechanical engineering industry in 1960, for example, the consumption of metal expressed in weight per unit of final product was on average more than 40 per cent higher than the corresponding figure for the United States.[8] And the gap tended to widen over time, for lack of sufficient incentive at the level of the enterprise to economise on raw materials, either in the short term (by stricter management), or, particularly, in the long term (by accepting the risks of innovation). This excessive intermediate consumption had a direct effect on the structure of investment: the activity of the building industry was orientated largely towards basic investment; similarly, the production of capital goods was directed more towards the sectors upstream of the engineering industries (notably energy) than to those downstream of them (sectors producing goods for final demand).

The wastage which is characteristic of the centralised model was thus the fundamental obstacle to any restructuring: the 'normal' functioning of this type of economy requires the production system permanently to reabsorb a steadily growing amount of resources, in the form of investment and intermediate consumption. Moreover, various aggravating factors tend constantly to cause unbalanced growth.

It is necessary first of all to underline the fundamental dissymmetry between the respective distribution conditions for the production of sectors A and B. Consumer goods are destined to be sold to the populace. The refusal to buy articles of too poor a quality or which do not correspond to people's needs has sometimes, since the end of 'absolute shortages', had the effect of seriously disrupting the growth of light industries (for example, in Hungary from 1954 to 1955, and in Poland from 1962 to 1963). There are no such constraints for the capital goods sector, since its products are distributed to the rest of the state sector by purely administrative processes, which is an obvious advantage from the planner's point of view! There is no *a priori* limit to the expansion of sector A. When the complementarities between different inputs are not respected, the normal reaction of enterprises is not to refuse surplus deliveries, but to ask for more of the products which are in short supply. Sector A can thus develop as a sort of 'enclave' within the national economy, destined to grow continuously, with a growing proportion of the available means of production being used to manufacture additional means of production.

In this case, the only obvious symptoms of imbalance will manifest themselves in sector A itself, when certain sectors, for one reason or another, fail to match the general rate of growth. The result is a permanent incentive to increase further the share of basic investment, for fear of jeopardising growth in all the sectors downstream (including the manufacture of armaments). Not only are the sectoral interests of heavy industry the best protected within the central apparatus, but it is always the deficits which appear in the basic sectors which, *de facto*, require urgent correction in the short term. The authorities are constantly preoccupied with easing the most threatening bottlenecks, with attending to the most urgent things first:

> In the present circumstances, the essential thing is to win time. . . . From the state's point of view, it is worth deliberately accepting a certain increase in the cost per kilowatt-hour, in order to gain time and to obtain within a short period the maximum increase in electricity production. This way of looking at the problem arises from the fact that we must, within a very short time, increase investment for the development of heavy industry, in particular the chemical industry, the steelworks and the non-ferrous metals industries.[9]
> (Speech by Khrushchev in June 1968 at the inauguration of the Kuibyshev hydro-electric power station)

It is inevitable that considerations of economy and efficiency are relegated to the background.

A few years later in Czechoslovakia, Ota Sik summed up the whole process in this way:

> More and more steel was needed for production in the engineering industries; new steelworks thus had to be built, which led to the launching of large-scale construction projects, which, in their turn, demanded more heavy machinery. And so on. . . . All sectors were working for each other . . . There was always a certain demand, covered by certain resources, but the final result for the populace was minimal.[10]

It was quite obviously the desire to escape from this Parkinsonian trend which was to lead, in the mid-1960s, to the centralised model itself being called into question.

The appearance of new distinctions

The general differences between the USSR and the people's democracies

The enormous disparity in size between the USSR and the people's democracies is enough to explain their very different problems, despite the similarity in economic policies and organisation.

1 In accordance with a very general law, the economies of the small and medium-sized countries of Eastern Europe were much more open to foreign trade than the Soviet economy.

Table 4.4 *Comparative levels of foreign trade* per capita *in 1965*

USSR	1	Hungary	4.3
Rumania	1.85	GDR	5.1
Poland	2.15	Czechoslovakia	5.3
Bulgaria	4.3		

(Indices with base: foreign trade *per capita* in USSR = 1.) Calculated from U.N. *Statistical Yearbook 1966*. The total of foreign trade in dollars (imports + exports) per head of population in 1965 ranges from 70 dollars (USSR) to 380 dollars (Czechoslovakia).

The difference in this respect between the USSR and the people's democracies was, in itself, nothing new, but it increased with the general development of foreign trade. Contrary to widespread opinion, the socialist countries played a large part, from this period onwards, in the rapid expansion of world trade; the share of the Comecon countries, including the USSR, in total world trade, which was only 7.8 per cent in 1953, reached 10.4 per cent in 1965, exceeding for the first time their share of the total world population.

Until 1965, all the Eastern European countries, with the exception of East Germany, had a higher rate of growth in foreign trade than the USSR. But in their case, this growth had a quite separate significance, since the degree of openness of these economies was structurally higher, and, moreover, had increased considerably since the war.

Table 4.5 *Imports as a percentage of GNP (Western definition), 1938-64*

	1938	1950	1964
Bulgaria	8	9	24
Hungary	5	6	17
Czechoslovakia	6	6	15
GDR	–	4	14
Rumania	4	5	12
Poland	3	6	10
USSR	0.5	2	3.5

Source: M. Ernst in JEC, 1966, p. 105. For pre-war period: 1938 or preceding or following year.

For small economies, engaged in a process of rapid industrialisation and in general poorly endowed with raw materials, imports are vital. Here again, there is a marked contrast with the USSR: raw materials and semi-manufactured products accounted in 1965 for the equivalent of 11 per cent of GNP (Western definition) in Bulgaria, 7 per cent in Czechoslovakia, 6 per cent in Rumania, 5 per cent in Poland, compared with only 1 per cent in the USSR. Despite the sustained increase in these imports, industrial growth was often slowed down abruptly at the beginning of the 1960s (in Czechoslovakia, East Germany and Poland) by a shortage of imported raw materials. In order to highlight the restricting factors, brief mention must be made of the terms of trade.

2 Just as in the Stalinist period, these terms were fundamentally different, according to whether the trade was between socialist countries, in which case it was controlled by government agreements, or trade with the 'capitalist world market', where everything is available, provided the necessary currency is obtainable, which poses the problem of export capacities.

However, the post-Stalinist evolution brought to light a new dissymmetry between the USSR and the people's democracies. The share of trade with the West in Soviet foreign trade did not stop increasing. In the people's democracies, on the other hand, the trend of the years from 1953 to 1955 was not repeated: the share of the Western market hardly changed in the ten years from 1955 to 1965; at the end of the period, by a curious reversal, it had become lower on average than for the USSR.

Table 4.6 *Share of trade with the West in total foreign trade (1955–65)*

	1955	1958	1962	1965
USSR	21.5	27	30	33.5
Six East European countries	30.5	31	28.5	31

The overall stability that can be observed for the people's democracies is the result of conflicting influences which balanced each other out: the attraction of the advanced capitalist countries was more or less offset by a 'voluntarist' policy of tightening the links between the European socialist economies. This policy was reflected particularly in a whole series of initiatives aimed at developing the activities of Comecon. The main stages were, firstly, the initial specialisation agreements made in the mid-1950s, which concerned the people's democracies in particular, secondly, the adoption in December 1959 of the Comecon charter (ten years after its creation), and then in 1962 the adoption of the fundamental principles of the international socialist division of labour. This last measure was a new attempt at economic stimulation in which the Soviet government was heavily involved: the plan behind the principles was for a sort of supra-national system of planning, which would finally integrate all the socialist economies. But immediate resistance from Rumania practically prevented any progress in this direction, by causing a severe crisis, which was resolved only by substantial Soviet concessions. The strength of the relations between the USSR and the other Eastern European countries was not, however, affected by it.

The continuing priority given to trade with the USSR was not, of course, unrelated to the balance of power (political and military) between the dominant country and its partners, but it can be explained much more directly by the almost irreversibly unequal dependency relationships that had been established between the Soviet economy and the more industrialised economies of Eastern Europe. Over the years, the USSR had become the great supplier of raw materials (and energy) for the whole of Comecon. As a result of the sustained efforts involved in the plans, the Soviet-type economies suffered from a chronic shortage of basic products; the parallel industrialisation of all the countries of the group had given rise, on the other hand, to a growing abundance of manufactured goods.[11]

Paradoxically, however, basic products, sold at prices close to the 'world price', were relatively cheap, whereas manufactured goods (including capital goods) were heavily over-priced, particularly in view of their quality: the price ratios in force within Comecon at the beginning of the 1960s thus by no means indicated that the USSR was systematically exploiting the people's democracies. However, in addition to this overall imbalance, the detailed price structure of foreign trade was very confused; for this reason, any trade agreement arose necessarily from a package deal, in which the partners were content to seek approximate, overall compensation for their mutual advantages and disadvantages. This state of affairs made any precise adjustment at the margin very difficult, and was an additional cause of inertia.

For the industrialised economies of Eastern Europe, any sudden re-orientation of their foreign trade would have involved an immediate cost and almost incalculably great risks. For this reason, the type of relationships that were established within Comecon were accepted as a basic fact, and the very bitter negotiations were concerned only with the terms of trade. The USSR put pressure on its partners in order to obtain their direct participation in the enormous burden of investment that it was accepting in order to increase its production of energy and raw materials. Poland, which received more than its fair share of support from the other people's democracies, demanded that the surpluses generated within Comecon be converted into gold and foreign exchange (which would have led, in the final analysis, to the USSR indirectly financing an increase in purchases on the Western market). These conflicting claims more or less cancelled each other out. The successive compromises were in general to the short-term advantage of the people's democracies, but their dependence on the USSR was only increased in the long term.

3 The overall increase in trade with the West up to 1965 was not particularly impressive. But the structure of imports shows that this trade was very important for the socialist countries (including the USSR), and the structure of their exports suggests some of the main obstacles to any greater expansion.

There is a striking difference between the structure of imports and exports. That of the socialist countries' exports to Western Europe closely resembled those of undeveloped countries: after twenty years of sacrifice in the cause of rapid industrialisation, the disparity with Western Europe in levels of development had not diminished at all, but had, on the contrary, increased.

Three particular items stand out in the list of imports. Firstly, grain:

Table 4.7 *Breakdown by product of inter-European trade (1964–5)*

	Eastern European imports from Western Europe		Exports from Eastern Europe to Western Europe		Trade between West European countries	
Foodstuffs	14.7		22.1		13.9	
meat and animal products		2.7		10.0		5.0
grain		4.8		2.7		1.5
Raw materials, fuel, metals	24.6		59		26.6	
Manufactured goods	58.8		16.9		54.9	
machinery		29.2		5.1		24.6
shipping		7.0		0.6		1.3
other transport equipment		1.8		1.6		8.3
chemical products		12.0		3.9		7.5
other manufactured goods		9.2		5.8		13.3

Source: *Bulletin économique pour l'Europe* (15), 1, 1966, p. 31. Approximately 2 to 4 per cent of the total cannot be broken down. The USSR is included in Eastern Europe, but Yugoslavia is not.

the grain shortage in the people's democracies went back to the 1950s; by about 1965, the USSR was no longer in a position to deal with it, as it had been in about 1958, and itself became a net importer in years of bad harvest. Secondly, chemical products: many sectors in the chemical industry had not yet made good their deficits. Finally and most importantly, imports of capital goods and transport equipment: the modernisation effort and the chronic obstacles to innovation within Soviet-type economies increasingly forced the socialist countries to turn to the capitalist countries, where technology was more advanced.

In the list of exports, there is an overwhelming preponderance of primary and semi-manufactured goods (fuel imports alone exceeded the total sales of manufactured goods, capital goods and consumer goods put together). The USSR and Rumania were better placed in this respect than the economies that were more industrialised, yet not so rich in raw materials.

Czechoslovakia was particularly hard hit by the widening technological gap with Western Europe. During this period, Czechoslovakia lost the position, that it still had at the beginning of the 1950s, as a net exporter of capital goods to Western Europe, and, in order to maintain a certain flow of exports, had to agree to enormous discounts (40 to

70 per cent on machinery sold in the Common Market)[12] in comparison with theoretically similar goods of Western origin. The inadequate export capacity of the people's democracies was without doubt the main factor inhibiting their trade with the West.

The growing diversification of national policies

Towards the end of the 1950s, the main differences between the people's democracies stemmed from their respective levels of development which were a legacy of the past: two advanced economies (East Germany and Czechoslovakia) had a clear lead over the two semi-industrialised economies (Hungary and Poland) and the two predominantly agricultural economies (Bulgaria and Rumania). Fifteen years later, despite the general increase in levels of industrialisation in Eastern Europe, the old distinction had lost none of its importance. But, as we have seen, the differences had largely changed to the disadvantage of the more industrialised countries, which had a slower growth rate in almost all sectors and increasingly serious problems in the functioning of their economies. On the other hand, an initially less advanced country, such as Bulgaria, had without doubt benefited from technical co-operation within Comecon, and from the specialisation agreements which guaranteed outlets for its new industries. As a result of these favourable conditions, the Bulgarian economy had by 1963 become a much more 'open' economy than that of countries like Greece and Yugoslavia (the amount of foreign trade per head of population was 300 dollars, as against 170 and 120 respectively). Rumania and Poland were at a level comparable with that of Spain (130 dollars per head of population). On the other hand, by 1965, the foreign trade levels of Czechoslovakia and East Germany had largely fallen behind that of Austria for example (380 and 360 dollars per head of population compared with 510): this imbalance reflects the double handicap imposed on the more industrialised socialist countries by the application of the centralised model and by the kind of specialisation allotted to them within the group.

However, similar basic conditions and problems do not exclude the possibility of solutions being sought in very different directions. During this period, economic policies began to diversify noticeably from one country to another, by deviating more or less on a particular point from the traditional Soviet model. From this, new differences arose, which cannot be explained adequately by the initial difference in levels of development.

1 Despite the constraints mentioned above, the strength of economic relations with the advanced capitalist countries of Western Europe and North America was to a large extent a question of political decision. The East European countries had very different levels of trade with the West, without there being any obvious link with their respective levels of industrialisation. Moreover, significant short-term variations reflected the particular political situation.

Table 4.8 *Share of trade with the Western industrialised countries (1958-65)*

1958		1962		1965	
Poland	37	Poland	31	Rumania	30.5
Hungary	27.5	Rumania	26.5	Poland	28
GDR	23	Hungary	21.5	Hungary	27
Czechoslovakia	19	Czechoslovakia	17.5	GDR	22
Rumania	19	GDR	17.5	Czechoslovakia	21
Bulgaria	11	Bulgaria	14.5	Bulgaria	17

The relative decline for Poland clearly illustrates the gradual loss of its uniqueness within the group after 1956, for political and economic reasons. But the greater weight of political factors is reflected even more clearly in the contrast between East Germany and Rumania: very marked changes – in opposite directions – had taken place in both countries within a very short space of time.

The whole future development of East Germany was determined by the historical circumstances of its creation. In about 1960, however, its economy was benefiting from the privileged conditions that the Federal Republic granted to inter-German trade: at that time, trade with the 'other Germany' accounted for more than half of the total foreign trade of East Germany with Western industrialised countries, which the East German government felt to be an unacceptable degree of dependency. The building of the Berlin Wall in 1961 was accompanied by a sudden brake: inter-German trade was reduced by 37 per cent (between the fourth quarter of 1960 and the first quarter of 1962), and trade with the rest of Western Europe by 13 per cent. The USSR then granted massive credit to East Germany, which in general supported Soviet positions in negotiations within Comecon.

At almost the same time, Rumanian imports from the West trebled at one go (between 1959 and 1961), and from then on Rumania reserved its most sought after export goods for the Western market. But Rumania's permanent deficit with the West was supported above all by the favourable conditions of payment obtained for its orders of capital goods. The Rumanian government would never have accepted such a high level of indebtedness but for its overriding desire to escape 'integration' within Comecon, to carry out its own strategy of autonomous development (which was actually very close to the traditional model of the Stalinist period) and to build up a powerful heavy industrial sector, whatever the cost.

2 There were also differences in the agricultural policies applied in Eastern Europe.

In Poland, agriculture remained largely in private hands, which set the country apart from the other socialist countries. However, this difference in structure did not mean that any priority was given at the beginning of the 1960s to the development of agriculture. Bulgaria, conversely, had been the first of the people's democracies to complete the main part of the collectivisation process, as early as the mid-1950s, and was thus emerging from the characteristic difficulties of the transitional phase. Throughout the whole of the period under discussion here, its agricultural policy was characterised by a sustained investment effort (for modernisation and intensification) and, particularly, by significant concessions to the peasants, whose income tended to approach the national average. The results were favourable in comparison with those of all the other economies of Eastern Europe.

Among the countries where the decisive phase of agricultural collectivisation was taking place at the end of the 1950s various methods were employed: these were rigid in Hungary and especially so in Czechoslovakia, where even greater efforts were made to limit the role of private plots than in the USSR, but gradual and much more flexible in Rumania and East Germany. The results obtained by the various countries were directly affected by these differences.

3 There are much greater similarities in industrial policy. The uniqueness of Hungary, which has already been mentioned several times, could still easily pass unnoticed; nevertheless, this difference became more marked, and constant efforts did in fact result in more balanced growth.

Because of the historical vicissitudes which characterised the 1950s (the imbalances of the Stalinist period, which reached their peak in the 1950s, the sudden deceleration of 1954–5, the upheaval of 1956 followed by a slow consolidation), the Hungarian leaders had been careful not to lapse again into the excesses of the earlier phase of 'forced industrialisation'.

Investment policy had remained relatively cautious. At the beginning of the 1960s, Hungary was the only East European country where the relative weight of investment in GNP did not exceed the maximum of the Stalinist period. The contrast is particularly clear if the share of the increase in GNP absorbed by the increase in gross investment in the ten years from 1955-65 is compared:[13]

Czechoslovakia	58%	USSR	45%
Poland	53%	Hungary	38%
East Germany	45%		

This fairly moderate overall increase resulted in lower priority being given to heavy industry. In this respect, Hungary again stood out, for

Table 4.9 *Percentage in heavy industry of the economically active population in the manufacturing sector (1950-67)*

	1950	1967	Difference
Hungary	60.3	55.1	− 5.2
GDR	68.0	69.6	+ 1.6
Czechoslovakia	51.0	61.7	+10.7
USSR	68.8	71.6*	+ 2.8
Poland	50.7	57.8	+ 7.1
Rumania	43.6	49.7	+ 6.1
Bulgaria	33.8	42.7	+ 8.8

Source: JEC, 1972, p. 232, and JEC, 1970, pp. 72-80.
* 1966.

two reasons: the share of light industry and the food industries in total industrial investment recovered at the beginning of the 1960s, against the general trend, and the actual evolution went further in this direction than had been planned.[14] The distribution of the industrial workforce also clearly reflected this evolution against the trend in other countries.

The aim of Hungarian economic policy from 1957 to 1965 was not only to modify the sector shares inherited from the Stalinist period, but also, and this was much more difficult, to redress the main distortions inherent in the centralised model: the sacrifice of quality to quantity ('production for production's sake') and abnormally high levels of intermediate consumption for a given amount of added value. Unable to rely on large reserves of labour and poorly endowed with raw materials and energy supplies, Hungary certainly had every incentive to economise on inputs and to make increased efficiency a top priority. But it succeeded better in this than the other socialist countries which faced the same problems and professed the same intentions.

Table 4.10 *Steel consumption in the Hungarian engineering industry: comparison with various East and West European countries (1960–5)*

	Steel consumption in kg per 1$ of production (1960)	Ratio between the increase in steel consumption and the increase in the value of production (1960–5)	Average export price of 1 kg of engineering products (1964)
Poland	0.61	0.94	0.74
Czechoslovakia	0.67	0.96	1.28
GDR	0.50	1.18	1.28
Hungary	0.45	0.78	1.54
Austria	0.37	0.72	1.74
Italy	0.28	0.96	1.93
FRG	0.18	0.76	1.80
France	–	0.73	1.80

Source: E. M. Snell in JEC, 1972, pp. 256, 253 and 288. The estimates of the value in dollars of the production of machinery and capital goods are taken from A. Bodnar, *Zycie Warszawy*, 12 March 1966, p. 3. The average export price of 1 kg of engineering products in 1964 was lower for the USSR (0.93), Bulgaria (0.65) and Rumania (0.63) than for Hungary.

In 1967, the total consumption of steel per head of population in Hungary (116 kg) was not only lower than in Czechoslovakia, East Germany, Poland and the USSR, but also than less industrialised countries than itself, like Rumania (207 kg) and Bulgaria (162 kg). The ranking closely matches that for *per capita* consumption of energy.

Table 4.11 *Total energy consumption per head of population (1967): comparison between Hungary and various East and West European countries*

GDR	5,344	Belgium	4,742
Czechoslovakia	5,133	FRG	4,650
Poland	3,652	France	3,634
Bulgaria	2,890	Austria	3,252
Hungary	2,546	Italy	2,436
Rumania	2,309		

Source: JEC, 1973, p. 285.

Admittedly, all these comparisons pose methodological problems, since they conceal the influence of many factors and in fact give only an order of magnitude. Nevertheless, the convergence of the conclusions is significant (all the more so since the data originate from different sources, which in no way intended to highlight the specificity of the Hungarian economy): Hungary seemed regularly to occupy an intermediate position between the Western economies and those of the other socialist countries. The anomalously high consumption of energy or basic products in the socialist countries (particularly East Germany and Czechoslovakia) in comparison with Western countries was significantly lower in Hungary. In other words, energy (or steel) consumption in Hungary was relatively low in relation to its position in the hierarchy of East European levels of industrialisation. And yet the difference was without any doubt due to industrial consumption (domestic consumption of electricity, which is an indicator of the standard of living, was, on the contrary, significantly higher in Hungary in 1965 than in Poland, for example, whereas several years earlier the opposite had still been the case). Hungarian industrial production thus consumed the least energy of all the Eastern countries, due both to judicious decisions on specialisation for a country poor in primary resources and to gains in efficiency which were beginning to make themselves felt in certain industries. Savings in energy, steel and cement reduce not only the level of intermediate consumption, but also basic investment needs.

A lower rate of investment than in the other socialist countries had little negative effect on the evolution of labour productivity. In this respect, Hungary was the only country which escaped the general decline in all the industrialised or semi-industrialised economies in Eastern Europe at the beginning of the 1960s. The effort of the Hungarian leaders, which, in fact, had only just begun, to increase 'modernisation investment' relative to 'capacity investment' provides a partial explanation.

Table 4.12 *Average annual growth rate of labour productivity (1950–67)*

	1950–60	1961–7	Difference
Hungary	2.8	3.6	+0.8
Poland	2.8	2.4	−0.4
USSR	4.8	3.3	−1.5
GDR	4.8	2.9	−1.9
Czechoslovakia	3.3	1.3	−2.0

Source: JEC, 1972, p. 62, supplemented for the USSR from JEC, 1968, and JEC, 1970.

The same contrast can be observed between the growth rate of agricultural or industrial production, which was similar in Hungary to the other countries of the group, and the growth rate of *per capita* consumption, where Hungary gained a quite clear relative advantage.

Table 4.13 *Consumption and retail sales (1955–64)*

	Level of *per capita* consumption			Volume of retail sales *per capita*		
	1955	1960	1964	1955	1960	1963
Consumption in Hungary as % of						
consumption in Poland	108	116	120	103	111	110
consumption in Czechoslovakia	73	78	84	68	79	85
consumption in GDR	76	72	80	–	–	–
consumption in USSR	–	–	–	119	125	131

Western source: M. Ernst in JEC, 1966, p. 62. Although Hungary lagged behind Austria and West Germany, the gap was smaller than for the other socialist countries.
Soviet source: Ia. Ia. Kotkovskii and O. K. Rybakov, translated in JEC, 1968.

The healthy state of Hungarian exports of manufactured consumer goods to Western Europe at the beginning of the 1960s was another encouraging sign: some products at least (e.g. leather goods) were of sufficiently good quality and succeeded in increasing their share of the market, at the same time as Czechoslovakia was encountering serious difficulties with similar articles.

These were certainly still only the first signs of recovery. Their importance must not be exaggerated, particularly as far as the standard of living is concerned (the gap between Hungary and Czechoslovakia and East Germany was still far from being filled, and the gap between Hungary and Western Europe continued to widen). The similarities with the other Soviet-type economies were still much greater than the differences. Moreover, one country at least was applying an economic policy of which some aspects were not dissimilar from Hungarian policy. That country was East Germany. Common to the two countries was the importance that they attached to balanced growth, to relatively moderate growth in investment (except between 1958 and 1961), and to adequate control over inflationary pressures (both a cause and a consequence of a more efficient banking system). The same constraints applied to the improvement of the standard of living: house-building, in particular, remained sacrificed to productive investment, in order to reduce the risk of imbalances and bottlenecks in the building and building materials sector.

On several points, the Hungarian evolution from 1957 foreshadows that of the East German economy after the reform of 1963, which is paradoxical in view of the respective levels of development of the two countries. The concentration of enterprises, for example, which facilitates the transmission of centralised directives and the exercising of control at an intermediate level of the hierarchy, accelerated rapidly in Hungary from 1960 onwards, as it was to in East Germany in the middle and at the end of the 1960s. Similarly, the drive to perfect a more balanced system of indicators of success, which was a point common to all the reforms which stressed the reduction of costs and the improvement of quality, was already relatively advanced in Hungary at the beginning of the 1960s. From this period onwards, Hungarian economic policy seemed to have turned the institutions of the centralised economy to best account by seeking systematically to limit the consequences of the distortions inherent in the model.

Thus real progress had been made in comparison with the 1950s. But the limits of progress were becoming more and more obvious: which led directly to much more radical new reforms being considered.

In order to understand the origin of the reforms of the 1960s, it is thus necessary to take into account both the fundamental problems common to all the Soviet-type economies and the historical conditions particular to each country.

From about 1962 to 1965, economic disappointments multiplied in all the Eastern European countries. The promises to improve the standard of living were not kept. Depending on the sector, the technological gap between Eastern Europe and the advanced Western countries remained stable, grew wider, or was recreated in new forms. And finally, the drop in industrial growth rates appeared as the most obvious symptom of economic difficulties.

It is no doubt necessary to be wary of the rather frequent tendency to draw exaggeratedly pessimistic general conclusions from the slightest slowing down or break in growth: it was, to say the least, a hasty conclusion to interpret the severe crisis in Czechoslovakia at the beginning of the 1960s, caused by an accumulation of errors and circumstantial factors, as a sign of the inevitable cessation of growth in the more developed Soviet-type economies. Similarly, to present 'the reforms' *en bloc* as a necessary development, corresponding to a certain stage in the evolution of 'productive forces', is a result of simplistic determinism: the distortions inherent in the centralised model make themselves felt at all stages of growth, and the desire to find a solution for them is above all a question of political decision.

The drop in growth nevertheless played an important role, since it helped greatly to force the leaders to admit that economic reforms were urgently necessary. The East German and Soviet governments were the first to go down this path. The initiative came from the top, and the consensus at the 'summit' was strong enough to overcome temporarily the resistance of vested interests in the bureaucracies. It was particularly remarkable that in the USSR a reform, of which the broad outlines had been drawn up under Khrushchev, was not called into question in 1964-5 as a result of the new direction, in contrast to many other aspects of Khrushchev's policy.

But if the wind of reform was at that time blowing in almost all the Comecon countries (except Rumania), it was not blowing with the same force everywhere. Poland, Czechoslovakia and Hungary were the three countries most open to the West, and had already carried through an initial series of reforms aimed at easing administrative controls and increasing the rights of the enterprise. The implementation of these initial reforms had demonstrated both the power of the recentralising mechanisms in Soviet-type economies, and the risks of any partial decentralisation conceived simply as a relaxation of constraints within the framework of the current model. The contradiction between increased autonomy for enterprises and the maintenance of tight planning, leading to an unbalanced investment policy, had been the direct cause of the failure of the reforms, while contributing to the worsening disequilibriums of the period from 1959 to 1962.

And yet, the evolution of the three countries was far from being parallel.

In Poland, there was profound bitterness after the hopeful beginning of the new regime. The return to the traditional orientations in almost all areas from 1959 onwards had a depressing effect on public opinion. Debates among economists were never as intense as they had been in 1956-7, nor was there the same climate of freedom from which they had benefited at that time. For its part, the government was reluctant to launch itself into new reforms, and was prepared to do so only in stages, each preceded by an experimental phase, in order to reduce the risks.

In Czechoslovakia, the seriousness of the crisis was reflected, at the beginning of the 1960s, in the more uneven pace at which developments proceeded. At the very moment when the government was completing the dismantling of the 1958-9 reform, and when the centralist backlash was reaching its culmination in about 1962-3, the majority of economists were coming to the conclusion that the failure of the reform was due to the fact that it did not go far enough along the road to decentralisation, and that the solution to all problems lay in re-establishing the mechanisms of the market. In a climate of exasperation, the most radical proposals were widely discussed: the contrast with East Germany is particularly striking in this respect.

Although expressed in a more moderate way, the criticisms made by Hungarian economists were just as radical in content. They denounced the policy of 'forced industrialisation' introduced at the beginning of the Stalinist period, and the impasse into which the Hungarian economy had sunk (F. Janossy was to suggest the term 'pseudo-development' to describe the technological gap which persisted despite the continuous increase in investment, and the permanent disparity between the increase in the standard of living and the rate of industrialisation); it was clearly stressed that the model in force was fundamentally to blame. Aware of the inadequacy of the adjustments outlined since 1957, the instigators of the Hungarian reform insisted on obtaining from the government, at a relatively early stage, an unequivocal decision on the basic options, for fear that the consistency of the plan would be jeopardised afterwards by compromises and half-measures. Since the situation was much less critical than in Czechoslovakia, it was in the end possible to prepare the plan carefully, and to implement it with calculated slowness: by postponing the coming into force of the 'new mechanisms', Hungary spared itself the demoralising 'false starts' which contributed to the sinking of the Czechoslovakian reform between 1965 and January 1968. The fate of the two projects, initially fairly similar in inspiration and content, was to be very different.

Part III
The reforms and their aftermath

5 Limited or fundamental reform?

It is still difficult today, because of an inadequate historical perspective, to assess the importance of the economic reforms implemented in the socialist countries in the middle and at the end of the 1960s. In the West, there has been widespread disenchantment among those who thought that the reforms heralded a decisive change of direction: nothing of the sort in fact happened. However, if a more reasonable attempt is made to judge the reforms according to their own aims, the reserve with which the subject is treated in all the socialist countries is in itself revealing: nowhere, except in Hungary, are the reforms of the 1960s considered as an essential milestone in recent economic development.

But to see these reforms merely as a temporary interlude would be to go to the other extreme. From time to time, the theme becomes topical again: one particular country announces, with more or less conviction, that the process is being relaunched, and this will doubtless be the case until the basic problems for which the reforms were to have been a solution are resolved. Besides, attempts which prove unsuccessful are not always unworthy of attention. A systematic analysis of the initial plan and its actual implementation may help us to define better the essential characteristics of the Soviet-type economies and societies, their capacity for adaptation and their resistance to change. While there are many similarities in the various national experiments, they developed in different ways; a comparative analysis thus seems advisable in order to bring out both the similarities and the differences.

Yet, the dominant approach among Western observers since the beginning of the 'Liberman discussion' has been to consider in a very general way 'the economic reform in Eastern Europe', as if there were only slight differences from one country to another. And indeed, everything seemed to point in the same direction: there were similar problems to be solved, the reforms took place at the same time, their general orientation was similar, each stage of their implementation was strictly controlled by the party, even the nomenclature was often very similar (from the New East German Economic System of 1963 to the New Hungarian Economic Mechanism of 1968). It was, of course, the development of the Soviet reform which was most closely followed in the West. For their part, economists in the socialist countries had excellent reasons for stressing the similarities of the different projects, rather than their distinguishing features: playing down the originality of their own endeavour was the first condition of success for the authors of the radical reforms, while the authors of the more conservative reforms rejected the very notion of a possible plurality of models in a socialist economy.

The process of 'normalisation' in Czechoslovakia was to be a forcible reminder of the limits of permitted differences; at the same time, the reform of economic mechanisms alone seemed to lose much of its importance. The concept of the reforms as an evolving process, and the insistence of governments on their 'open' nature, as a reaction against the 'dogmatism' of the Stalinist period, turned out to be illusory. They were often used simply to justify a series of experiments and half-measures, which, even if they were presented as temporary arrangements, tended to become permanent. In all countries the reforms were at least partially halted, as a prelude to being more or less explicitly challenged. Today, just as fifteen years ago, there remain very strong similarities among all the Soviet-type economies: it is enough simply to mention the decisive influence of the party agencies at all levels of decision-making, the direct control of large-scale investment, the development of specialisation agreements within the Comecon framework, the centralised determination of prices and the very strict control of the evolution of wages, and the priority implicitly given to guaranteeing employment over the requirements of mobility and profitability.

This initial impression of uniformity needs clarification and qualification. But it must be stressed immediately that the gradual convergence that characterised the later phase does not mean that there were no fundamental differences from one country to another in the initial reform plans. The systematic minimisation of these differences led to certain Western analysts making errors, but of widely differing kinds. The most widespread error initially was to consider 'the reform', taken as a whole, as the beginning of a conversion to 'market socialism'; it was more or less hesitant, more or less held up by the resistance of the 'bureaucrats', but inevitable in the long term as soon as a breach had been opened in the centralised economy. This interpretation was almost immediately contradicted by developments in the USSR in particular, and thus gave way to a very different interpretation, which saw all the reforms as purely empirical, partial corrections, decided on under the pressure of circumstances. It no doubt had to be acknowledged that some reforms went further than others, which was to be explained, for example, by the balance of power between 'pragmatists' and 'dogmatists',[1] but in the final analysis they were all the result of 'more or less pronounced Libermanism' (H. G. Schaffer).

It is certainly necessary to 'classify' the reforms, from the most limited to the most radical, but any attempt to do so comes up against several difficulties.

The reforms did not all have the same outcome. The progress of the Czechoslovakian reform was characterised by dramatic reversals, which means that separate consideration must be given to the hesitant initial phase from 1965 to 1967, the explosive period from January to August 1968, the one-year interval after the Soviet intervention, when the economic reform seemed to be forging ahead, and the final phase of normalisation from the autumn of 1969 onwards. Even apart from this extreme case, there was always a time-lag between the successive stages of the process, from the proposals by economists for reform to their actual implementation, *via* the texts which set out the general principles and the laws and decrees which put the reform into practice. A separate classification ought logically to be drawn up for each stage: in Poland, for example, a real gulf separated the positions taken by the leading economists from the very cautious concept which finally prevailed; in Bulgaria, an initially radical plan in the end led only to very partial changes.

Another, even more serious difficulty is that there is no single *a priori* criterion for drawing up such a 'classification'. Each reform was more or less far-reaching in a particular area (the orientation of day-to-day production, investment decisions, access to foreign markets). A complete inventory of similarities and differences could well lead to an impasse, by putting what is essential and what is of secondary importance on the same level, and by suggesting, falsely, that there is a continuous gradation between the different plans.

Our approach will be quite different, since we shall rely on the notion of the 'model' forming a consistent whole which has been the main theme in the first two parts. This will lead us to isolate a small number of main criteria, that are closely linked, to the extent that they all directly reflect the underlying model. These criteria are, firstly, the conditions of access for enterprises to the means of production (i.e. was rationing maintained or abolished), secondly, the nature of the regulators used to guide their decisions, thirdly, the incentive formula, fourthly, the principles of price determination and, finally, the type of economic organisation. Remarkably, these different criteria, taken as a whole, all point to the same conclusion as to the 'limited' or 'radical' nature of the reforms contemplated in each country. Moreover, some anomalies are purely superficial. The importance of 'decentralised investment', for example, can be assessed either according to the financing criterion ('decentralisation' often amounting to little more than deducting from the profits made by an enterprise the necessary funds for investments decided by higher authorities), or according to the actual decision-making level; a classification based on the first criterion often contradicts all the indicators of relative decentralisation, but adopting the second, undoubtedly more significant, criterion is often sufficient to make them tally.

It is true that several plans for reform contained internal contradictions, often of crucial importance. These are 'unstable schemes', of which it is impossible to say whether they were more or less far-reaching than a limited but consistent reform (of the East German type, for example). Their implementation led rapidly to intolerable consequences. Thus any relaxing of the control over product range was disastrous for consumers, as long as the incentive system did not first and foremost reward enterprises for satisfying demand more adequately. Similarly, the more widespread use of profits as an indicator of success was incompatible with arbitrary and rigid prices. In the absence of new and efficient regulators, even the partial decentralisation of investment came into conflict with all the planned balances; and so it went on. The factors which seemed to be the most innovatory were to be neutralised almost as they were introduced. As we have seen, the 1950s offered several examples of half-measures which proved to be impracticable, and the experiments of the 1960s confirmed without doubt that partial decentralisation is impossible if it is conceived as a compromise solution or a mere relaxing of constraints, without the restoration of market mechanisms and control by the market.

Consequently, the analysis must first of all concentrate on that closely interdependent group of elements which defines the 'model' or 'economic mechanism'. On the other hand, there is a much less strict correlation between the more or less radical nature of the reforms and the spread of the private sector, the desire to open up the economy to the West, the degree of political liberalisation or even the position given to trade unions. There is no *a priori* reason to assume that the economic reforms had to be accompanied by abrupt discontinuities in all respects in the evolution of the different countries.

Yet it is impossible to avoid the question of why the reforms of the 1960s, even the initially radical ones, did not succeed more in bringing about profound changes in economic structures and patterns of behaviour, and why, in the final analysis, they had so little influence on political, social and cultural developments. Is it enough simply to mention the influence of the Stalinist past, and the need for a long transition to dispel the consequences of the centralised model? Experience also shows that an internally consistent plan for economic reform is not in itself a sufficient condition for long-term success. Resistance to certain social implications, more or less consciously underestimated at the outset, was without doubt a decisive factor. Nor could a decentralising reform in a Soviet-type economy be compatible with just any economic policy. A return to unbalanced growth could well prove fatal to it: faced with unforeseen tensions, the most expeditious solution is always to re-establish direct controls, and it is a deeply ingrained reflex. The reforms thus remained precarious and vulnerable, long after they had been successfully incorporated into the economy. In fact, time was not on their side: their success depended on their ability to produce tangible results rapidly, before the initial enthusiasm had faded, yet without going beyond the limits fixed by the basic options common to all the communist regimes.

The common ground

The general aims of the reforms were basically the same in all the countries. In each of them, efficiency was to be improved, technological development to be accelerated, and 'extensive' growth was to give way to 'intensive' growth. A more rapid improvement in the standard of living – after the cruel disappointments of the early 1960s – was also a major aim of the reforms, and without doubt their ultimate objective. There was nothing fundamentally new in that. If the reforms of 1963–8 represent a turning point, it is certainly not because of the adoption of these long-proclaimed grand aims, but only because of the desire to overcome a certain number of obstacles, the cause of which was becoming increasingly clear.

The diagnosis of the factors preventing both improved consumer satisfaction and intensive development was, to a certain extent, the same in all the countries. Bureaucratic interference in the day-to-day running of enterprises was harshly condemned everywhere. Attacks were made on the stifling proliferation of controls, on the stupidity of dictating to enterprises even the strictly technical decisions within their scope, on the arbitrary fixing of planned targets and on the excessive alterations made to plans as they were being implemented. The term 'administrative management methods' (as opposed to 'economic methods') appeared often in official declarations, in the USSR, East Germany, and the other countries, with clearly pejorative connotations.[2] At the same time, there was much stress on the unique role to be played by initiatives taken by the enterprise itself. 'Nobody can know better than the enterprise', stressed Gomulka, 'its own hidden economic reserves and how to put them to use.' But what the enterprise alone knows, it can also very well conceal: an end therefore had to be put to an incentive system which encouraged enterprises to haggle over targets and to reduce their real potential. Hypercentralisation (labelled 'bureaucratism') was also judged to be responsible for the maladjustment of production to consumer demand: too many administrative screens separated the producer from the final consumer, and the enterprises had no means of gauging precisely the requirements of its customers. The logical conclusion of this analysis[3] was to recommend the development of 'direct links'.

However, in no country was the fundamental problem of the reforms put in terms of arbitration between the preferences of the central authorities and the individual preferences of consumers. It was considered self-evident that the reforms had both to find a remedy for the consequences of hypercentralisation and to strengthen the ascendancy of central planning. The countries which opted for more radical reforms – Czechoslovakia and Hungary – were as vigorous as the others in asserting the importance of the second aspect: 'As to its effects, the new system of management will be more centralised than the present one, which is, from more than one point of view, centralised only in appearance. . . . The new system of management is necessary precisely for the greater fulfilment of the central will.'[4]

The improvement of planning methods

Nowhere was the improvement of planning techniques seen as a means of replacing political decision by the authorities with economic calculation.

On the contrary, the improvement was to allow central planning to fulfil its role as an instrument of political decision-making. In order that the national economic plan might no longer be a mere juxtaposition of 'more or less co-ordinated' sectoral plans, it was proposed in Hungary that in future there should be a strict obligation for alternative plans to be drawn up at each level of the planning process; the Planning Office would itself submit to the political authorities several alternatives 'involving differences of opinion on fundamental points of economic policy and indicating different strategies' (Ganczer in Friss (ed.), 1969, ch. IV). Thus a political decision was to be both the starting point (in the form of general directives) and, particularly, the end of the planning process. The Hungarian example is especially significant: even a reform clearly centred on the decentralisation of the day-to-day running of the economy could go hand in hand with increased centralisation as far as the collecting of information, the process of drawing up the plan and the essential decisions were concerned.

These last, by definition, implied long-term choices. This is why the long-term (fifteen- to twenty-year) and five-year plans were stressed; in future, they were to have priority over the annual plans. The FYP provided certain guarantees of stability, to the advantage of enterprises, through methods which depended on the type of reform adopted: in East Germany, the main tasks to be carried out over the planning period were to be communicated to enterprises, whereas in Hungary, the main fiscal and other regulators were to be fixed for three to five years.

But these long-term concerns were accompanied by a need for increased flexibility. The precise problem was to 'link the long-term stability of the aims underlying development with flexibility in the carrying out of tasks . . . in the framework of the annual economic plan . . . with a view to obtaining the best possible relationship between stability and mobility in planned economic development' (Wolf, 1966, in *Eastern European Economics*, Summer 1967). There was no longer any question of systematically ignoring uncertainties, of planning without taking into account the many variables that were outside the authorities' control (weather conditions, the economic situation abroad, the evolution of consumer demand). Thus the plan was for targets to be fixed in the form of margins, for reserves at all levels to be created, and for alternative plans to be drawn up, so that the broad outlines of a strategy drawn up at the beginning of each period could be followed, while at the same time making it possible to adapt to the requirements of the situation.

Strengthening and reform of the incentive system

The insistence on the role of material incentives had such an important place in the official presentation of the reforms that it was sometimes believed that they had been 're-discovered': as if bonuses of all sorts were not already an important element of the traditional system! The reconciliation of the interests of the individual, of the enterprise and of society appeared as a *leitmotif* in the outline of the aims of the various reforms. 'The optimum relationship between planning and initiative must be established, with maximum co-ordination of the interests of the enterprise and its workforce, and those of society as a whole' (Bachurin, 1968, in *Problems of Economics*, April 1969, p. 12). These were old problems, well-known to countries like Poland that had already made one or even several attempts at partial reform: 'Until now, all reforms carried out in the socialist countries have been attempts to rationalise the economic mechanisms so as to avoid conflict' (Lipowski, 1968, in *Eastern European Economics*, Autumn 1969).

However, the reforms of 1963–8 marked a turning point, to the extent that the problem of the inefficient incentive system was from then on discussed as a product of the system of planned management, and not in terms of a denunciation of the individual faults of enterprises with a tendency to cheat. If the system of regulation was unable to reflect accurately the wishes of the planner, and if the regulators functioned in the wrong way, it was intolerable to appeal to the 'moral conscience' of the managers of an enterprise, without attempting to change the system.

In fact, it was not so much a question of strengthening as of re-orientating the incentive system. Particular emphasis was to be given to worker participation in the collective performance of the enterprise (as opposed to the individual performance of workers paid according to productivity). And from now on, profits appeared as the main criterion used to measure this collective performance. From 1963 onwards, the East German reform gave profits a 'decisive role' as an 'economic lever' in the new system of planned management. Profits were officially defined as

> the reflection of the collective efforts and the good management of socialist producers . . . The development and implementation of modern methods . . . the reduction of costs, the improvement of quality, adapting production to needs and good marketing must

> create profits, whereas any violation of these social necessities will cause losses to be made.[5]

Almost all the reforms set up funds for each enterprise (a profit-sharing fund, a fund for social measures and a development fund), linked at least partially to the amount of profit and sustained by deductions from profits.

It remains only to assess the precise significance that can be attributed to profits as an indicator of success in a Soviet-type economy. Profits are without doubt an aggregate indicator *par excellence*, but can they be a simple, objective norm, of uniform application, which enables the old system of rewarding enterprises for exceeding more or less arbitrary production targets, that were constantly revised on the basis of the results obtained, to be abolished? The fate of the reforms depended to a large extent on the answer to this question. Precise conditions must be met if profits are to measure correctly the net social contribution of the activity of an enterprise. Any increase in the importance of profits and of the 'indirect' regulators (the basic aim of which is to influence decisions made by enterprises, through the total amount of profits) is conceivable only if the nature of prices, their role in a planned economy and the method by which they are determined are fully redefined.

The rehabilitation of 'commodity and money relationships'

The persistence of commodity and money relationships – Marx had forecast their disappearance in the first phase of the construction of socialism – had imperceptibly ceased to be considered as an undesirable feature of the economy, even if care was still taken to justify them:

> We have observed [wrote W. Ulbricht[6]], that socialism is not a brief transitional phase in the evolution of society, but constitutes a relatively autonomous social and economic development in the historical age of transition from capitalism to world communism .... For this reason, the categories of the social economy which, from a structural point of view, are similar to those of the capitalist economy (money, prices, profits etc.) [can only be] seen as a necessary evil that must be eliminated.

However, the real question was not the justification of money and prices, which had never really been challenged since the period of war communism, but rather to enable them to fulfil their role in accordance with the 'economic laws of socialism'. And to that end, it was urgently necessary to put an end to the disorder in the system of prices, which robbed monetary calculations of any meaning.

The problem of prices was thus the crucial problem of the reforms of 1963–8, since it was at this point that the two main lines of reform converged: the strengthening of central planning, and the reduction of the centralised management of enterprises through indirect methods.

1 At the end of laborious discussions on the 'law of value', which had been going on in the USSR since the end of the 1950s, the theoretical solution of prices 'proportional to value' (taking into account only labour costs) was dismissed in all the socialist countries. The various price reforms carried out at the end of the 1960s tended systematically to include in prices an element of profit calculated in proportion to the (monetary) value of fixed and circulating capital, in order to 'transmit to purchasers more accurate information on the social conditions of production' (Sztyber, 1969, in *Eastern European Economics*, Winter 1970–1, p. 91). In a way, this was an extension of the notion of 'socially necessary expenditure', in that it took into account the degree of capital intensity: thus 'the criterion for decisions on investment plans becomes, at the same time, the basis of price determination' (Sztyber, 1969, in *Eastern European Economics*, Winter 1970–1, p. 91).

The same preoccupation with 'economising on capital' was to lead – often without waiting for the implementation of the prices reform – to the introduction in all the countries of a 'tax on fixed and circulating funds'. A tax of this kind was implicitly equivalent to making enterprises pay interest on the productive capital made available to them by the state. Judged immediately to be one of the most innovatory aspects of the reform, this measure created a stir in the West that was no doubt out of proportion with its true theoretical and practical importance.

Studies by mathematical economists (particularly Soviet ones) had without any doubt contributed to the adoption of these measures; but they were implemented as a result of an empirical compromise. For fear that many enterprises would be penalised for earlier, excessive investments that they had not decided on themselves, the idea of making the tax rate (6 per cent) equal to the true economic cost of the capital, corresponding to the minimum level of efficiency required for new investment (of the order of 15 per cent as a rule), was abandoned; and, in addition, there were to be a whole series of exemptions for certain sectors. The same empiricism prevailed when it came to determining the element of profit to be included in prices, which was in theory proportional to the total amount of capital, but which was in fact variable according to sector and product, so that there was not too much deviation from existing situations. At least capital was in theory no longer free for enterprises.

In the mining industries, an important step was taken towards fixing prices on the basis of marginal cost: it was admitted that it was necessary to establish a single price 'on the basis of expenditure recorded by enterprises functioning normally, but working in the worst natural, mining and geological conditions' (Gabyshev, 1969, in *Problems of Economics*, July 1970). This led to a levy proportional to their relative advantage being deducted from all the other producers, under the name of 'fixed payment'.

2 The concern with greater price flexibility was much clearer proof of a new approach than the discussions on the theoretical 'formula'. The former practice – infrequent general revisions, separated by long intervals – was widely condemned. It was admitted that 'even the most perfect reforms cannot solve the problem once and for all', and that the price structure would in future have to be continuously adjusted, particularly in the sectors where the acceleration of technological progress was a priority aim. 'We thus need a much more dynamic price structure than in the past . . . [in order to] reflect the constant changes in the proportions of value or in the conditions in which value is produced' (Reilher and Schierz, 1965, in *Eastern European Economics*, Summer 1967).

It was admitted more or less explicitly that demand, which no formula for calculating prices on the basis of production costs can, by definition, take into account, had at least to exercise an influence on the day-to-day adjustment of prices. The notion of an equilibrium price emerged, even in the countries which did not opt for the general reintroduction of market mechansims.[7]

The constant adjustment of prices was not, however, limited to the pursuit of instant equilibrium in accordance with a static concept. All the countries stressed the need for long- or medium-term planning of prices. Projected wholesale price indices by product group, included in the FYP, were to aid the calculations of the planner himself, and also those of enterprises. By combining price planning and a stable incentive system, enterprises were to be given the chance to plan further ahead, in accordance with their increased powers of decision and responsibilities.

The apparent similarity and the basic options of the reforms

An increased role for profits among the indicators of success, greater price flexibility, the development of 'indirect', as opposed to 'administrative' methods of managing enterprises: these have been picked out as the main aims common to all the reforms, and they give them an undeniable kinship. Yet care must be taken not to overestimate a whole series of similarities which are, in fact, well within the basic options of the model: measures that on first sight seem similar often hide fundamental differences.

This is the case with the profit indicator. There was no doubt a basic agreement to prevent profits being appropriated by a private capitalist, or even by the staff of an enterprise; the higher authorities always maintained their right to control how profits were used, since they at least determined how profits were to be allocated. If profits have a place in a socialist economy, it is as a criterion of efficiency. The role that can be given to them in the incentive system depends very much on how accurately they reflect the efforts made by an enterprise. Their significance in this respect varies completely according to the actual extent of centralisation: is the enterprise able to choose its suppliers and production methods? To what extent is it responsible for its investments? Is there competition among enterprises in the same sector for the placing of orders with customers? And, above all, is adjustment to demand – in other words, quality assessed from the point of view of the user – a determining factor in the producer's profits? If none of these conditions is met, if profits continue to depend basically on factors unconnected with the efforts of the enterprise, how can it be possible to persevere with the original intention of making profits the sole criterion, or even the basis of the incentive system?

Similarly, price flexibility was considered desirable in all countries. But how was this flexibility to be guaranteed? By a free system of price determination, after the necessary conditions for the re-establishment of market mechanisms had been created? Or, on the contrary, by maintaining the principle of centralised determination? And if there was a movement towards a combination of the two, or the development of new formulae, such as part of the task of price determination being delegated by the central authorities, what was their precise significance, particularly from a dynamic point of view: would such a system prove capable of functioning? In what direction would it tend to evolve? As long as the rigidities inherent in the traditional system of price determination persisted, it was unthinkable to allow enterprises the freedom of determining their own activity; and, in particular, the range of goods to be produced had still to be imposed, in one way or another. Any questioning of the need for 'bureaucratic interference' is thus proof of a superficial analysis.

The same ambiguity appears again in relation to the 'indirect' methods ('economic' methods) of managing firms. In all cases, the aim was to make possible, on the basis of certain parameters (prices, wages, rate of interest, taxation), decentralised economic decision-making at the level of the enterprise, in order to reduce the amount of work involved in the system of planned management, without, of course, any idea of meeting the broad targets laid down by the central authorities being abandoned. But it is clear from what has gone before that the essential point is to know how the parameters were fixed:[8] was the decision taken solely by the central authorities, or were there also, in addition to a small number of strategies available to the planner, a large number of parameters determined by the market? A distinction can be made between two broad types of reform, which differed in two main ways.

The first difference was in the extent to which the scope of political or administrative decision-making was widened. In the limited reforms, their scope continued to include all economic activity; in the fundamental reforms, the principle of planning by directive continued to apply to all priorities (and in this respect, there was no precise pre-established list) defined by the central authorities, but it was recognised that there existed a vast 'zone' (comprising essentially the multitude of detailed decisions relating to consumption) within which no specific social preferences operated; within this zone, the authorities left the direct adjustment of supply and demand to market mechanisms.

The second difference was in the principles by which the system functioned. In the limited reforms, any process of adjustment required a specific intervention by the higher authorities; in the 'fundamental' reforms, the centre influenced and guided the market, but refrained as far as possible from any direct interference in the actual processes; even the targets given priority by the state were normally to be achieved by means of the market.

The main differences and the distinguishing features of the two main types of reform

The presentation of the reforms

It is true that all the governments – except in Poland and Rumania – spoke of 'fundamental' economic reforms, and stressed the difference from the many administrative reorganisations of the past, which had always had disappointing results.

In the majority of cases, this did not prevent ritual homage being paid to the services rendered by the traditional planning system, and its 'objective necessity' in the previous stage of development was explicitly reaffirmed. For example, if we are to believe one senior official in the East German planning commission, there was nothing in the reforms which resembled 'a repudiation of the economic principles of socialism that have been observed until now, or a correction of so-called errors' (Wolf, in *Eastern European Economics*, Summer 1967). In two countries, on the other hand, the mistakes of the past were bitterly denounced: in Czechoslovakia, of course, even before 1968, but also in Hungary. The works of I. T. Berend sought the origin of the fundamental imbalances that were affecting the Hungarian economy in the Stalinist past, and tried to correct the statistical falsehoods of the 'Rakosi era'. F. Janossy questioned the persistence, despite recent watering down, of the policy of 'forced industrialisation', 'like an old liaison which is maintained by force of habit and which will end only if a new love comes to take its place' (Janossy, 1969, in *Eastern European Economics*, Summer 1970). The sudden hiccups in production suggested to G. Peter an unflattering comparison with an athlete who takes drugs and whose performances suddenly collapse. In more moderate terms, the main authors of the reform suggested quite explicitly that the model then in use was responsible for the situation. I. Friss, for example, stressed that the slowing down of growth was not inevitable ('it is certain that the shortcomings of our planning system and of our methods of economic management have contributed to it') (Friss, in *Acta Oeconomica*, 1967, vol. 2, p. 4), just as, for B. Csikos-Nagy, director of the Prices Office, the lack of adjustment to demand and reductions in quality were not to be considered as accidental failures, since these negative phenomena 'arise basically from the old mechanism' (Csikos-Nagy in Friss (ed.), 1969, ch. VII, p. 16).

It was around the notion of the model that the basic contrasts between the countries crystallised.

It is true that not all the Hungarian authors were in agreement on the precise definition and delimitation of the different models of the socialist economy. A. Hegedus, for example (Hegedus, in *Acta Oeconomica*, 1970, vol. 5), proposed three distinct models: management by the administration, full *khozraschët* (management based on monetary indicators, quite close to the type of reform that East Germany was trying to introduce), and, finally, autonomy for enterprises accompanied by control by the market. B. Csikos-Nagy, like most of the Hungarian economists, confined himself to a simpler distinction between a 'pure planned model' (based on direct orders and the detailed breakdown of the targets contained in the plan) and a model based on a 'consciously regulated market' (in which the interaction between planned regulation and the market was to guide the national economy). At least there was general agreement that a very clear decision as to the kind of model had to be at the root of the reforms. And throughout the whole of the preparatory phase, efforts were made systematically to compare 'the two different types of socialist economy: the economy based on direct detailed orders, and the economy based on the working of a consciously controlled market' (Schweitzer, 1968, in *Acta Oeconomica*, 1968, vol. 3, p. 336).

An entirely different approach prevailed in those countries where the notion of the plurality of socialist models was implicitly or (increasingly) explicitly impugned. In East Germany, the reform, dictated by the scientific exigencies of the development of 'the' planning system, could well be presented on occasions as a sort of middle way: 'The New Economic System is the practical negation both of the bureaucratic methods of management, formal and administrative, and of the concepts of the working of socialist economies that are inspired by the market economy.' But it was clear that this latter type of solution was ruled out as a matter of principle: 'The concept, sometimes expounded even by socialist authors, according to which it is necessary, in the development of the socialist system of planning, to choose between two models – the centralised administrative model and a decentralised market economy – seems excessively schematic and only offers a choice between two equally inadequate solutions' (Wolf, 1966, translated in *Eastern European Economics*, Summer 1967). From 1968 onwards, the crisis in Czechoslovakia brought with it increased attacks in the USSR and in East Germany against 'market socialism', an 'undeniably anti-Marxist' concept; these attacks were in fact aimed at all supporters of the decentralised model, those people who 'while seeming to demand the elimination of the shortcomings in the development of socialism, are in fact seeking consciously or unconsciously to send the economy sliding down the road to the abandonment of its basic advantages, by borrowing to a greater or lesser extent capitalist methods' (Eremin, 1967, translated in *Problems of Economics*, August 1970).

The role of the market

It was acknowledged in all the countries that the market in a socialist economy had to be at the service of central planning. But within this general statement there were very wide divergences.

In Czechoslovakia and Hungary, a general agreement had been established as early as the preparatory discussion phase (1964–5) to make the increased role of the market a fundamental guiding principle. The essence of the reform was 'to link the planned central management of the national economy to the active role of the market' (Fekete, in Friss (ed.), 1969, p. 70): a close link of this nature was the only possible foundation for the autonomy of the enterprise.

The market was to fulfil a double function: the detailed adjustment of supply to demand and the control of planning decisions.

It is indeed hard not to acknowledge that purchasers (final consumers or enterprises) are more competent than any administrative agency to judge whether a product is suited to their specific needs. For this reason, the reform was to aim at 'reunifying the processes of production and realisation', in order that enterprises might be 'guided more and more by the judgements of the market' (Csikos-Nagy, in *Acta Oeconomica*, 1970, vol. 5). In other words, only a prices system influenced by the market could supply producers with detailed and constantly up-dated information on the requirements of consumers, and at the same time encourage them to react in an appropriate way.

As prices lose their purely administrative nature, the market becomes suited to the no less essential function of control allotted to it. The words of Ota Sik, 'Market relationships help to ensure that the labour expanded in the enterprise tends to be socially necessary labour' (Sik, 1967, p. 186), echo those of B. Csikos-Nagy: 'Decisions taken in the sphere of production must be justified in the sphere of exchange' (Csikos-Nagy in Friss (ed.), 1969, p. 186). That being the case, why should the decisions of the central planners not be subject to this control? The market thus has the function of 'revealing and correcting planning errors' (Sik, 1967, p. 272). If, for example, the cost of a large-scale investment project has been underestimated at the outset, the central authorities have to have the means of knowing *ex post* the real cost of their decision. However, this in no way implies any ***automatic*** correction by the market: the final decision would always be made by the political authorities.

The clarity of the basic concept of the Czech and Hungarian reforms is in contrast to the ambiguity of the East German, Polish and Soviet reforms. It is true that 'market relationships' were no longer condemned as a matter of principle. The change to the notion of 'sold production' (unsaleable goods were no longer counted in production, which was an astonishing innovation!), the insistence on 'direct links', on 'contracts' or 'planned orders' are proof of similar preoccupations to those of the Czech and Hungarian leaders, but do not mean, for all that, that market relationships were to be even partially re-established. Consequently, it was inevitable that the 'direct links' (between producers of consumer goods and commerical organisations) came very close to the traditional planned contracts, putting partners designated by the administration into contact with each other, with the sole aim of settling the details of a transaction decided on by an outside agency. In theory, the 'orders' that enterprises were to obtain from the planning agencies certainly implied an element of competition; but, even supposing that the system were to function as planned, any competition was completely asymmetrical, since the only spokesman for the producers was the administration to which they were answerable.

Micro- or macro-economic planning?

This was not a separate 'option' from the previous one, but rather a corollary of it. In the countries which had decided on radical reform, the normal functioning of the market required, however formidable such a change might appear, that micro-economic planning be abandoned. That it was retained in the other countries was a direct result of their opposition to the market as a principle of regulation.

However, the distinction in this respect no longer seems to be as clear-cut, to the extent that all the countries attempted to reduce the level of supervision of enterprises. In the USSR and in East Germany in particular, the number of specific production targets in the central plan was reduced, as were the number of compulsory indicators for enterprises and the number of planned balances drawn up at the highest level. In East Germany, developments in this direction had gone so far that it had become possible, by 1966, to wonder whether the East German economy was on the way to a decisive transformation of its *modus operandi*, a question to which we shall return. It is sufficient to observe here that the system of '*Kontingente*' – delivery slips linking the purchaser to a vendor designated by name – was maintained for basic products; if, on the other hand, the number of balances drawn up at ministerial level was reduced to 'only' a few hundred (at the height of the reform), it was as a result of a kind of delegation of power to the intermediate agencies in the economic hierarchy, the 'associations of enterprises' (cf. p. 142), which had been made responsible for several thousands of balances. As for the rest, the implementation of the reforms was to offer many opportunities to verify the basic lesson of the earlier attempts at reform made at the end of the 1950s: the limits to decentralisation within the framework of the model in force, and the strength of the endogenous processes of recentralisation.

In Hungary, on the other hand, a sort of 'moment of truth' was reached at the end of the first phase of preparatory studies, when the main committee responsible for drawing up the plan asked the authorities of the Hungarian Socialist Workers' Party to make a clear decision as to whether detailed planning at the level of the enterprise should be maintained or abolished. R. Nyers seems to have played a decisive role, by winning acceptance within the central committee (at the November 1965 session, two years before the introduction of the reform) for a new concept of planning by directive: 'Formerly, the mandatory nature of the plan was interpreted to mean that it was obligatory for each of the particular targets or indicators in the plan to be fulfilled, whereas now we have come to consider the complex entity of the economic plan as a compulsory directive for economic action' (Nyers, in *Acta Oeconomica*, 1966, vol. 1, p. 19). I. Friss rightly saw this as the basic originality of the Hungarian reform: 'In contrast with the earlier situation, and with the reforms introduced in the other socialist countries, enterprises in our new system no longer receive any compulsory target or quantitative indicator' (Friss (ed.), 1969, p. 13).

This is in marked contrast with the first phase of the Czech reform, which lasted until 1967, during which it was thought possible to introduce a radical plan by gradual steps. The whole system of administrative-type planning was still in place, and it was often difficult to distinguish any difference between its new 'information only' function and its old function of planning by directive. E. Loebel expressed the general disappointment of reforming economists at the time, when he stated: 'The principle of autonomy for the enterprise, which is the fundamental principle of the new system, has in practice been eliminated.'[9] In order for the decisive step to be taken, the political turning point of January 1968 was necessary. The action programme of the Czech Communist Party, adopted on 5 April 1958, decided clearly in favour of autonomy for enterprises: 'Enterprises faced with the requirements of the market must have freedom of decision in all questions directly concerning the management of the enterprise and must be able to react creatively to the needs of the market', and at the same time announced 'a complete transformation of the role of the plan which, from being an authoritarian device, becomes a programme of economic policy for the efficient development of the economy'. Thus the close interdependence of the main guiding principles of the reform – autonomy for enterprises, the influence of the market and the slimming down of the central plan – was at last fully recognised.

The principles and methods of the incentive system

The fundamental principle of the centralised model is that enterprises are rewarded according to their fulfilment of planned targets. In all the countries where micro-economic planning remained, this principle was never really challenged – even in East Germany – by the increased role of profits or profitability. Profits passed to the state, but a part of them was deducted in order to create various funds for the enterprise (used to finance respectively the payment of bonuses, social and cultural measures for the personnel, decentralised investment by enterprises and the setting up of reserves); this 'deduction' depended on extremely diversified and complex norms, which in fact left all power of assessment to the supervisory authorities. Moreover, since enterprises could still have arbitrarily determined minima or more or less advantageous compulsory tasks imposed on them, the persistence of the traditional bargaining relationships could be foreseen.

In contrast, the incentive system adopted in Hungary appears relatively simple. The enterprise kept the profits it had made, after the deduction of taxes for which it was liable to the state; the only compulsory norm concerned the distribution of the total amount of pre-tax profits between the profit-sharing fund and the development fund (for investment purposes) which were then taxed by different methods. Despite many vicissitudes in the practical implementation, which left a wide margin for the supervisory authorities to influence the bonuses of their firms, the basic principle at least was not called into question: incentives were no longer linked automatically to the fulfilment of a series of compulsory targets.

As early as 1967, Czechoslovakia – as well as Bulgaria – had seemed on first sight to be going much further in the reform of the incentive system, by adopting as 'maximand' not profits (the difference between the income of the enterprise and all its production costs, including wages) as in the USSR, East Germany or Hungary, but gross income (the difference between receipts and production costs other than wages), as in Yugoslavia. Much was at stake: the replacement of profits by gross income would enable the authorities' control over wages to be abolished. Indeed, in the traditional system, the tax on profits encouraged enterprises to inflate wages (included in production costs); if, on the other hand, gross income became the essential indicator and the basis for taxation, these manipulations would become pointless, and the enterprise could in theory be left to allocate its gross income (after tax) as it saw fit, for the payment of wages or bonuses, or for other purposes. But, in practical terms, this radically simplified system was doomed to immediate failure. As in Hungary, the risk of inflation necessitated 'exceptional measures' to slow down the rise of individual incomes, often by the use of methods in blatant contradiction of the spirit of the reform. And, above all, in the conditions that then prevailed, 'gross income' was much too loosely connected with the efficiency of an enterprise (or with the merits of its personnel) to provide the basis for any increased differentiation between individual earnings; in this sense, the redistribution carried out by the supervisory authorities was no doubt usually justified. But the systematic neutralisation of the effects of the new incentive system could only result in 'the perpetuation of economic backwardness' – in the words of the document published in April 1968 by the Czech Communist Party – that is, in the paralysis of the reform.

Economic organisation: strengthening of the intermediate levels of the hierarchy or competition among enterprises?

1 The increased responsibilities given to the 'associations of enterprises' (the eighty 'Vereinigungen Volkseigener Betriebe', or VVB) were the

keystone of the East German economic reform. They date back to 1958, when the sector management agencies were abolished and re-christened VVB. But, as a consequence, they tended to become more administrative in character. 1963–4 was a turning point: the VVB became part of the system of '*khozraschët*', with profits as the main indicator of success and incentive; at the same time, they were to become the mechanism for a policy of 'deconcentration', aimed at lightening the burden of the national planning agencies, while guaranteeing them more effective control of economic activity.

As far as the enterprises were concerned, the strengthening of the VVB was synonymous with increased centralisation. Using their knowledge of the enterprises under their jurisdiction[10] – which were decreasing in number as a result of amalgamations – the officials of the VVB were better able than the central authorities to judge the results of each enterprise and to assess the material rewards or promotions that its managerial staff deserved. Their direct knowledge of production costs in their sector enabled the VVB to exercise, in the name of the central authorities and according to norms fixed by them, a certain amount of 'delegated' power in the determining of prices. Investment decisions were almost entirely entrusted to them (under the control of the ministries and the banks), with enterprises not even retaining the right to dispose of their depreciation funds. Finally, and above all, the associations of enterprises played an essential role in the to-ings and fro-ings up and down the hierarchy (ministries, VVB, enterprises) which resulted in the development of the central plan, incorporating contracts between enterprises; for thousands of products, the adjustment between needs and resources was carried out under the supervision of the VVB, whose task it also was to convey the impetuses emanating from the central authorities.

Following the example of East Germany, Poland, Rumania, Bulgaria and Czechoslovakia also gave a pivotal role to the associations of enterprises or to equivalent organisations. In Poland and, particularly, in Czechoslovakia, the supporters of real autonomy for enterprises were very quickly driven to denouncing the conservative influence of the associations and their omnipotence as a serious threat to the reforms; the impression of continuity with the past was reinforced by the fact that former officials of the central administration often found themselves in charge of the associations. The swing against the prerogatives of the associations which occurred in Czechoslovakia at the beginning of 1968 certainly confirmed their incompatibility with the logic of the radical reforms, which were orientated towards the market and the development of competition.

Hungary, on the other hand, very quickly opted for a type of economic organisation 'comprising two basic decision-making levels: the state and the enterprise' (Hetenyi, in Friss (ed.), 1969, ch. II, pp. 63-4). Two, and not three: 'The new system does not include sector plans, nor decisions at sector level.' This did not, of course, mean the abolition of all planning of long-term development in each sector; but, in order to encourage enterprises to conform to such planning, the central authorities would rely on 'economic considerations rather than on arguments of authority and prestige' (Hetenyi, in Friss (ed.), 1969). While the 'functional' powers of the central agencies (Central Planning Commission, the ministries of finance and labour and the Prices Office) were widened and clarified, there was no longer place in theory for the intermediate supervisory authorities. And although associations of enterprises existed in Hungary as in the other East European countries, they were very different: set up on the initiative of the enterprises themselves, they carried out, in flexible ways, the functions that the member enterprises agreed to entrust to them; membership was optional.

It was in the USSR, as well as in Hungary, but for very different reasons, that the strengthening of the associations met the strongest resistance. The industrial ministries, re-established in 1965 after the *sovnarkhoz* interlude, opposed any encroachment upon their own decision-making powers, for fear that the associations would in turn begin to behave in an autarchic manner; a certain number of those already in existence were dissolved in the years following the reform of 1965. However, this divergence from the East German model did not subsequently widen: from 1970 onwards, there was a growing trend to strengthen the industrial complexes and the associations, particularly in 1973. Like the development in the opposite direction that occurred in Czechoslovakia in 1968, the reversal that took place at that time in the USSR clearly shows that the functional principles characteristic of each type of reform imposed their own kind of economic organisation.

2 In the mid-1960s Czech and Hungarian economists were unanimous in their praise of the virtues of competition.

> Competition gives the purchaser freedom of choice, safe from any economic constraint. . . . Competition begins at the production stage in industry. . . . It involves prices, range of choice, quality and provisions for delivery. The reform foresees the gradual development

> of competition, not only among different enterprises, but also among different activities in order to obtain the purchasing power which appears in the market. (Frenyo, in *Acta Oeconomica*, 1967, vol. 1, p. 93)

Even so, competition really had to be capable of playing the role attributed to it in the plan for reform.

Here again, very clear decisions of principle were taken in Hungary. The system of allocation by the administration, 'which gave rise to an enormous bureaucracy' (Nyers, in *Acta Oeconomica*, 1969, vol. 4, p. 9), was abolished and replaced by a 'commercial mechanism based on direct and, in principle, free market relationships among enterprises' (Gado, in Friss (ed.), 1969, p. 109). The former storage and distribution organisations became commercial wholesale enterprises which had to prove their viability in the face of competition. Industrial and agricultural producers gained the right to sell their production directly, and, in return, the commercial wholesale and retail enterprises were to be free to choose their suppliers.

But the actual introduction of competition was not compatible with just any kind of industrial structure. It was clear that competition had no place in a hierarchical economy in which the associations supervised production in each sector and contolled sales: the declared intention of promoting competition in Czechoslovakia from 1965 onwards was thus doomed to failure. However, the absence of compulsory associations in Hungary was certainly not a sufficient condition for the re-establishment of competition; the very high degree of concentration reached by Hungarian industry by the beginning of the 1960s (the number of state industrial enterprises had fallen in 1967 to 807, and those with more than 1,000 workers accounted for more than 80 per cent of the total) was a no less formidable obstacle. The economic reform was accompanied by a perceptible reversal of this trend in some sectors, but the overall change was quite restricted, since most of the amalgamations were irreversible.

As a consequence, the restoration of a minimum of competition had to be basically dependent on certain 'peripheral' developments. There were various attempts to encourage private initiative, particularly in the service sector (building maintenance, car repair, dry cleaning); the number of self-employed craftsmen and retailers, which had been falling continually at the beginning of the 1960s, began to increase, without, however, reaching the same relative importance as in East Germany.

The remarkable development, following upon the reform, of the secondary activities of the agricultural co-operatives, particularly in the building industry, was much more significant. Finally, the central authorities tried to stress the competitive nature of foreign trade. Exports to the socialist countries, stipulated in the long-term agreements, were put out to tender. About a hundred large enterprises had direct access to the international market. And the retail trade in particular was authorised to request additional imports of consumer goods, in order to prevent national producers from abusing their monopoly position; without allowing itself to be restricted by balance of payments difficulties, the government had no hesitation, after 1968, in actually using this solution both as a means of adjusting supply and demand and of putting pressure on producers.

However, the fact remained that the obstacles of the re-establishment of competition had been seriously underestimated at the beginning, and we shall see what an influence this initial mistake had on the fate of the Hungarian reform.

The principles of price determination

In this respect, comparative analysis brings out both clear differences in the approach to the problem (the Soviet and Hungarian approaches clearly illustrate the two opposite poles), and also common constraints which arise from maintaining a balance between supply and demand. It is hardly surprising, therefore, that the solutions actually applied have a certain similarity.

1 The problem of prices can be summed up in three basic questions: who determines prices (what decision-making centre(s), or what mechanism)? How are they determined? And what are the functions of the prices thus determined?

Paradoxically, the debate on prices remained centred for a long time on the second question, since it was implicitly assumed that the central determination of prices was self-evident, and since a clear answer to the third question had always been refused. In the USSR, the heart of the problem still seemed in 1965 to be to perfect a 'formula' that could 'more accurately' express production costs (socially necessary inputs). Liberman's proposals even helped to turn attention away from the key question of equilibrium prices; Liberman himself came to terms quite easily with the inevitable limitations on the autonomy of enterprises made necessary by imperfect prices. Thus the Soviet wholesale prices reform of 1967 had only limited objectives: it was aimed at reducing the most obvious discrepancies between prices and production costs, and at reducing the number of sectors and enterprises operating at a loss. This was indeed a minimum condition for the implementation of the reform, but not a sufficient condition for the establishment of a real system of 'management by prices'.

In Hungary, as B. Csikos-Nagy clearly explains in an article entitled 'The two phases of the debate on prices in Hungary' (*Acta Oeconomica*, 1966, vol. 1, p. 255), the problem of prices had for a long time been posed, as in the USSR, independently of any reference to the model and the possibility of changing it. The decisive turning point came when the economic reform was being drawn up. It was realised then that 'the unsuitability of the prices system was not an accidental defect in the old system, but the inevitable corollary of it' (G. Peter, in *Acta Oeconomica*, 1967, vol. 2, p. 35). If there were so many aberrant disparities, without any economic or political justification whatsoever, between costs and the prices in force, it was because prices were 'extraordinarily rigid and unsuited to the harmonisation of supply and demand. The extremely wide scope of price determination by the state – it affects more than one million products – makes it impossible to determine correct relative prices' (Nyers, in *Acta Oeconomica*, 1966, vol. 1, p. 27). More fundamentally, the idea emerged that it was the absence of any control by the market, in a system of allocation in kind, that caused the chaos in the prices system.

The problem of prices was thus entirely rethought with a view to the reform of the economic mechanism: it became clear that it was not a question of 'choosing a prices system', but first of all of 'defining the relationship between the plan and the market'. The function of prices was not simply to adjust demand to a predetermined supply, but was to give an orientation to the production process: 'There must be economic unity between production and sales, in such a way that short-term decisions taken by enterprises are fundamentally determined by the needs and value judgements of the market' (Gado, in Friss (ed.), 1969, p. 109).

The Hungarian reform thus involved an unequivocal decision: it was necessary 'to put an end to the administrative prices system' (Csikos-Nagy, in *Acta Oeconomica*, 1966, vol. 1, p. 264), i.e. to centralised price determination. Once the changeover had been successfully completed, the central authorities would have to avoid as far as possible any direct interference, and allow the economy to function 'with the help of a prices mechanism which adequately reflects the economic processes operating in the market' (Csikos-Nagy, in Friss (ed.), 1969, p. 148). On the other hand, this in no way prevented the state from conducting a prices policy; the turnover tax, in particular, was to regain its normal function of expressing properly justified social preferences, instead of being determined residually as in the old system.

2 Although the basic principles were very far apart, the difference seems on first sight to be much less obvious when their implementation from one country to another is compared. All the countries had inherited a profoundly distorted prices structure at the end of the Stalinist period. But no government wanted to take the risk of an upheaval in retail prices with fearsome social consequences, which would endanger the standard of living and would not fail to rouse the populace against the reforms; retail price increases were thus limited as much as possible (in Hungary and Bulgaria, the main examples were certain food products for which prices at the production stage had been considerably increased), and for the time being any reform was limited to wholesale prices.[11] The distortions in the structure of wholesale prices were no less serious than for retail prices, and there was no question of relying on the 'market' to correct them 'spontaneously', which would have triggered off intolerable disturbances to the activity of certain sectors. The reforms of wholesale prices were thus carried out according to the traditional procedure, that is, using centralised calculations based on production costs declared by enterprises. They differed from one country to another in the theoretical 'formula' adopted (inspired more or less directly by Marx's 'production prices'), but above all in the extent of the deviations from this formula that had to be accepted for many reasons, and also in the firmness with which the price-determining agencies were able to resist the pressures from enterprises to obtain excessive increases.[12] But these were simply differences of degree, rather than of kind.

The true nature of each reform is more accurately reflected in the choice of procedures laid down to guarantee the future 'flexibility' of prices and their constant updating. However, comparisons are not made any easier by the multiplicity of price categories, which, under very similar designations, could have a very different meaning; there were 'ceiling' prices, 'supervised' prices (both of which invariably tended to be fixed at the permitted maximum), 'calculated' prices (determined by an intermediate agency or by the manufacturing enterprise itself, but on the basis of imposed norms), and 'free' prices (whose real meaning changed completely according to whether they were the result of bilateral bargaining or true market relationships, and according to the kind of controls to which, despite their name, they still remained subject). We shall limit ourselves to the essential characteristics in discussing the USSR, East Germany and Hungary.

In the USSR, the refusal to abandon prices to the influence of supply and demand was constantly reaffirmed, but attempts were made to delegate certain powers, although this was not to be to the benefit of the ministries; the State Prices Committee opposed that, for fear of excessive inflation in the rates of profitability, by alleging that the risks of bottlenecks would be the same as at the central level. Thus, 'it is not a question of transferring the right to determine the price from one administrative agency to another, but of creating the conditions under which enterprises can be left to fix prices themselves' (Stinin, 1968, translated in *Problems of Economics*, April 1969). But we must not be deceived by this apparently radical decentralising formulation: the intention was not to transfer any decision-making power to enterprises, but to enmesh them in a network of detailed norms, with the aim of covering in advance all possible cases, on the basis of scientifically determined 'technico-economic parameters'. The formidable difficulties raised by such an attempt will be analysed later.

For its part, the East German reform delegated a large part of the work involved in price determination to the enterprises, and particularly to the VVB, on the condition, of course, that they complied with strict rules. In particular, the VVB were responsible for enforcing the principle of 'dynamic prices', which required that prices should be reduced in accordance with a reduction in costs, as soon as the rate of profitability exceeded the planned maximum by a certain percentage. This system assumed that the VVB, although dependent on their enterprises, and with a stake in their results, would behave like an administrative agency with the general interest at heart, and not like a monopoly seeking to maximise its own profit.

Neither in the USSR nor in East Germany did the reforms of wholesale prices have any effect on retail prices: the turnover tax, which corresponded to the differences between these two sets of prices determined independently of each other, operated as a sort of screen, which both isolated producers from the influence of final demand and prevented changes in production costs having any direct repercussion on retail prices.

In Hungary, the government took a calculated risk by partially freeing prices immediately after the reform of wholesale prices (which took place at the same time as the introduction of the new economic mechanism, on 1 January 1968).

Free prices largely prevailed for the products of the processing industries (consumer and capital goods). But these 'free' prices were, so to speak, embedded between the fixed prices of the basic products, on the one hand, and the equally rigid wholesale prices on the other. Centralised price determination for energy and the main raw materials is not incompatible with the functioning of a 'market economy'. On the other hand, the maintenance of strict control over retail prices posed problems, all the more so since there had not been any preliminary reform of retail prices: apart from a few adjustments made in 1966 and on 1 January 1968, the Hungarian government had resigned itself to 'crystallising' the prices structure in force on the eve of the reform, despite all its imperfections. The unification of the prices system, which was a fundamental element in the Hungarian 'new mechanism', was thus postponed to a later stage of the reform.

Table 5.1 *Distribution of total turnover in Hungary by pricing system (1968)*

Wholesale prices	Free prices	Supervised, ceiling and fixed prices	
Agricultural production prices	10	90	
Raw materials and semi-manufactured goods	28	72	
Manufactured goods	85	15	
Retail prices		**Flexible regulation***	**Strict ceiling or fixed prices**
Foodstuffs	12	27	60
Clothes	25	54	21
All goods	23	27	50

Source: R. Nyers, 'Hospodarske Noviny', 25 July 1969, whose information has often been reproduced, for example by W. F. Robinson (Robinson, 1972, p. 59).
* Increase limited to 5 or 10 per cent according to product group.

On the other hand, the introduction of foreign exchange multipliers was a significant step forward towards taking into account price variations abroad: importers paid, and exporters received, the actual price in foreign currency, multiplied by a uniform coefficient (corresponding to the average purchase cost of the foreign currency: e.g. 40 forints for one rouble, 60 for a dollar). This system was not intended to bring about a reorientation of Hungarian foreign trade, and the immediate effects of its implementation were to a large extent neutralised by the widespread use of subsidies. But at least it ensured that any change in foreign markets would automatically be felt in future by Hungarian enterprises, unless the government decided otherwise, by introducing new subsidies. Thus real innovations existed side by side with the ubiquitous 'transitional' arrangements which tended to perpetuate the state of affairs prior to the reform: the real question was whether these seeds would succeed in developing as planned.

Summary

It is generally accepted that the various economic reform plans of about 1967 can be classified in the following way (going from the most fundamental reforms to the most limited): Hungary, Czechoslovakia, Bulgaria, East Germany, Poland, the USSR and Rumania. An attempt will be made here to clarify the significance of this classification, by situating each of them in relation to the two poles represented by the two most coherent reforms, that in East Germany and that in Hungary.

1 The East German reform was the most systematic attempt to improve the centralised model. Its aim was to strengthen the ascendancy of planned management, by relieving the upper levels of the economic hierarchy of the tasks of day-to-day management. It was based on the principle of delegating a wide range of powers to intermediate agencies, the 80 VVB that were responsible for implementing the decisions of the central plan and were able to supervise the enterprises under their jurisdiction more efficiently than the central authorities. Neither regulation by market mechanisms nor competition had any place in this economic organisation. The centralised system of allocation of the means of production was reorganised, but the principle of it was not called into question: the adjustment of flows took place in the preparation of the central plan, under the responsibility of an agency at an appropriate level of the hierarchy, according to rules fixed by higher authorities and, if necessary, under their direct supervision. The reduction of the number of compulsory indicators for enterprises and the increased use of monetary and financial mechanisms were both considered desirable, but the conditions for a radical simplification of the incentive system, using the 'profit' indicator as a basis, were far from fulfilled, whatever the initial intentions in this respect might have been. The meaning of

profits was particularly ambiguous when applied to the VVB, which, among other things, were responsible for assisting in the constant up-dating of prices, together with the reduction of production costs.

2 Like the East German reform, the aim of the Hungarian reform was to gain real control over development, by means of more detailed and more efficient central planning. But the reform involved such a radical transformation of the principles by which the economy functioned that it must be interpreted as an attempt to introduce another model of the planned economy. The 'new economic mechanism' in Hungary was based on the reintroduction of market mechanisms as regulators of the activity of enterprises; at the same time, it reintroduced the possibility of direct adjustments based on the judgement of the market – within the limits compatible with the macro-economic targets of the plan. Decentralisation was not to mean the relaxing of constraints (i.e. a reduction in the number of compulsory indicators . . .), but that control by the market would replace them. The re-establishment of a minimum level of competition, by means suited to each sector, was thus a fundamental requirement of the reform: only under this condition could profits play the role allocated to them, that of acting as a criterion for the allocation of bonuses and as the foundation of gradual wage differentiation by enterprise. The internal consistency of the plan is thus undeniable. For all that, the transition to the decentralised model was not an easy task: the industrial structures that had developed during the previous phase (large enterprises predominating in a small economy), the desire to minimise the social risks (priority was to be given to guaranteeing jobs and to keeping retail prices stable), and the ambiguous implications of the reform for the distribution of income and of decision-making powers all contributed to the weakening of the initial enthusiasm and to making the reform more vulnerable to any external threat.

3 The Soviet, Polish and Rumanian reforms were carried out in a much less determined fashion than in East Germany, but were similar to the East German reform.

The eventual lack of impact of the Soviet reform does not mean that the initial plan was more limited than in East Germany. The initial stress on direct links, the intention of replacing the centralised system of allocation with a wholesale trade in the means of production and of 'decentralising' a part of the investment process, and mistrust of the autarchic behaviour of the associations of enterprises could have brought about a radical reform. What the Soviet leaders seem to have lacked (as indeed did Liberman himself) was a clear understanding of the preconditions that had to be satisfied before enterprises could be granted even partial autonomy. In rejecting any regulation by the market, and allowing ministries direct supervision of enterprises, the Soviet reform was doomed to maintain the centralised system of management for enterprises in almost as detailed a form as before (only the really redundant orders, probably less numerous than was generally thought, could be eliminated). In this respect, the effort to develop 'economic' or 'indirect' methods was a deceptive simplification, since it made it necessary to strengthen the centralised system of price determination, without the system becoming precise enough to make it possible to dispense with the traditional agencies of economic management. The subsequent turnaround in favour of the associations amounted to an implicit recognition that, within the framework of the centralised model, only the type of reform introduced in East Germany made deconcentration viable.

For its part, the Polish economy, from the end of the 1950s until the present day, has experienced a long series of abortive attempts at reform. Those at the end of the Gomulka period (1965-70) were carried out with an obvious lack of conviction. The usual tendency in the decentralising phase to abolish certain compulsory indicators was accompanied by ill-co-ordinated changes in the incentive system and in economic organisation. In 1970, in fact, Poland was as far from having achieved deconcentration of the East German type as it was from having achieved decentralisation of the Hungarian type. Moreover, the general weariness caused by the lack of progress from the incessant half-measures was an increasingly serious handicap for any subsequent reform. It was for this reason that Gierek, at the beginning of the 1970s, tried in the first place to rectify the situation by means of a change of direction in economic policy (concessions to wage-earners and to peasants, simultaneous increase in consumption and investment through a massive increase in imports and Western credit): as in Rumania, though in a different context, the increased emphasis on foreign trade and credit was a substitute for rather than a complement to institutional reforms. A few attempts to grant greater autonomy to the 'large economic organisations' (WOG) were cut short one after the other.

Until the 1970s, Rumania remained the only country that questioned the actual principle of overall economic reform. Yet the industrial groups in Rumania were in many respects the counterparts of the VVB in East Germany, since they were also largely responsible for supplies of materials and equipment, for sales and for the distribution of production programmes among their enterprises. The strengthening of their powers from October 1971 onwards increased the similarity with the East German reform.

4 The fate of the Czech and Bulgarian reforms was so different that it might seem strange to put them together.

Nevertheless, in both countries – as in Poland after October 1956 – there had been at the outset, in about 1964–5, a wide-ranging, open and free debate (which in Bulgaria even went so far as the occasional acceptance of references to Yugoslavia). Influential economists firmly developed a plan for a radically decentralist reform, as in Hungary, without incurring the disapproval of the political authorities. But, in Bulgaria as in Czechoslovakia, the general outline of the reforms, drawn up in 1965, was so vague – another resemblance with the Poland of 1957 – that it anticipated all the half-measures of the 1966–7 period. The plan to abolish the centralised system of allocation, to accept the partial free determination of prices under the influence of supply and demand, to link wages directly to the evolution of the gross income of the enterprise (which both countries chose to make a basic indicator), and to develop the role of the banking system, is certainly proof of an attraction towards the decentralised model, but which was far from reflected in a coherent set of measures to implement the plan. Among many other limitations and ambiguities, the powers given in both Czechoslovakia and Bulgaria to associations of enterprises would have been sufficient in themselves to jeopardise any plan for a reform of the Hungarian type: the way was thus prepared for a process of gradual recentralisation which became apparent in both countries as early as 1967, that is, almost as soon as the reforms had been implemented.

It was in 1968 that the course of the Czech and Bulgarian reforms diverged fundamentally.

In Czechoslovakia, the arrival in power, at the beginning of 1968, of the Dubcek government, led not only to an almost desperate attempt to open the way as quickly as possible to a new, radically decentralist economic reform, but also marked the starting point for a powerful spontaneous movement which looked as though it would transform the whole of social, cultural and political life. The hopes placed at that time in 'socialism with a human face' had a far greater impact than the purely economic decisions of the period, which had hardly begun to make themselves felt by the summer of 1968.

In the final analysis, it is of very little importance that the plan for a Hungarian-type reform survived for a little over a year after the occupation of Czechoslovakia in August 1968, or that attempts had at first been made to 'institutionalise' the workers' councils set up in 1968 rather than abolishing them. The disparity between the exceptional difficulties of that period in all areas and the very strict conditions outside of which a decentralist reform has no chance of success was so wide that no attempt will be made in the context of our comparative study to draw any conclusions from developments in Czechoslovakia after 1968.

The crisis in Czechoslovakia was also to sound the death knell of the Bulgarian reform. From July 1968 onwards, the central committee of the Bulgarian Communist Party broke with the decentralist impetus of the reform by taking very decisive measures, in contrast with the usual forms of gradual recentralisation: the industrial ministries were placed under the direct supervision of a committee for economic co-ordination; their own powers *vis-à-vis* the enterprises were strengthened; and the number of compulsory indicators was increased from five to ten. This 'second stage' of the Bulgarian reform was completed on 1 January 1971, with the reorganisation of the 'economic associations' which were almost halved in number, and which became responsible for supplies, sales and the implementation of the plan by their enterprises.

The end of this process was that, at the beginning of the 1970s, only two distinct types of reforms remained: the East German type, aimed at a rationalisation of the centralised model, and the Hungarian type, based on the decentralised model. In the countries which tried to challenge the centralised model without opting decisively for a radical reform, most of the innovatory elements had been submerged, and the strengthening of the intermediate decision-making levels, modelled more or less on the East German example, remained the principal difference with the situation before the reforms.

In order to illustrate the basic distinction brought out in this chapter, we shall continue our analysis of the Soviet, East German and Hungarian reforms, and attempt to assess more accurately the results of each of them, by answering the following three questions: – Was there a real reform? Was the incentive system really substantially modified? Was there a reduction in centralised management and increased powers of decision-making for enterprises (or, where appropriate, for the intermediate levels of the hierarchy), in accordance with the original plan? – Was the reform viable? Was it able to survive the tensions, disequilibria or conflicts which might have arisen from its implementation, either

immediately or in the long term, or which might even have occurred for quite unconnected reasons?
– Was the reform effective, i.e. capable of bringing about in the long term a better adjustment of production to final demand and a more rapid increase of individual and collective consumption?

6 The USSR and East Germany: the remains of the reforms

The Soviet and East German reforms have been described as 'limited' reforms, since their aim was not to transform the model in use. Nevertheless, the implementation of the central plan by indirect methods is in itself an extremely ambitious project. 'Perfect indirect centralisation', as defined, for example, by Novojilov, would involve the production units themselves being allowed to take their own decisions, but in conditions that would necessarily lead to the result decided on in advance by the central authorities who had fixed the criteria and the parameters. Or, to take up the image of one of the chief officials of the Hungarian national planning office, O. Gado: 'Indirect management . . . must resemble that trick by the conjuror who offers a pack of cards to the audience and asks them to take one, although he is sure that the card he wants will be chosen' (Gado, in Bognar, 1969, p. 90). On first sight, this was a problem common to all the economic reforms of the 1960s, since the aim of all of them was to change to methods of 'indirect' management. But the size of the problem, and even its nature, varied greatly, depending on whether an attempt was being made simply to ensure that the decisions made by enterprises conformed overall to the national economic plan (as in Hungary), or whether the aim was to use indirect methods to implement every detail (enterprise by enterprise) of a plan which remained micro-economic in character. Although there were already considerable difficulties in the first case, there was every likelihood that they would be insurmountable in the second. Soviet mathematical economists were the first to decide that it was inconceivable, in the foreseeable future, that the functioning of the economy could be formalised and a totally automated system of centralised economic management set up.

Although 'perfect centralised calculation' might be impossible, progress could still be made in that direction. But it is impossible not to be struck by the relative lag in the development of mathematical studies of planning in the USSR in particular, in comparison with Western countries, or even with Hungary. Moreover, this lag persists, particularly if the actual application of mathematical methods is considered. Such a lag is not fortuitous, nor can it be adequately explained *a posteriori* in terms of resistance from 'vested interests', at the level of the ministerial management agencies, for example. The evolution of planning techniques is determined by the very nature of the model. As J. G. Zielinski noted:

> There seems to be a paradoxical relationship between the extension of central planning and the corresponding planning techniques: the wider the scope of central planning (and consequently the more difficult its tasks), the more it must have recourse to rudimentary planning techniques . . . The result is that the extension of central planning predetermines the planning techniques that can be used and on which the quality of the calculations in the plan depends. (Zielinski, 1969, p. 286)

It is no doubt slightly exaggerated to state that planning techniques are 'predetermined' in this way, since, despite everything, there has been continuous progress in each country since the pioneering days of the first FYPs. But there does exist a fundamental relationship between the multitude of detailed decisions that must be made in a system of planned management, and the persistence of empirical methods for making essential adjustments as the need arises. Thus the choice of model is obviously not without significance in determining the planning methods used, and recent experience certainly confirms the idea of a sort of negative correlation between the exigencies that the type of organisation chosen places on the planning system, and the ability of the system to respond appropriately.

Conversely, the absence of any spontaneous correcting mechanism, in the event of a planning error, for example, explains to a large extent the incomplete and precarious nature of reforms of the Soviet or East German type. Since a specific intervention remained essential in the event of an unforeseen difficulty, it would generally seem more expedient to send a directive (or a 'recommendation') to the enterprises concerned, rather than act indirectly by manipulating the economic regulators. And often, even, in order to avoid the increased risks of errors arising from poor adjustment of the indirect regulators, it would be considered advisable to retain, for information purposes only, the system of direct supervision of enterprises. Thus this type of reform is in fact characterised by the superimposition of two management systems, which is practically irreconcilable with the avowed intention of cutting back the administrative apparatus of planning.

In every country, the results of the reforms were far removed from the initial plan. In basing the analysis on the internal logic of the centralised model, our intention is not to minimise the importance of purely ideological factors, nor the resistance of the bureaucracies under threat (or which thought they were under threat) of losing their prerogatives: their role is self-evident and unanimously recognised. Nevertheless, it is still necessary to explain what very real problems quickly gave rise to the counter-offensive by the supporters of the traditional system, who had been more or less reduced to silence during the phase in which the reform was dominant; in other words, how and why the search for greater economic efficiency in the direction indicated by the reforms was abandoned, even though it remained the major preoccupation of the leaders.

The lessons of the Soviet reform

The incompatibility between autonomy for enterprises and the retention of the system of centralised allocation

1 More flexible supervision of enterprises and a widening of their financial responsibilities were the aims of the Soviet reform of 1965. On the other hand, its effect on the supply system for materials and equipment – the key institution of the centralised model – had not been clearly defined at the outset. The implementation of the reform was to commit the system in three different directions: (1) the unification of the allocation system under the aegis of Gossnab (state committee for the supply of materials and equipment), (2) the development of stable 'direct links' between enterprises and (3) the introduction of a wholesale trade in producer goods. The first of these three directions was synonymous with greater centralisation (the aim was to thwart the autarchic behaviour of the intermediate agencies, the industrial ministries or the regional agencies), but the other two would seem at first sight almost to indicate that the centralised model was to be called into question. This juxtaposition of 'centralist' and 'decentralist' measures was very characteristic of the Soviet reform: subsequent developments rapidly allowed their respective impact to be assessed.

The reorganisation of the supply system, which had become essential after the abolition of the *sovnarkhozy*, took place from 1965 onwards. It involved the setting up of a very complex hierarchy of supply agencies under the control of Gosplan. This system was organised on both functional (by product group) and regional lines. The increased weight of this whole apparatus was reflected in the increase in personnel, which had almost stabilised at the beginning of the 1960s, but increased rapidly again after the reform.[1] Moreover, the unification was far from complete. Gosplan had the task of approving the planned balances for the 2,000 most important products (which, in 1967, represented 22 volumes totalling 11,500 pages). And above all, despite the concern to avoid duplicating tasks, the industrial ministries, which had been re-established in 1965, increasingly regained important responsibilities. In 1968, the federal list of products subject to planned balances still amounted to more than 16,000 products, and, in 1975, approximately 20,000. These impressive totals alone clearly show that the system of centralised allocation underwent no fundamental change.

This was the framework into which the 'direct links' had to be fitted. The authorities had recommended on several occasions (notably in a decree of April 1969) that these links be extended, always with limited effect. The very term 'direct links' may well be misleading; in fact, the enterprises concerned did not have the initiative since the higher authorities – the supervising ministries and the supply agencies answerable to Gosplan – took the decision to link a particular purchaser to a particular producer. This was hardly more than an extension of a formula already applied in the capital goods sector to the relationships between the consumer goods sector and commercial enterprises, and the change from the traditional procedure of planned contracts was probably very slight. The only new element was a desire to guarantee enterprises a certain degree of long-term stability. But in this respect there was a wide gap between intentions and reality: how was it possible, in the Soviet system, to prevent the necessities of day-to-day adjustment from overriding the long-term commitments of any one enterprise, and was it conceivable that a producer would give precedence to his commercial obligations over obedience to his supervisory authorities?

The aim adopted from 1965 to 1969 of 'gradually setting up a planned wholesale trade in production goods' turned out to be even more ambiguous. Unless capital goods were put on sale freely, the transfer of responsibilities to the local agencies of Gosplan was of purely administrative significance only; on the other hand, the abolition of rationing, even though it was only gradual, would involve a radical transformation of the model. It is true that the following years saw the development of a network of 'wholesale shops', which by 1973 totalled

740 points of sale, but they had hardly anything to offer other than small pieces of equipment, spare parts and work clothes; total sales, which were barely 3 per cent of the turnover of Gossnab, included goods sold only on presentation of an allocation slip: thus the wholesale trade could only function with marginal sources of supply (e.g. surpluses from enterprises), or be reduced simply to one form among others of the system of administrative allocation. The fundamental obstacle to its development was the impossible task of getting hold of a significant quantity of goods that had not been allocated within the centralised model.

The measures taken in April 1969 to establish the direct links and the wholesale trade were the last step of the Soviet reform. As early as the end of 1968, the attacks had been multiplying against anything that resembled market socialism, and any real extension of the reform became impossible. From the plenum of December 1969 onwards, positions hardened further. Faced with the proposal by 'certain academic economists' to give enterprises the right to choose their customers and suppliers, a senior official in Gosplan no longer had any hesitation in declaring in 1973: 'This apparently innocent proposal in fact conceals the abandoning of centralised planning and a return to market relationships. . . . If purchasers were allowed to choose the supplier most advantageous to themselves . . . the functioning of enterprises would be disrupted.'[2] In fact, the practical men in the economic administration had a better understanding of the logic of the model than the innovators who supported gradual transformation; the system of centralised allocation was a necessity as long as prices and production targets for each enterprise continued to be fixed by the administration.

2 What, then, remained of the initial intention of increasing the scope for enterprises to take their own decisions?

Decentralisation of investment had, from the outset, been considered only within very strict limits; the financing of an increasing part of planned investment did not in itself involve any sharing of responsibilities. However, a development fund had been set up in every firm, and that enabled additional investment for modernisation purposes to be made. But how were these funds to be used within a system of centralised allocation? Where could the enterprise find the equipment that it really needed? It soon became evident, after the disillusion of the first years of the reform, that 'decentralised' investment by enterprises had to be integrated, in one way or another, into the national economic plan, with a consequent right of control and powers of arbitration for the supervising authorities.

Enterprises were hardly any freer as far as day-to-day production decisions were concerned. The rationing of inputs was sufficient to exclude any spontaneous modification of production methods. However, incentive based on profits increased the temptation for enterprises to reorientate their production structure to suit their own interests as far as possible, to the detriment of users: the supervising authorities then had no option but to reintroduce a very detailed specification of the range of goods to be produced, in order to prevent the activities situated downstream from being completely disrupted. In general, the gradual reappearance of the compulsory indicators that had been abolished, at least in theory, was one of the outstanding characteristics of the post-reform period. The standard list appended to the FYP for 1976-80 contained twenty compulsory indicators for each enterprise without counting the subdivisions and additions; a few redundant indicators did not reappear, but the list was made longer by indicators which had not existed before 1965, and which were evidence of new preoccupations to which we shall return.

For their part, the managers of the units of production suffered much less from the lack of autonomy than from the unstable conditions in which they had to work. Once again, the promises of the reform had not been kept: the incessant modifications to the plans while they were being implemented were an eternal subject for complaint. But it is difficult to see how the supervisory authority, should one of its enterprises under-perform, for example, could avoid altering the obligations of the other enterprises, in an attempt to maintain as far as possible the planned balances for which it was responsible. The frequent breakdowns in the supply system, which intermittently paralysed the activity of any enterprise or workshop, were more than ever a major source of disruptions within the Soviet economy. Even in the USSR of the 1970s, a priority user had to fight hard for the privilege of obtaining regular deliveries of the planned supplies to which he was entitled. The non-priority enterprises had no reason to abandon their traditional habit of over-stocking, which aggravated shortages and brought about a redoubling of direct controls.

Just as before 1965, the functioning of the Soviet economy depended on administrative management methods: this was both a cause and a consequence of the failure of the profit-based incentive system.

The incompatibility between profit-based incentives and the arbitrariness of prices

1 The various funds set up for each enterprise (profit-sharing fund, social and cultural funds, development fund), sustained by a share of profits, were the most tangible and lasting result of the 1965 reform.

However, total payments made to the various funds still represented only a fairly small proportion of total profits, in comparison to the contributions to the budget (6 per cent on average of industrial profits in 1965, 12 per cent in 1968, 18 per cent in 1977).

But the efficiency of the incentive system was particularly weakened by its complexity. The following formula is a very simplified form of the one fixed at the outset for the setting up of the profit-sharing fund:

$$F_1 = S(xr + yt)$$

where S is the enterprise's wages fund; r the percentage increase in production sold (or, alternatively, the increase in profits) in comparison with the previous year; t the rate of profit as a percentage of capital; and x and y norms fixed by the sector management.

This formula had the advantage of establishing a balance between its two component terms, one of which (xrS) depended on the rate of increase, and the other (ytS) on the level of profitability: thus an enterprise suffering from an initial handicap, but which started to recover, would benefit particularly from the first term; on the other hand, the efficient enterprise which had already reached its maximum potential retained the benefit of the second term. At the same time, in order to encourage enterprises to prefer a tight plan, the planned increase in sales or profits was more profitable than an unplanned increase achieved by exceeding the targets. Different norms and parameters were fixed for the two other funds. The system certainly did not lack ingenuity! As it was put into practice, however, new faults kept being revealed in the system, and each distortion caused the proportions to be changed or correctives to be introduced. For example, the indexing of payments to the wages fund – a logical step in order not to penalise labour-intensive industries – proved to be a serious disincentive to making economies in the labour force, and had to be changed. And so it went on . . . The result was that the formulae were constantly diversifying, and became so complex that the reactions of enterprises to a variation in the parameters became virtually unpredictable.

2 The authors of the 1965 reform had good reason to shrink from

the decision to make the incentive system simpler and more uniform, and based directly on profits. In the Soviet-type economy, profit levels continued to be dependent above all on factors unconnected with the efforts of the enterprise and also on the skill with which the enterprises of a particular sector, with the complicity of their supervisory authorities, succeeded in having excessively inflated production costs accepted as the basis for the calculations of the agencies responsible for price determination.

The results of the 1966-7 reform of wholesale prices were revealing in that respect. The aim of the reform was to eliminate losses in certain sectors, while leaving the general level of prices unchanged, but the result was an average increase of 8 per cent, and, in particular, an unexpected and considerable increase in profitability in some sectors where it had already been high at the outset (precision engineering, electro-technology). There was an overall increase in industrial profits of 25 per cent between the first quarter of 1966 and the first quarter of 1967, and a further one of 48 per cent in the following twelve months: it would be very bold to see this as a propitious effect of the economic reform, encouraging enterprises to double their efficiency! For various reasons, of which the main one was undoubtedly the constraint of leaving the level of retail prices unaltered, the idea of unifying rates of profit was abandoned, not only among sectors, but even for similar products within the same sector. General policy considerations might just possibly explain the retention of a profit rate for agricultural machinery that was half that for precision instruments, but hardly the fact that in the clothing industry, for example, the rate of profit varied according to article from 1.4 to 92 per cent. In any case, the result was that the same enterprise commonly found itself having to produce different articles varying greatly in profitability. The wider the gaps became, the more incentive there was for the enterprise to deviate from the product range laid down, and the stricter the supervisory authorities had to be in their control.

Thus the fundamental problem was the arbitrariness and rigidity of prices, which usually prevented any clear significance being attributed to the disparities in profitability. The initial intention of correcting all the distortions in the system by making profits the principal indicator of success presupposed a price mechanism able to guide enterprises in the direction desired by the planner. However, the prices arising from the 1966-7 reform still did not fulfil any of the necessary conditions: they did not balance supply and demand; their structure ratified many divergences from the structure of production costs, and most of these divergences did not reflect the specific preferences of the planners any more than those of consumers; in short, any spontaneous correcting mechanism was quite out of the question. It would have been unthinkable in these circumstances to allow profits to play the role assigned to them *a priori* in the incentive system.

Thus after the reform of 1965, it was as if it had been recognised that all the financial regulators (prices, taxes and profits) were incapable of ensuring that production conformed to demand, and as if their function had been limited to encouraging the most economic use of available resources. But even in this respect, they seemed to inspire only limited confidence. This was not unjustified: for example, the 6 per cent tax on fixed and circulating capital (significantly lower than the efficiency norm for investments) had not put an end to pressure from enterprises to obtain as much investment as possible. A further reason for the lack of confidence was the continuing tendency to over-stocking, with enterprises seeking above all to protect themselves from the risks of a breakdown in the supply system. In the same way, the general tendency to 'hoard labour' could not be considered irrational when it was the only way of countering the changes in the rate of production made necessary by the irregularity of supplies.

In any case, the fate of each enterprise remained in the hands of its supervisory authorities, who distributed investment, fixed more or less easy and more or less profitable targets, and laid down all the parameters of the incentive formulas applicable to each category. Even the frequent modifications to targets during the period of the plan, which had been considered to be an abuse of authority which seriously disrupted the functioning of an enterprise, were in a sense inevitable in a system which contained no other element of flexibility; and they also made it necessary to correct at the same time, and in each individual case, the application of the pre-established incentive norms. Direct, overall assessment by the supervisory authorities was undoubtedly the only way of avoiding glaring injustices, but it reduced to nothing the guarantees of stability that the reform was supposed to bring to enterprises.

Thus uncertainty remained at all levels: uncertainty for enterprises as to the reactions of their superiors in the hierarchy, and uncertainty for the authorities as to the real potential of the production system. While the day-to-day functioning of enterprises was affected by it, it was innovation which, in this context, posed the particularly difficult problems.

Innovation: the crucial problem in centralised economies

1 There is very strong resistance to change within the Soviet economy. That the system functions at all, despite the jolts and breakdowns in supply, is due to the regular renewal from one year to another of the main connections between customers and suppliers. If the hazards of the incentive system do not have intolerable effects on individual earnings, it is because a large proportion of the bonuses tend to become almost automatic in fact, even if not established by right. Every worker is virtually certain to keep his job. The rigidity of prices, linked to the way in which they are determined by the administration, is both a stabilising factor and a brake on innovation. The waiting period necessary for the introduction of a new price is sometimes sufficient to delay the launching of a new product. More often, enterprises do everything within their power to continue producing old products, for which the assimilation costs have been absorbed for a long time: the fixed selling price automatically guarantees increasing profitability, as production costs go down. Long runs become particularly advantageous when the producer, under cover of a minor innovation, succeeds in gaining from the outset a high 'temporary price', on the basis of production costs declared for the first year, which the overworked price determination agencies subsequently allow to be perpetuated, thus giving certain enterprises a level of profitability out of proportion with the accepted norms. The result, paradoxically, is an excessive increase in the number of 'new products', in an economy in which the level of innovation is in fact particularly low: in the mid-1960s at least a third of the production of the mechanical engineering industries was benefiting from these temporary prices.

The central authorities have tried to act against this laxity. With regard to price determination, as to the supply system, the 1965 reform aimed at increased centralisation. The State Prices Commission, set up in 1965 and attached to Gosplan, then directly to the Council of Ministers, brought together a large part of the powers exercised until then by the *sovnarkhozy*, the local authorities and various ministries. It was directly responsible for determining the prices of 85 per cent of the total value of the production of heavy industry and 50 per cent of that of light industry, as well as the retail prices of all widely sold consumer goods. It also promulgated mandatory 'methodological instructions' ('Methods of determining the wholesale price of new consumer goods', drawn up in 1969 and revised in 1974). The reform as a whole tended to associate flexible and constantly adjusted prices with centralised determination, as a safeguard against abuses. The approach to the ensuing problem of innovation was to penalise obsolete products by regularly reducing their price from year to year.

But this method of so-called 'graduated' or 'sliding' prices usually proved inadequate. The evolution of production costs, which varies greatly according to product and enterprise, is very difficult to predict. A sudden, pre-planned and uniform reduction in the price of old products may well cause a shortage of certain products for which there are no better substitutes; in this case, there is all the more encouragement for enterprises to put forward 'pseudo-innovations', with the sole aim of benefiting from a more advantageous price. In fact, it is the very principle of the permanent centralised adjustment of prices that lacks realism, since its aim is neither more nor less than to replace the pressure exerted by competition with that exerted by price determination agencies; as a result, each price – and there are millions of them – might be compared to a clock without a mechanism, whose hands have constantly to be advanced manually.

Price determination is an onerous task. The price reform of 1967 was the result of six years' work by several thousand specialists; it led to summaries totalling 38,000 pages, or, according to other sources, to 2,500 lists of prices, some of which exceeded 300 pages in length; and nobody seems able to clarify the exact number (ten million?) of prices determined at various levels of the economic administration. In the two years after the price reform (1967-9), the State Prices Committee published 830 additional lists for machinery and instruments alone, and in 1972 it fixed 300,000 new retail prices. But even greater efforts would be necessary if there were to be a constant up-dating of all prices which took into account all inter-relationships. The prices fixed by the administration have remained as rigid: the prices of fuels and energy, for example, did not change between 1967 and 1979 (with the result that by 1979 almost all enterprises in the sector were functioning at a loss). The revision that was expected to be completed by January 1982 will have been the first overall revision since 1967. The officials of the State Prices Committee are the first to recognise that they are inundated with work, and their conclusions agree with those of the officials in the supply system: 'It is wrong to imagine that prices must guarantee the equilibrium between supply and demand. The task of balancing supply and demand . . . is the responsibility of the planning agencies' (V. Sitnin),[3] and there is all the more reason for the much more delicate task of encouraging technical progress to be dependent on direct intervention.

2 The reform of 1965 should have created a more favourable context for innovation, both by giving enterprises a long-term perspective and by abolishing the relative advantage of producing old products, and by creating a 'buyers' market' in which the simple fact of being able to sell his production normally was sufficient incentive for the producer. But, since these targets were hardly achieved, as we have seen, innovation still required specific incentives.

These incentives first of all involved the determining of the price of new products. The 'instructions' of 1969 and 1974 were aimed at limiting abuses and easing the task of the supervisory agencies, by establishing a simple principle: the price of the new product was to be fixed in such a way that the increase in efficiency arising from the innovation should be divided between the producer-innovator and the client enterprises. The only question that remained was how to measure the increase in efficiency (if only to eliminate bogus innovations), and how to effect the division. It was here that the difficulties began.

In actual fact, no economic system succeeds in every case in ensuring the best possible compromise between the immediate diffusion of increases in productivity and their complete retention by the producer, which are both equally to be avoided. But the Soviet approach eliminates *a priori* one essential element in any correct solution: the direct assessment of quality by the user. The administration, or research institutes answerable to it, reach a judgement in his name. The price of new products is determined as much as possible by the technico-economic parameters method, which consists of defining all the 'objective', measurable characteristics of each type of product, which together are supposed to express its 'useful effect', and of drawing up 'standard relationship coefficients' between the technico-economic parameters and production costs. The price can thus be calculated (except in the case of 'entirely new' products with no close substitute) on the basis of the price of the old product, corrected directly in accordance with the evolution of the parameters.

This method, which was improved in 1974, although its broad outlines remained unchanged, leaves many problems unsolved, starting with the still indispensable up-dating of the price of old products (if this is not done, all the faults of the initial price system will automatically be transferred to the prices of the new products, and can only get worse as time goes on). It is cumbersome to implement: how can gradual improvement in quality be reflected in prices if the slightest change requires a decision by the administration? L. Maizenberg acknowledges that 'Prices are not changed until a whole series of improvements has profoundly altered the technico-economic parameters of a product' (Maizenberg, 1970, translated in *Problems of Economics*, February 1971). The producer thus has no incentive to introduce gradual small improvements, which have a minimal effect on the parameters used by the administration, but which are important from the user's point of view. Much hope seems to have been placed in the setting up of an automated data processing system for prices, both to increase the number of parameters taken into account and to shorten waiting periods; but the simple fact that this programme, launched at the beginning of the 1970s, is not due to be completed until the end of the 1980s says a lot about the difficulties of all kinds that have to be overcome. And above all, even an exhaustive summary of all the qualities of the product, and the working out of adequate measures and an ideal weighting would not resolve the basic difficulty, i.e. that a particular product does not have the same 'use value' for all its users: the technico-economic parameters method, without a free choice of supplier, necessarily requires certain enterprises to pay a higher price for products whose 'superior quality' in no way corresponds to their actual needs.

The fundamental error is undoubtedly to tackle the problems of quality and innovation independently of adjustment to demand – but can it be otherwise within the framework of the centralised model? The first step seemed to be the replacement of 'gross production' by the 'production sold' indicator in the reform of 1965: the production of totally unsaleable goods would no longer give a right to bonuses. But the persistence of the 'seller's market' and the compulsory attachment of each enterprise to suppliers designated by the administration practically robbed this change of any significance. The customer for the goods produced can only appeal to the administration, and the changes in his favour to the legislation on contracts introduced in 1967 were limited in their effectiveness, since the State Arbitration Commission was inundated by the vast number of disputes (tens of thousands each year) and the difficulties it encountered in locating responsibilities.

The different types of *ad hoc* measures, which are being increasingly used in conjunction with the regulation of prices in order to encourage technical progress and the improvement of quality, all depend on a direct assessment by the administration. The fixing of increasingly numerous and rigid norms of quality, in an unprecedented attempt to extend indefinitely the scope of what can be measured, is merely an attempt to avoid the issue. 'The introduction of new techniques' figures high on the list of compulsory indicators for the period of the 1976–80 plan. It is the same as far as specific incentives are concerned. The 'fund for the assimilation of new techniques', set up in 1961 and reactivated at the time of the reform, has never functioned as planned, because the administrative procedure for granting subsidies is extremely cumbersome. The concern with quality now means that enterprises which reduce their production costs by using excessively cheap raw materials are penalised (the economies made in this way are subtracted from the total profits used to calculate bonuses), and also that bonuses are allocated in accordance with the 'proportion of high quality articles in total production': the first measure may well discourage perfectly justifiable substitutions, and help to make the level of profits even more arbitary and conventional, determined retrospectively by the administration (which is the last straw); the second encourages producers to lay siege to the supervisory agency (OTK), whose job it is to award the seal of quality without the least concern for the needs of the user. The final possibility is to award a special bonus to the enterprises which have incurred neither a fine nor any complaint that they have failed in their contractual obligations; this is a common sense measure, actually implemented during the five-year period from 1976 to 1980, but which for all that seems no less of a strange last resort.

The 1979 reform

In July 1979, a 'readjustment' of the economic mechanism marked a new attempt to correct these chronic deficiencies. Whether it was a continuation of the 1965 reform (the official presentation) or confirmation of its failure, the 1979 decree did not herald a change of direction, but was part of a process that had begun a long time before, and the few relative innovations are revealed only on close examination. Admittedly, the dominant preoccupations of the leaders have certainly changed since the time when everything was subordinated to maximum growth in production: savings in material resources, in investment and especially in manpower are now obviously uppermost in their minds; the economic cost of delays, discontinuities and disequilibria of all sorts is clearly perceived. But the need to encourage enterprises to exceed their targets (by 'mobilising', and at the same time revealing, their 'hidden' reserves) has not, for all that, disappeared. The principle of the 'counter-plans' method, which was introduced in certain sectors from 1971 onwards and which, in the 1979 decree, it was intended to extend much further, is very reminiscent of an earlier reform in Czechoslovakia at the end of the 1950s: the enterprise is rewarded according to the gap between the targets assigned to it (yearly targets within the FYP) and the more ambitious targets that it fixes itself in its counter-plan. This formula is as arbitrary as the traditional practices: in order to give an advantage to an enterprise, the supervisory authorities have only to fix moderate initial targets for it which it will have no difficulty in exceeding. Moreover, to judge by all the precedents, its efficacy is likely to be very limited (unless priority enterprises are authorised to take advantage of their more ambitious targets in order to obtain extra inputs, which would then make it a serious source of disequilibrium). Although the counter-plans method is to become widespread for the 1981-5 period, it appears to be for want of anything better, as if all possible formulae had already been considered. Similarly, the change to a net production indicator (standard value added) creates an impression of '*déjà vu*', since the first experiments in this direction go back at least fifteen years. This is at best a very indirect encouragement to economise on raw materials, which is proof of the lack of confidence in the effectiveness of the profitability indicators which are supposed to have the same kind of effect.

And yet the insistence of the 1979 decree on the development of profit-sharing and financial autonomy is obviously a continuation of the 1965 reform. The reference to profitability is present everywhere. The principle of *khozraschët* now applies at all levels of the hierarchy, up to and including the ministries. The financing of the research and development institutes is to be by means of contracts, with payment to be made on final receipt of the commissioned project. The material and technical supply agencies must also balance their expenditure and income, and so on . . . Financial autonomy is also to increase 'at the bottom'. Within enterprises, there is a plan for the determination of individual wages to be decentralised at the level of the shift team, so that everyone has as direct an interest as possible in increasing labour productivity. Within certain limits, a reduction in manning levels leads to special wage increases. It is also hoped that the doubling of social security contributions will further encourage enterprises to economise on labour. All this is part of a logic of economic management based on profitability. More generally, each aspect of the behaviour of an enterprise must have a financial justification, and add to or subtract from its profits: for example, there are provisions for a bonus if investments are completed early and for a penalty for any delay in the deliveries schedule.

What, then, gives rise to the general impression that the 1979 decree is a retreat from the underlying aim of the 1965 reform, if not from its actual implementation? What has disappeared in the interim is first of all the intention (which may be merely an illusion) of radically simplifying the economic management system by means of the 'unifying' role of profits. In 1979, on the other hand, profits were 'exploded', segmented *ad infinitum*. Each element of the profit now has a different status according to its origin. Thus profits achieved over and above the planned target are acquired by the firm up to a limit of 50 per cent (encouragement); but the proportion is reduced to 25 per cent once the excess reaches 3 per cent (relative penalisation). Profits attributable to improvements in quality benefit from a preferential rate of payment (70 per cent). Conversely, deductions are made from profits arising from articles deemed to be 'second class', or simply from highly profitable products manufactured in long runs (without, for all that, any discount on the price paid by the user). In cases of excessive price increases or deliberate reductions in quality, the corresponding profit is to be confiscated. In general, the administration retains complete freedom to exercise any discrimination it wishes, and to determine itself, often retrospectively, the 'true' level of profits.

The 1979 decree also confirms the rediscovery of the basic characteristics of the centralised model that had been temporarily forgotten at the time of the 1965 reform: incentive must never override the need to obey directives, and its influence must be exerted within the framework fixed by the planned constraints. This is the reason for the increased calls for discipline: labour discipline, financial discipline, price discipline (it has been announced that 4,500 price control commissions are to be set up). It is the responsibility of the enterprise to adhere strictly to the maximum authorised manpower levels, the constraints on the range of goods produced and the deadlines assigned to it. The exact number of compulsory indicators, which had mostly already been restored a few years after the 1965 reform, no longer has much meaning, since they encompass all aspects of the activity of an enterprise, starting with technological development; confidence in the latest 'technico-scientific' norms imposed from outside in order to force the rate of progress seems stronger than ever. But, in order for the constraints to be effective, it is still necessary to ensure that the planned economy has a stability that has been lacking until now, and it is precisely in this area that the 1979 decree is intended to be an essential milestone, by setting out the principle of the absolute primacy of the FYP. The operational targets are to be fixed for five years by the annual sections of the FYP (any downwards revision is submitted to the Council of Ministers for authorisation); these targets are to be made concrete by long-term direct links between enterprises in accordance with contracts drawn up under the aegis and responsibility of the ministries which plan even the price of fashion goods five years in advance! The total amount of the incentive fund is also planned for the duration of the five-year period. Any flexibility in wholesale prices is deliberately excluded during the interval between two plans. The 1979 decree, if it is fully implemented, ought thus to give the Soviet economy an unprecedented degree of rigidity; if not, the intention of giving firms if not increased autonomy, then more stable operating conditions, will once again remain a dead letter.

Shortly after the beginning of the 'Liberman discussion', A. Nove wrote: 'The attempts to control production by controlling prices are not only impracticable but illogical. If the central authorities know exactly what must be produced, the simplest way of obtaining it is to issue clear and unequivocal instructions, and there is no need to act indirectly . . .' (*Economics of Planning*, 3, 1963, p. 19). By challenging from the outset the principle of adjustment based on market relationships between enterprises, the Soviet authorities condemned the 1965 reform to introduce only uncertain and precarious changes. Consequently, there has never been any question of replacing direct orders to each enterprise with 'control by means of prices', but rather of combining the two; and it was not long before the balance swung in favour of the directives. The concept in force today is based more than ever on the idea that, through 'scientific' planning, it can be 'known exactly what must be produced' and how to produce it, in the smallest detail, five years in advance.

In these circumstances, the nature of the economic organisation that is called upon to act as a link between the central authorities and the units of production acquired decisive importance. Although hostility towards 'market socialism' has never ceased, the East German reform was followed with interest in the USSR from 1963 onwards, and favourably assessed. Yet the VVB, the linchpin of the East German New Economic System, still had no counterpart in the USSR at the beginning of the 1970s. The main resistance was at the level of the industrial ministries: the grouping together of enterprises could well weaken their decision-making powers if it resulted in a redefinition of the boundaries between sectors and the prevention of autarchic behaviour. A complete reorganisation was, however, decided on in April 1973, in accordance with a complex plan comprising several 'decision-making levels', which were basically associations of basic producers (bringing together several enterprises to make single factories), and federal associations (which replaced the sector management departments in the ministries). This reorganisation was still a long way from being completed six years later; the decree of July 1979 forecast that 'the setting up of production associations as basic levels will be completed within the next two or three years'. At the top, the 'reform' might very well be limited to rechristening the existing sector management departments 'federal associations', by making them conform strictly to the principle of '*khozraschët*'. Even in this case, however, the changes introduced to the middle and lower levels of the hierarchy are not insignificant: (1) they tend to ease the task of the central authorities, by reducing the number of people they deal with directly, and thus the number of directives they have to issue; (2) the production units can be supervised and guided 'more closely' (for example, as far as the distribution of production programmes, regulation of bonuses and the allocation of funds for technical development are concerned), due to the more precise knowledge that an intermediate agency can acquire; (3) they fit into the process of concentration that has been going on for a long time, but which is less advanced in the USSR than in the other socialist countries. This evolution corresponds logically to the decision to develop and reinforce centralisation. In any case, it gives added interest to the study of the results obtained in East Germany after the introduction of the New Economic System.

The lessons of the East German reform

The gradual introduction of reforms into the Soviet-type economies has almost always triggered off recentralising mechanisms right from the early phases of their implementation, with the result that the initial plan has had little chance to function properly before being completely altered. The East German reform is an exception. Its various elements were introduced one after the other, very gradually, between 1963 and 1969. The brakes were certainly applied from time to time, and this was prematurely interpreted as a blocking of the reform (for example, when the suicide of its main author, Apel, was followed by the re-establishment of the industrial ministries in December 1965), but, on the whole, the dynamic of the reform was maintained until the end of the 1960s. The results obtained within the framework of the New Economic System also served in 1979-80 as a springboard for an attempt to stimulate growth, aimed at accelerating the modernisation of priority sectors. The reform could not withstand the tensions and imbalances caused by this change of tempo, and collapsed very suddenly from the beginning of the 1970s.

The ascendant phase (1963-8)

1 This phase was characterised by a tendency both to limit direct orders and to increase the role of profitability and financial regulators.

The number of specific production targets imposed on enterprises was continuously reduced. The rationing of the means of production was made more flexible and continued only for a few products in short supply. Controls on employment and wages were similarly relaxed. Before the reform, manning levels, the total wages fund and the average wage were fixed for each enterprise, although this last factor was implicitly determined by the two preceding indicators; in 1966, this redundant indicator was abolished, and, by 1969, only the wages fund was still fixed.

The incentive system depended increasingly on profits, but the changeover was not without hiccups. After an initial attempt in 1964, it became necessary to abandon the use of profits from 1965 until the completion of the prices reform; but, as M. Keren points out: 'the very fact that it was necessary to banish profits for about a year proves that they had acquired an important place among the factors influencing management decisions, both at the level of the VVB and of the enterprises' (Keren, 1973*b*, pp. 565-6). Once the new prices came into force from 1967 onwards, profits acquired an undeniable pre-eminence among the indicators of success. The principle of profitability was also applied, for example, to institutes of applied research, which played an increasing role in the East German economy: they had to finance their own activities by means of contracts with enterprises, and thus had a direct interest in the productivity of their own research.

Profits made by enterprises became more and more directly their source of investment funds; but the replacement of budgetary financing by self-financing did not in any way mean that the central authorities had renounced control over investment. The conditions under which investment was carried out had undoubtedly changed even more than the system of finance. Enterprises, forced to pay the tax on fixed capital even before the new capacity entered into production, had every incentive to keep a close check on the carrying out of investment for which they were responsible. Above all, the banking system, which had been reorganised in 1967, exercised increased responsibilities in the finalising of projects. The specialist sections of the new industrial and commercial bank examined each investment project both from the point of view of its adherence to the plan, and from the point of view of its economic value and its prospects for financial profitability. They were at liberty to reject or have altered ill-conceived projects, and to vary the rates of interest (up to 12 per cent), according to the degree of risk involved and the relative priority attached to the prospective investment. Thus the total amount of profits made became the basis of the banks' own incentive system, just as it was for enterprises.

2 Thus it is clear that East Germany went further than most of the other socialist countries towards the reinstatement of economic calculation, which is why, by about 1968, there were many apparent resemblances with the Hungarian reform. But rather than interpreting the East German reform as a concession to the logic of the market, it must be seen as an original attempt to establish an overall model of a socialist society, described as the 'developed socialist social system'. It was in this spirit that the VIIth Congress of the SED, in April 1967, changed the name of the New Economic System (NES) to the Socialist Economic System (SES). Ulbricht forcefully restated his thesis that socialism was a relatively autonomous socio-economic form, and not merely a phase in the transition from capitalism to communism.[4] The semi-official adoption in 1969 of a new manual entitled *The Political Economy of Socialism and its Application in the GDR* symbolised the new concept of the role of East Germany as the most developed socialist country.

The nature of the system in force in about 1968 should not be misunderstood. The drawing up of the plan was based very largely on outlines provided by the production units themselves, but these outline plans were not implemented until they had been approved by higher authorities. Thus the micro-economic nature of planning was not called into question. Financial indicators took over to a large extent from direct orders in volume terms, but it was self-evident that 'the parametric elements of the New Economic System function only within the framework of the constraints of the physical planning system' (Granick, 1975, p. 150). Each production unit continued to receive several compulsory indicators (physical and financial) which had to be adhered to completely as a condition for the allocation of bonuses in a more effective way than in the past. The influence of profitability was thus exerted only within clearly defined limits. The obligation to go through the state banking system for all transactions meant that the economy remained open to scrutiny.

If the East German economy underwent substantial changes between 1963 and 1968 (in contrast to the Soviet economy), it was above all because a new division of tasks and more effective centralised management had been made possible by the strengthening of the intermediate decision-making levels, that is, the 80 VVB and the 50 specialist banking sections, of which each one was the appointed banker of one, two or three VVB. The first duty of the banks was to ensure that the investment priorities laid down by the plan were observed, and they had all the necessary powers to that end. But most of the regulatory functions that had hitherto been carried out by the central administration now fell to the VVB. These included the drawing up of a large number of planned balances, the adjustment of the norms for wage increases and the bonuses allocated to each enterprise to take account of the difficulty of the targets and the changes in the course of the year, the covering of the deficit of certain enterprises and the redistribution of the depreciation fund. To the extent that detailed investment decisions were partially decentralised, it was the VVB that benefited and not the enterprises. Finally, applied research, which in the USSR at this time had to be linked either to enterprises or to ministries, usually found in East Germany an appropriate position at the intermediate level of the VVB.

3 For several years in succession, until about 1968, the NES operated with satisfactory results. The constraints applying to the range of goods produced were less strict, but producers tried on the whole to respond to the needs of their customers; rationing of the means of production had become more flexible without causing even temporary shortages; the system even contained a certain margin of flexibility, which meant that, should the need arise, additional, unplanned demand could be satisfied, for export, for example; and modifications to targets imposed on enterprises in the course of the year were less frequent. Credit for these results must go above all to the policy of moderate growth which prevailed after the crisis at the beginning of the 1960s caused by excessive investment: from 1964, the government resolutely gave priority to steady growth over rapid growth; accumulation was kept within reasonable limits, and the 'reconstitution of the reserves' became a major preoccupation. The effects of the change to less tight planning were very

apparent at the level of the enterprise. Managers were very pleased[5] to be able to admit openly that they had reserves, without risking an immediate increase in their targets . . . on one condition, however: they were not to exceed the plan by too obvious a margin. And this is undoubtedly the fundamental point. Exceeding the targets was no longer really encouraged, and almost all managers of enterprises or VVB took care not to do so, even where profits were concerned, which were the main determinant of bonuses; there was in any case no question of sacrificing the other compulsory indicators to the maximising of profits, nor of risking for that reason a conflict with the purchasers of their products by imposing on them a range of goods they did not want. There even seemed to be a tacit agreement between the managers of enterprises and their staff to avoid any significant exceeding of productivity norms, particularly if it was to be the result of an intensification of the work effort (Granick, 1975, p. 190), since the strict arrangements for the control of wages (the prevention of inflationary pressures was more than ever a priority aim in East Germany) did not allow workers to be adequately rewarded.

It is thus understandable that the recovery and consolidation of the East German economy achieved from 1964 onwards gave renewed confidence to the East German leaders, without seeming to them to be a satisfactory result; they thus tried, from 1967-8 onwards, to redirect the course of the reform in order to put it at the service of a particularly vigorous policy of structural transformations.

1969-70: the turning point

1 Right in the middle of the 1966-70 FYP there was a real change of tempo, symbolised by the new watchword 'do not just fulfil, exceed'. In 1968, the targets in the annual plans were increased for GNP, industrial production, labour productivity, and, above all, for imports of capital goods and for investment (the plans for 1969 and 1970 provided in quick succession for an annual increase of 11 per cent in investment). Enterprises were once again encouraged to exceed priority targets.

This very clear change of direction in economic policy is reminiscent in certain respects of what had happened in Czechoslovakia and Poland ten years earlier: there was the same refusal to consider the possibility of a conflict, even in the short term, between the sudden rapid expansion in investment and progress in consumption, the same wish to depend on recent institutional reforms to obtain 'by the shortest possible route' an acceleration of economic growth, which had to meet all needs. However, the aim was no longer to re-establish overall priority in favour of heavy industry, but above all to accelerate technical progress. The research and development effort was suddenly stepped up.

Table 6.1 *Research and development expenditure as a percentage of national income (1960-70)*

	1960	1965	1968	1970
GDR	1.8	2.5	3.0	3.9
Czechoslovakia	2.4	3.3	3.3	3.8
Hungary	1.7	2.3	2.4	2.4
USSR	2.7	3.8	–	4.1

Source: *Etude sur la situation économique de l'Europe en 1971*, 2nd part, p. 130.

The new strategy was to concentrate maximum effort in a selective way on the key targets on which the development of the rest of the economy depended. The priority given to 'structurally decisive' projects related particularly to automatic control systems, electronic data-processing equipment and the production of precision scientific instruments. Attempts were also made to hasten the introduction of new raw materials (synthetic fibres, plastics, petrochemical products and light-weight construction materials). The reference to the 'most advanced level of world technology' became the decisive criterion for the allocation of investment loans.

2 This new strategy directly affected planning methods, economic organisation and the implementation of the reform.

At first sight, it was a logical consequence of the decisions taken since 1963: the aim now was to transform the economy according to the logic of the reform. What was more in keeping with the principles of efficiency and profitability than the priority given to technological modernisation?

And indeed, there was a vigorous attempt to restore order to the price system. Whereas the revision of prices carried out in 1966-7 had been of the most traditional kind, East Germany moved in 1969 towards the 'production prices' formula (which means that the element of profit included in prices had to reflect capital intensiveness). Any attempt at a new general reform of prices was abandoned for the immediate future, since the intention was to put into practice a policy of 'dynamic prices', a sort of permanent updating, by means of which increases in productivity were intended to be reflected as they occurred in the formation of prices. The implementation of this was largely the responsibility of the VVB who were given the task of establishing about three-quarters of the prices; although the VVB acted on the authority of the central administration and were subject to strict norms, this was nevertheless a new extension of their responsibilities.

The incentive system was also adapted to the requirements of the new phase. Thus it was planned to refund to producers for a year the equivalent of the 'loss of profit' caused by the reduction of prices, in the form of a reduction in the tax on profits. Moreover, all incentive indicators and norms for 1969-70 were fixed as early as 1968, in such a way as to protect enterprises against the 'ratchet effect' (the increasing of targets in accordance with progress made). In the April 1970 programme, it was planned to give enterprises and the VVB stable bases for calculation for the whole of the five year period from 1971-5, in accordance once again with one of the fundamental aims of the New Economic System, which was to lengthen the time-scales of production units.

But the April 1970 plan was cancelled in the autumn of 1970, and this abandonment was only the outcome of a process that had begun two years earlier with the return to tight planning.

As early as 1968-9, the new approach of technological development involved 'selective centralisation of the management of key sectors' (*Etude sur la situation économique de l'Europe en 1969*, 2nd part, p. 78) that had been given priority in the distribution of credit, of the means of production and of highly skilled personnel. Essential decisions (concerning, for example, the introduction of automated data processing systems) were worked out by a working party attached directly to the Council of Ministers. Experts in the Ministry of Science and Technology drew up in detail a number of different plans for each 'structural complex'. Once the central authorities had taken their decision, all the agencies concerned were obliged to implement the 'structurally vital plans'. They were given priority in the allocation of capital goods in short supply. The bank was obliged to release the necessary credit, and to relegate criteria of profitability to the background. Enterprises received new compulsory indicators regarding the mechanisation and automation of nationally important manufacturing.

The concentration of enterprises, after a phase of relative stability which lasted until 1967, increased again very rapidly from 1968 to 1970. The main feature was vertical integration, with the development of complexes whose basic function was 'to co-ordinate within a single organisation the various stages of development and manufacture leading to a final product' (Granick, 1975, p. 142). The final producer was thus made responsible for organising the earlier stages of production; smaller enterprises were gathered around the complex and formed with it 'a chain of co-operation'. The most important complexes, with the research institutes that were linked to them, were the direct responsibility of the Council of Ministers, without being attached to a VVB.

At this stage, therefore, the East German economy was characterised by a real reform of planning methods (now based on the requirements for final products, as opposed to the traditional practice, for which the starting point was the production of intermediate goods), and by the retention or the reappearance of the dominant features of the centralised model: direct supervision by the central authorities of the main production units, concentration in their hands of the important decisions, and the 'shock absorber' role of the non-priority sectors. To be more precise, the basic originality of this period was, to use the expression of D. Granick, the evolution towards a sort of industrial 'dualism'. It was as if the authorities considered 'extreme centralisation' indispensable to technological modernisation, but without forgetting that a system of planning based on detailed physical quantities is inefficient if applied to the whole of the economy. This is the reason for the contrast between the re-establishment of direct management methods with regard to the priority sector (producing the essential goods, or '*strukturbestimmende Erzeugnisse*') and the much greater autonomy enjoyed by production units in the remaining sector; thus the influence of criteria of profitability was not eliminated, but practically restricted to the non-priority sector, which had to make do with aggregate planning, for want of anything better (Granick, 1975, p. 161). However, it very quickly became evident that this was an unstable equilibrium.

3 In accordance with a familiar process, the acceleration of investment firstly caused construction deadlines to be extended and an increase in the number of incomplete investment projects. However, thanks to reserves built up in the preceding years, to much use of overtime and to withdrawals from the non-priority sectors (such as house-building), the whole priority sector was able to maintain a rapid rate of growth, often in excess of targets, throughout 1969. But it was not long before bottlenecks began to multiply in many different manufacturing industries. The reduction in basic energy investment to the advantage of the new leading industries was eventually reflected in shortages of electricity in particular, which, in their turn, affected the growth of the priority sectors themselves; to take a single example, in 1970, the electronic

and electro-technical industries, which had the very highest priority, were 4.1 per cent below the target in the annual plan. 1970 was thus a year characterised by breakdowns in the supply system and failures to honour contracts, by a general failure to meet production and investment targets, and by a worsening of the foreign trade deficit. Without being comparable with that in Czechoslovakia in about 1963, the economic situation was worrying enough to bring about a new and sudden change of direction on the eve of the 1971-5 five-year period.

The questioning of the New Economic System

The disruptions in the East German economy in 1970 were directly caused by the acceleration of investment and the attempt to make good within a few years an often considerable technological gap. They could conceivably have been corrected by a return to less tight planning, accompanied by a policy of modernisation and restructuring that did not try to cut corners. In fact, there was both a very clear policy change in this direction, with a sudden brake on investment from 1971 onwards, priority being given to building up reserves again, and less ambitious targets being fixed, and also an implicit challenge to all the basic orientations of the NES. It is true that the principles of the reform were not officially repudiated. The exact significance of the change of direction in 1970-1 is open to debate (were the seeds of it not contained in the decisions taken in 1968-9? And in any case, even at the height of the NES, enterprises had still been obliged to draw up and pass on, 'for information only', the old compulsory indicators that had been abolished), there may have been questions about its durability (certain observers believed it was only a phase[6]), but there can be no doubts about its reality. The replacement of Ulbricht by Honecker a few weeks after the first steps towards recentralisation gave it an undeniable political significance. East Germany seemed to have given up the attempt to open the way to a new type of socialist economy, in its capacity as the most advanced country in the group. The manual *The Political Economy of Socialism and its Implementation in the GDR* was abandoned and replaced by a Soviet manual – as before, symbolising the fundamental decision to align even more closely with the USSR.

1 The tensions and imbalances in the economy first of all made it necessary to annul contracts already agreed between enterprises. The number of balances drawn up by the central administration was greatly increased in 1971-2. In 1971, it was decided to freeze prices for the

entire duration of the 1971-5 FYP (the events in Poland at the end of 1970 no doubt played a part in this). Strict controls were planned in order to thwart the disguised increases in prices to consumers. There were stricter and more detailed controls on prices and employment. The main aim was to stabilise the *level* of prices in the face of the inflationary pressures that appeared in about 1970. But the process of putting order back into the *structure* of prices (the change to prices of the 'production price' type; the principle of 'dynamic prices' reflecting productivity increases) was at the same time interrupted.

Under these circumstances, the return to the detailed fixing of the range of goods produced, in the form of monthly production targets, was perfectly understandable, in view of the rigidity of prices. Contracts between enterprises tended once again to become merely a method of carrying out the national plan, rather than the basis on which it was constructed. The procedures of administrative allocation (made concrete by the granting of delivery slips) regained their essential role in the maintenance of planned balances. These balances were precarious and often achieved 'on paper', in accordance with the old practice, by arbitrarily reducing the intermediate consumption norms for non-priority users (i.e. a decrease in inputs, without any corresponding reduction in planned output).

At the same time, profits lost their pre-eminent position among the indicators of success. Not only were they supplanted by the indicator of production sold, which received the greatest weighting in the calculation of the bonus fund, but the disillusion with and mistrust of an incentive system based on profits were reflected in all sorts of measures. The November 1971 decree on prices forced enterprises producing consumer goods to manufacture a minimum proportion of relatively cheap articles. From 1972, a performance fund was set up alongside the bonus fund with the specific aim of encouraging increased labour productivity, savings in the use of raw materials and improvements in quality, with separate payments for each of these headings. This need for direct and separate intervention by the administration both in order to maintain ordinary cheap production and to encourage good quality is very characteristic of the model. Profits now at most provided the main source of finance for an enterprise's planned investment, and this certainly did not mean that enterprises had any decision-making power with regard to this planned investment; from 1972, moreover, if enterprises did not reach the planned level of profits, payments to the budget were automatically reduced (by 50 per cent from 1973) so as to safeguard planned investment. Conversely, additional profits made by breaking the discipline of the plan were confiscated: in other words, as M. Keren stresses, the administration gave itself full scope to decide for itself the profit level of each enterprise (in Bornstein (ed.), 1973).

It should be noted finally that in 1972 the bulk of the private or semi-nationalised industrial enterprises, which had been one of the original features of the East German economy since the Stalinist period, were nationalised.

2 Consequently, from the beginning of the 1970s, 'indirect encouragement of an enterprise's own initiatives gave way to strong pressure for strict fulfilment of centrally fixed targets' (Leptin and Melzer, 1978, p. 132). Today, there are more compulsory instructions than at the beginning of the 1960s, on the eve of the reform. Similarly, the idea of a single indicator of success seems to have been abandoned; directives issued in 1975, for example, distinguished twelve categories of criteria of efficiency, which left unsolved the problem of their respective weighting.

The freeze on prices to consumers has been renewed in successive plans. However, the problem of prices has continued to be very topical. The fixing of the price of new products brings into play complex administrative procedures, superimposing a series of controls carried out at different levels of the hierarchy; the approach is much the same as in the USSR, which is based on taking into account use value through the determination of technico-economic parameters, with increases in productivity divided up in favour of the innovator (70 per cent for the producer, 30 per cent for the purchaser). But it was above all the massive increase in the price of imported raw materials, including, from 1975 onwards, those imported from the USSR, that led to a major disruption. After the increase had been absorbed by means of subsidies, it was decided to reflect it in wholesale prices from 1976 onwards. The result was a renewed undermining of the unity of the prices system: the same product was sold at a much higher price to industrial users than to consumers; the prices used to express the planned indices (1975 constant prices) were again separated – as before 1967 – from actual everyday prices; the increase in costs was more or less offset by tax reductions differentiated according to enterprise. In fact, there was much greater reliance on specific incentives to economise on raw materials (involving guarantees against the ratchet effect) than on direct reaction by enterprises to the increase in the price of inputs according to the profitability criteria.

The return to less tight planning in 1971-2 was only partially maintained. The deterioration of the international situation seemed to encourage the fixing of relatively ambitious targets, particularly in order to export more and offset the reductions in the terms of trade. The official line recommended 'tight, but realistic plans'. Thus the last FYP (1981-5), contrary to the general trend within Comecon, fixed a growth rate target that was slightly ***higher*** than the results of the previous five-year period. Moreover, there was every encouragement to exceed targets, but, in order not to disrupt supplies, attempts were made to integrate any overshooting in advance into the planned evolution. For this reason, it was decided in 1974 to adopt the counterplan method (using the corresponding targets in the FYP as the basis for reference, as in the USSR). The results were limited, for the same reasons as in the USSR: whatever promises were made, enterprises feared that the authorities might make increased demands, in one way or another, should they be imprudent enough to reveal their 'reserves'.

3 The measures taken in 1971-2 thus marked the end of the NES, and not merely an eclipse. Yet the present situation is not simply the one that prevailed before the reform. There have been two principal gains from the reform.

The first of these is an economic organisation in which the intermediate levels of the hierarchy continue, despite the fluctuations between decentralisation and tighter controls, to relieve the central administration of a large part of the tasks of day-to-day management. Between 1978 and 1980 there was a major restructuring, with the widespread establishment of combines, which were to take over the role of the VVB. The actual significance of this process had varied from sector to sector: in extreme cases, the combine may simply be a new title for an already existing VVB.[7] But in general, the aim was to replace the old principle of horizontal grouping with vertical integration. The criticisms made today of the VVB (that they were too bureaucratic and tolerant of price increases) reveal above all their inability to solve the eternal problem of Soviet-type economies: the adjustment of inter-sector deliveries. The aim of changing to a system of organisation based on the combines was to internalise supply relationships as far as possible and to minimise any kind of external dependence: 'Within the combine, the most important phases of the process of reproduction are co-ordinated, beginning with research and development, followed by the projecting and self-sufficient production of rationalization means, leading to production itself.'[8] Thus the engineering industries are to have their own foundries and power stations, the shoe industry is to produce its own leather, and the ship-building industry its own electronic machines,[9] even if this means multiplying duplicate jobs and diseconomies of scale. There is particular emphasis on the self-sufficiency of the combines in plant and equipment, and on their responsibilities with respect to innovation. The combines were strengthened to the particular detriment of the autonomy of the integrated enterprises: the director-general of the combine nominates the managers of enterprises, and he is empowered to alter the production tasks of an enterprise, to redistribute its plant and equipment, to centralise its financial means (retained profits and depreciation funds), and to regroup all research and development, professional training and market research at the level of the combine; he is completely responsible for the organisation of deliveries within the combine and for the fixing of internal prices, the implementation of innovation programmes and the fulfilment of obligations towards the other Comecon countries. These responsibilities were given to the combines with the aim of reducing the control by the administration of day-to-day management, but the reform cannot be interpreted in terms of decentralisation. The uninterrupted process of concentration (the number of enterprises decreased from 11,000 in 1970 to little more than 6,000 in 1978, and in 1980 110 combines were responsible for 90 per cent of industrial production)[10] made the task of selective centralisation easier. Detailed targets are still fixed for the final production of the combines, but not for internal deliveries; they have no rights over their foreign currency revenue from exports; and, above all, it is clearly laid down that the central authorities can in the future redefine the boundaries of the combines in accordance with the national priorities of the policy of technological innovation.

There appears to be a second, irreversible gain from the past fifteen years: efficiency has become a permanent top priority target. The 'role of science and technology in the development of the productive forces' recurs as a leitmotif in official declarations and texts. An increasing share of GNP is devoted to research and development. Preference is given in principle to investment for modernisation over investment for increasing capacity. The incentive system for enterprises is no longer biased towards the maximum growth of gross production: in 1980, both East Germany and the USSR experimented with the widespread introduction of indicators of the value added type, and there are in addition many specific incentives to economise on raw materials; the East German economy was *relatively* well prepared to tackle the current phase of restrictions. The banking agencies have maintained an important role in the implementation (but not, of course, the formation) of investment policy, at the stage of preparing and assessing projects. Progress has been made towards standardising the rate of tax on capital at 6 per cent and the elimination of exceptions granted to certain sectors. The fixing of relative prices was an attempt to take better account, as far as possible, of use values (the differentiated increase in the price of fuels in 1976 was a real step forward in this respect). Another interesting development is that the purchaser's point of view has begun to be taken into account during the price-fixing procedures, thus giving the purchaser some control over the process.

The basic problems which brought about the reform have thus been alleviated or partially corrected, but not eliminated. Although the system of organisation based on the combines solves some of the problems caused by inter-firm relationships, it aggravates others; firms whose production was shared among several main customers do not fit easily into the new structure, and there is every possibility that there will be a return within a few years to a sector-based organisation, accompanied by denunciations of the wastage caused by the autarchic policy of the combines. Energy consumption (*per capita* or per unit of production) remains abnormally high in East Germany, compared, for example, with the Federal Republic. The fundamental importance attached to the stability of price levels is an obstacle to necessary readjustments. In particular, prices to consumers are almost completely rigid; the official index continues imperturbably to 'deny' the existence of any inflation, and subsidies have reached gigantic proportions. In these conditions, the gradual refinement of the financial regulators – a truly never-ending task – is still far from reaching the point at which the resurrection of the NES might become possible. As for the direct pressure exerted by the administration on producers, even if it helps the modernisation of some backward firms, there is much more doubt about its ability to 'force' innovation on the part of leading firms.

However, for reasons largely unconnected with the 1963 reform, the East German economy remains the most advanced socialist economy, and one of the best managed. An analysis of its recent performance will help us to assess the amount of progress that can be achieved within the centralised model.

The evolution of the economic policies and the overall performance of the Soviet and East German economies

The immediate cause of the reforms of the 1960s had been the marked drop in the growth rate. They were followed by a distinct, though short-lived, recovery in this respect, particularly in the USSR: the growth rate in the output of goods in 1980 (2.0 per cent) was the lowest in Soviet history, and the results for 1982 are likely to be equally bad. On the other hand, the East German economy is resisting the world crisis well and maintaining regular growth.

Table 6.2 *Evolution of the average annual growth rate of the net material product, USSR and GDR (1961–81)*

	GDR	USSR
1961–5	3.5	6.5
1966–70	5.5	7.8
1971–5	5.4	5.7
1976–80	4.1	3.6
1981–5 (plan)	5.1	3.4
1981	5.0	3.2

Source: Official statistics, quoted from *Economic Survey of Europe. Statistical Yearbook, Member countries of Comecon.*

However, it was not the slowing down of growth that we had identified as the basic problem of Soviet-type economies, but rather the technological gap, poor labour productivity and, above all, *the permanent disparity between progress in production and the degree of satisfaction of final needs*: thus we shall attempt to assess recent developments from this point of view. The repeated disappointments in this area are a cause of increasing concern and even exasperation for the leaders, as witnessed, for example, by Brezhnev's outburst at the 25th Congress of the CPSU against officials 'who have not been able to overcome their view of consumption as something of secondary importance . . . [who] have not understood that it is of fundamental economic and political importance, directly linked to the implementation of the decisions in the programme of the party'.[11]

But the official declarations stressing the importance attached to improving the standard of living have not until now had any decisive effect on the distribution of GNP: in the long term, the share of consumption has not increased at all since the reforms; and it is still too early to assess whether the recent slowing down in investment (which has been particularly rapid in the USSR) marks the beginning of a lasting

Table 6.3 *Distribution and final uses of GNP, USSR and GDR (1965-77)*

	1965	1977
USSR		
Distribution (in %) of final uses of GNP (Western definition)		
Individual and collective consumption	55.3	54.9
Capital investment and defence	35.2	39.2
Administration and miscellaneous	9.5	5.9
East Germany		
Distribution (in %) of NMP		
Individual consumption	71.6	68.2
Collective consumption	8.5	10.7
Accumulation	19.9	21.1

Source: for the USSR, estimations by I. Edwards, M. Hughes and J. Noren, JEC, *Soviet Economy in a Time of Change*, 2 vols, 1979.

reversal. Calculated in American prices, the share of fixed investment in Soviet GNP was estimated to be 31.1 per cent in 1976, compared with 16.4 per cent for the USA.[12] Although such comparisons can only give an order of magnitude, one thing is certain: despite this enormous investment programme, the backward sectors have still been unable to overcome their chronic difficulties.[13]

Agricultural policy

Agricultural difficulties are a problem of quite different dimensions in the USSR – where, in 1965, about a third of the total workforce worked in agriculture (just over 20 per cent in 1980) and where the grain shortage constantly returns to the forefront of topicality – than in East Germany – a highly industrialised country, where agriculture has reached a technical level comparable with that of Western Europe and where the share of agricultural employment was little more than 15 per cent in about 1965, and 10 per cent today.

Like Khrushchev twelve years earlier, Brezhnev vigorously criticised the restrictions on private farming as soon as he came to power; the 'agricultural reform' decided on at the plenum of March 1965 anticipated the industrial reform by seven months. It was reflected notably in facilities to restore private livestock (the results of which were to be immediately noticeable) and by an increase in agricultural production prices, in the form of a 50 per cent price rise in sales in excess of quotas.

This was a return to the system of 'double prices' that had been in use before 1958 (its problems seemed to have been rather quickly forgotten), but it was now being applied in a very different spirit: instead of appropriating compulsory deliveries, the aim was to encourage additional deliveries. The tax system was adjusted in favour of the poorest *kolkhozy*. As a result of these measures, the payment of a guaranteed monthly wage to *kolkhozniks* became more widespread and took the place of residual payment according to the system of workdays.

The drive to improve agriculture, agreed on in 1965, was not a flash in the pan. Soviet agricultural purchase prices have been increased many times in the past fifteen years; and since prices to consumers have hardly been increased, the state has had to pay enormous and steadily increasing subsidies. The trend has been the same in all the socialist countries, starting with East Germany: thus, since the Stalinist period, there has been a complete reversal in the relationship between agriculture and the rest of the economy. At the same time, considerable progress has been made towards parity between peasants' incomes and the average income of other categories of the population.

The general trend to gradual alignment with the social security benefits system for wage-earners and the relaxation in the USSR in December 1974 of the discriminatory system of internal passports for *kolkhozniks* were also proof of a new frame of mind.

The priority now given to agriculture, at least in the USSR, is shown even more clearly in the impressive increase in agricultural investment.

Table 6.4 *Share of agriculture as a percentage of total investment, USSR and GDR (1961-80)**

	USSR	GDR
1961-5	19.6	13.0
1966-70	23.2	14.6
1971-5	26.2	12.6
1976-80	25.7	10.8
1980	25.5	10.1

*Including, for the USSR, some unproductive investments in the agricultural sector, but not including investment in industrial sectors supplying agriculture.
Source: D. Carey in JEC, 1977, p. 590, continued for 1976-80 from official statistics.

The complementary increase in investment in the sectors linked to agriculture (fertilisers and agricultural machinery) meant that, in the USSR, the intensification effort could advance on a broad front. The central regions are no longer disadvantaged. The trend towards exceeding the planned level of agricultural investment will no doubt be confirmed in the course of the present five year period. Here again, there is a striking contrast with the Stalinist period: in order to make up for its slow development, Soviet agriculture now benefits from a massive injection of resources from the rest of the economy. Although the share of agricultural investment in East Germany is lower than in the USSR and going down, it nevertheless remains about five times higher than in West Germany (2.4 per cent of total investment for the average of the period from 1971 to 1975).

Have these efforts been reflected in the results obtained? The growth in Soviet agricultural production since 1965 seems both to be fairly rapid (particularly in comparison with the end of the Khrushchev period) and excessively irregular. To a large extent, of course, these fluctuations can be explained by natural conditions, and some comfort can even be drawn from a comparison of the two most catastrophic years, 1963 and 1975: the 1975 grain harvest was more than a third greater than that of 1963, and 7.5 per cent higher than the 1961-5 average. But poor weather conditions are obviously not an adequate explanation for recent results: for the first time, there has been an absolute fall in Soviet agricultural production in three successive years, 1979, 1980 and 1981. The most obvious symptom of failure is the constantly enormous disparity between planned targets and the results achieved, particularly in view of the level of investment and subsidies. The same is true in East Germany, where agriculture has stagnated: the level of vegetable production reached in 1974 was not attained again until 1980, and the targets for the present five-year period are surprisingly low.

The disparity between the means and the results thus makes it no longer possible to concur with the judgement made by R. Clarke in 1968: 'The list of changes introduced, and the results obtained, are ample proof that the real reform in the Soviet economy . . . has taken place in agriculture and not in industry' (Clarke, in *Soviet Studies*, October 1968, p. 178). Although there has certainly been a major reversal of economic policy, the change is of a purely quantitative nature. Agriculture remains subject to management by the administration, which in the USSR and East Germany involves compulsory and detailed planning of all aspects of production. It is true that there are slight differences between the two countries. The co-operatives and even the state farms in East Germany do not suffer from the gigantism that has tended to become more pronounced in the other countries (notably in the USSR with the gradual assimilation of the *kolkhozy* to the *sovkhozy*).

But the similarities are greater. Between 1972 and 1974, East Germany transformed the remaining 'flexible' type co-operatives into 'advanced' co-operatives. And above all, it opened the way to the development of the vertical integration of the agricultural and food processing industries, in the form of 'complexes' bringing together agricultural producers, processing industries and distribution agencies. The USSR went determinedly down the same road with the June 1976 decree on agro-industrial integration. This was a logical development, but it offered little hope of a solution to the fundamental difficulties linked to the application of the centralised model to agriculture.

Industrial policy and openness

The importance attached to the production of consumer goods (regularly referred to in East Germany as the 'principal aim' of the implementation of the plans) was not limited to declarations of principle. In the USSR, the period under consideration was marked by exceptionally similar growth rates for sector A and sector B industries from 1966-70, by the fixing, contrary to tradition, of higher targets for sector B than sector A in the 9th and 11th Soviet plans (1971-5 and 1981-5), by the constantly favourable readjustments towards consumption introduced in 1971 in the East German FYP, and by the Soviet decrees of January and February 1977 which aimed to give real priority to consumer goods and services.

It is thus necessary to look closely at the actual evolution of the production of industrial consumer goods (sector B) and of capital goods (sector A).

Table 6.5 *Ratio of sector B growth rate to sector A growth rate, USSR and GDR (1961-81)*

USSR	1961-5	1966-70	1971-5	1976-80	1981-5
planned	0.79	0.90	1.04	0.86	1.02
actual	0.67	0.99	0.83	0.79	–
GDR	1961-5	1966-8	1969-71	1971-5	1976-80
actual	0.78	0.84	0.64	0.87	0.83

Source: *Etudes sur la situation économique de l'Europe*

The growth rate in sector B was consistently lower than that for sector A in both countries. In the USSR, it did not prove possible to maintain the almost parallel growth of the years from 1966 to 1970.

The aim of a more rapid increase in sector B, the main feature of the 1971-5 plan, was not achieved, and it was abandoned in the following plan, no doubt by necessity rather than choice. During the five-year period from 1976-80, both in the USSR and East Germany, investment increased more than planned, but even this was not enough to bring about the planned growth in the net material product.[14] There is no guarantee that the priority given to sector B in the current Soviet plan will be adhered to any more closely, and perhaps in a few years' time the 'law of priority growth of the means of production' will be 'rehabilitated', as it was in 1976. Even in East Germany, where recent developments have been more favourable to consumption, there has been an almost uninterrupted decrease in the share of light industries and food industries in total industrial production.

The more rapid growth of sector A industries is determined, at least in an initial analysis, by the structure of investment.

Table 6.6 *Distribution by sector of total industrial investment, USSR and GDR (1961-80)*

	Energy electricity	Metal industries, engineering and electrical industries	Light industry and food processing
USSR			
1961-5	30.2	30.2	16.9
1966-70	29.4	32.0	17.9
1971-5	28.6	29.6	17.0
1976	28.9	33.9	16.2
1976-80	29.6	31.1	15.8
1980	31.9	35.0	15.7
GDR			
1961-5	36.7	27.2	13.4
1966-67	29.0	29.0	15.7
1968-70	18.2	31.6	16.9
1971-5	25.8	27.6	18.0
1976-80	23.3	31.8	17.3
1980	23.1	36.0	20.6

The distribution of investment in the USSR seems astonishingly rigid. The relative weight of the basic sectors (energy, iron and steel) is still as heavy, which certainly confirms that this is a fundamental constraint, for reasons already elaborated. The share of the chemical industries (9.9 per cent in 1979), which was a priority sector at the end of the Khrushchev period, has hardly increased in ten years. Finally, the share of light industries, despite a few short-term fluctuations, remains low and has not tended to increase at all since 1970. The evolution in East Germany is much less consistent. The sudden squeeze on basic investment (particularly in the energy sector) from 1968 to 1970, to the benefit of those sectors which had priority for modernisation purposes, was an obvious cause of the imbalances of 1970–1, and a large increase was urgently needed from 1971 to 1972, and then again in 1977. However, there is also a parallel and lasting trend towards a relative increase in investment in the consumer goods sector. This increase is still limited, but nevertheless significant. In return, it has been necessary to reduce the priority given to the leading industries (the growth rate in the chemical, electronic and electrical engineering industries by 1980 hardly exceeded that of the engineering industries as a whole), while increasing the dependence of the East German economy on foreign sources of energy and raw materials.

East Germany has undoubtedly a greater interest than any other country in Eastern Europe in long-term agreements within the framework of Comecon in order to safeguard its essential supplies of basic products, to find a market for its exports of capital goods and to orientate its development accordingly. This is the reason for the support given by the East German government to the USSR for the adoption and implementation of the Complex Programme (July 1971), aimed at relaunching the economic integration of the member countries of Comecon. This has been reflected since 1976 in the inclusion in the long-term plan of each country of a special chapter dedicated to the development of international co-operation among the socialist economies. The continued pre-eminence of trade within Comecon enabled East Germany to soften and reduce the effects of the world increase in the prices of raw materials. This relative advantage is, however, offset by participation in Soviet investment in the mining of raw materials and by increasing imports of capital goods within the framework of the Comecon specialisation agreements (in about 1975, machinery and capital goods accounted for almost 40 per cent of East German imports from Comecon). Nor is it enough to prevent East Germany having a large and lasting foreign currency deficit, at the same time as facing a loss in real terms corresponding to the fall in the terms of trade, so that the volume of exports has to be increased at all costs in order to limit the overall deficit. However, the result is that the East German economy, like the Czech economy, and for both economic and political reasons, finds itself more and more tied to Comecon; the trend towards an increased share of trade with the

West has remained much less marked over a long period – except for a sudden increase around 1978-9 – than for the other socialist countries, the USSR included.

Table 6.7 *Share of trade with the Western industrialised countries in total foreign trade of USSR and GDR (1965–81)*

	1965	1970	1975	1977	1979	1981
GDR	22	22	26	25	31	27
USSR	21	22	33	33	34	35

Source: *Bulletin économique pour l'Europe.*

East German trade with the West is characterised by a product structure that is very different from that of Soviet trade.

Table 6.8 *Share of machinery and capital goods in total trade of USSR and GDR with the Western industrialised countries in 1975*

	Imports	Exports
GDR	21.7	19.1
USSR	36.9	5.1

Source: *Bulletin économique pour l'Europe.*

The satisfying increase in East German exports of machinery and precision equipment to Western Europe is proof of the at least partial success since 1965 of the modernisation effort. There is a much more obvious imbalance in the case of the USSR. Together with the grain shortage, the urgent need for technological modernisation is the most powerful incentive for increasing trade with the West. The very marked improvement in the terms of trade from which the USSR has the good fortune to benefit as an exporter of oil and mining products and as a large gold producer helps to make the foreign indebtedness tolerable. The importing of Western technology operates, as it were, as a substitute for economic reforms, but this is quite obviously a very inadequate solution, and a serious symptom of failure.

The evolution of the standard of living

The economic difficulties of the beginning of the 1960s had had a serious effect on the evolution of standards of living. At the end of the 1960s there was a greater recovery in consumption than in production. But the recovery linked to the reforms was hardly a lasting one.

Table 6.9 *Evolution of average annual growth rate of real wages, USSR and GDR (1961-81)*

	USSR	GDR
1961-5	3.0	2.7
1966-70	5.0	4.2
1971-5	3.7	3.7
1976-80	2.9	3.0
1981	2.1	–
1981-5 (plan)	2.8	–

As is well known, Soviet consumption levels remain low. There has been undeniable progress in some areas: *per capita* consumption of meat, which had been almost stagnant at the beginning of the 1960s, improved fairly consistently in the ten years from 1965 to 1975; consumption of consumer durables, now including cars, is increasing rapidly. But in many areas, the slowing down of the 1970s is very pronounced. Agricultural failures in particular jeopardise any increase in the overall standard of living.[15] In other areas, isolated efforts at recovery often have questionable effects: thus the development of the production of consumer durables as 'by-products' of heavy industry resulted, at the beginning of the 1970s, in the manufacture of thirty-five different models of washing machine in thirty-five factories (only eleven of which were specialised), answerable to nine different ministries.[16] The exceptional effort to improve services and distribution, announced in the decree of February 1977, will at best enable a few glaring deficiencies to be alleviated somewhat (shopping centres are to be opened and packaging and storage problems alleviated). Above all, it is the qualitative imbalances and the mismatching of the production of complementary goods which weigh heavily on daily life: what is the use of being able to buy cameras without films, transistor radios without batteries, or spoons but no knives? In the middle of the 1970s, the picture in this respect, according to protests published in the Soviet press, is 'more or less the same as ten or fifteen years ago' (Schroeder and Severin, JEC, 1976).

The situation in East Germany is significantly better. The important thing is not that the East Germans still have the highest standard of living of all the socialist countries, but rather that the imbalances are less pronounced and the rate of increase relatively sustained and regular.

The evolution of the 1970s is characterised by a rather unusual trend for planned consumption targets to be exceeded[17] despite unfavourable circumstances (agricultural difficulties, foreign trade deficit); the disparity with the level of consumption in West Germany has ceased to widen since 1965.

As far as housing is concerned, both the USSR and East Germany have a considerable gap to make up, although the problem is less acute in East Germany because of the static population level. Until the end of the 1960s, the house-building programme was very inadequate in both countries. The present situation reveals a much greater contrast between the two, in favour of East Germany and to the detriment of the USSR.

Table 6.10 *Indices of house-building (averages 1961-5 = 100)*

	USSR	GDR
1958	105	–
1961-5	100	100
1966-70	106	86
1971-5	109	113
1976-80	99	158
1981	96	177
1981-5 (plan)	–	170

N.B. The indices are calculated according to the number of units constructed, except for the USSR between 1958 and 1966-70 (calculated according to the total area constructed in millions of m^2). The average area of new units is lower in the USSR than in the GDR (52.4 m^2 and 60.3 m^2 respectively). The index does not include 'renovated' units for the GDR.

In the USSR, house-building constantly lags behind the targets of the annual and of the five-year plans, which are themselves frequently revised downwards. In the long term, there has been a spectacular decline in the house-building programme. In 1958, the share of housing in total Soviet investment had reached 25 per cent, and the number of units finished in 1960 had been almost 2.6 million. At the end of two decades of decline, the share of housing is only one-eighth; in 1979-81, the average annual number of units completed fell below 2 million for the first time. And the minimum health norms relating to the habitable area per person drawn up in 1928 by the Soviet government had still not been achieved half a century later. For its part, East Germany had for a long time allowed its housing stock to grow old, but since 1971 there has been an undeniable improvement in the situation.[18]

Thus in the last fifteen years, the Soviet and East German economies have had to their credit appreciable growth in quantitative terms, without for all that succeeding in raising the standards of quality necessary for an improvement in the standard of living. Progress in this respect has been limited, and its connection with the reforms of the 1960s far from obvious.

The comparison outlined above also highlights a series of significant differences, almost all to the advantage of East Germany. There are many explanations, basically of an historical nature, including the technical and scientific potential inherited from the past, the role of 'the shop window of socialism' that fell to East Germany because of its exposed situation, and even certain consequences of the emigration to the West (enabling competent young men to accede to all positions of responsibility). The initial high level of development is an inadequate explanation of current progress, since the 'international socialist division of labour' seems rather to operate in favour of the less developed countries, such as Bulgaria. On the other hand, the political vulnerability of East Germany has certainly helped to win agreement, after the events of 1968 in Czechoslovakia and of 1970 in Poland, for a policy of moderate and more balanced growth; the recent evolution of the Comecon countries confirms that the basic choice for the communist governments is between forced acceleration of growth and greater satisfactions of needs, as the post-1956 evolution in Hungary had already shown.

It would be wrong to call such a recovery an 'economic miracle', given the relative backwardness in almost all areas in comparison with West Germany. But it does illustrate the margin for improvement available to the Soviet-type economies, even in the absence of any fundamental reform, and it is an encouragement not to overestimate the elements of relative inefficiency inherent in the centralised model. Moreover, only a much more serious economic situation than the one currently pertaining in the USSR itself could make it necessary for its leaders to make radical changes to the economic organisation, and thus risk confrontation with the vested interests at all levels of the hierarchy.

7 Hungary: the reform that survived

As we have seen, the aim of the Hungarian reform clearly was to institute a new model, linking planned management with the active influence of market mechanisms. It was conceived of as a qualitative change, the touchstone of which was the abolition of direct orders to enterprises. It was based on an overall analysis of the interdependencies that underlay the model, and on the political will to introduce immediately at least the minimum changes necessary to reach the point where the reforms would become irreversible.

The problem of putting an end to a system of centralised allocation and of re-establishing market equilibria is not without analogy with the problems of reconstruction in a post-war period. But the difficulties are on a quite different scale. The centralised model had been in use for almost twenty years and, together with the 'forced industrialisation' policy, had moulded the economic structures and influenced mentalities. The managers of enterprises were more inclined to plead their cause with the administration than to take risks, more used to struggling to get hold of the necessary means of production than to winning marketing outlets. Any economic reorganisation decided on at the top was viewed with mistrust by the populace as a whole; if the reform were to threaten jobs or the purchasing power of wages, it would be discredited before having had a chance to produce the long-term advantages expected of it. Caught between contradictory requirements – maintaining economic balances and reassuring the populace, without at the outset jamming all the mechanisms designed to correct the earlier distortions – the Hungarian leaders had only very limited room for manoeuvre.

The setting up of the reform

The preparatory measures

The strategy of the reform was fixed in March 1966, when the central committee declared itself in favour of the simultaneous introduction of the main measures of the reform: 'The new mechanism consists of a certain number of complementary elements which cannot have a beneficial influence on the economy unless they are implemented together. This is why the various fundamental elements of the NEM must come into force on 1 January 1968 after serious preparations which require time.'

Those responsible for the Hungarian reform were not under the illusion, which was fairly widespread in Czechoslovakia in about 1965-6, that the NEM could be relied on to 'clear away the debris of the old system'. Thus there was no question of freeing the process of price formation and waiting for equilibrium prices to emerge from a process of spontaneous adjustment, since the result might well be chaotic fluctuations. Thus during 1966 and 1967 preparations were made for a prices reform based as in the past on centralised calculations and the use of data collected before the reform, because this was the only way that a start could be made on implementing the reform on 1 January on the basis of a new and relatively consistent price system.

During this phase, the Hungarian leaders had no hesitation in using as much as possible the opportunities for direct intervention offered to them by the centralised model, in order to correct certain imbalances inherited from the earlier period. The urgent need for an agricultural recovery, in particular, seemed to justify an exception to the principle of simultaneous implementation. The measures taken from 1965 to 1967 (guarantees and facilities for the cultivation of private plots of land, the increasing of agricultural production prices) were not particularly original, but they were enough to trigger off a cumulative process, whereby peasants' income and agricultural production increased. From 1966 onwards, the co-operatives no longer received compulsory production or sowing targets (except for wheat); in 1967, the law on co-operatives permitted them to choose freely the method by which they sold their produce. The agricultural reform thus foreshadowed and prepared the way for the implementation of the NEM.

Meanwhile, however, the government had to resign itself to unpopular measures, by passing the increase in production prices on to the consumer.

The year 1966 was marked by a series of retail price increases (bread, meat, groceries, domestic coal and urban transport). The regime approached this critical phase with extreme caution. In a way that is at first sight paradoxical, but which is not at all unusual, the imminent economic reform was accompanied, in about 1965-6, by a tough line on political, ideological and cultural questions. The trade unions, however, were allowed to become, within certain limits, the spokesmen of the discontent caused by the price increases. By acting in time and supplying the necessary explanations, the Hungarian leaders succeeded quite well in avoiding the impression that rises aimed at eliminating the consequences of past errors (beginning with the backwardness of agriculture) were linked too directly to the reform.

In the capital goods sector, different measures were taken in order to maintain the essential balances in the period immediately following the reform. Since it had not been possible in 1966-7 to avoid an excessive increase in investment, the annual plan for 1968 contained provisions for this increase to be halted. The recovery of the balance of trade, which occurred in 1965-6, allowed a 'precautionary' increase in imports of raw materials and capital goods. Finally, a quota system (a more flexible version of centralised allocation) was maintained for thirty capital goods in short supply; to these were added a small number of import and export quotas, the aim of which was to maintain supplies to the domestic market. It was, of course, self-evident that enterprises that were 'inefficient', but whose products remained essential, would not be suddenly closed: subsidies covered their financial deficit.

Thus all precautions were taken to prevent the abolition of the rationing of the means of production from causing intolerable imbalances. The only question was whether the priority thus given to safeguarding these balances might compromise the effectiveness of the reform.

The implementation of the reform in 1968

The immediate reduction in the personnel of the sector management departments (from 30 to 60 per cent according to ministry) reflects most clearly the desire for irreversible change that existed in 1968.

The results of the first year of the reform were, on the whole, favourable. The introduction of the NEM did not cause any major disruption. There was still full employment. The reform of industrial production prices had been a success, and the partial freeing of prices had practically no inflationary effect (except in the construction industry); the extra increase in profits (in comparison with the norms laid down for the calculation of new prices) had been much more moderate than in Czechoslovakia, or in the USSR. There was a satisfactory increase in GNP and industrial production, without causing any external imbalance. It had been almost disconcertingly easy to abolish the directives system and to replace allocation by the administration with commercial relationships (e.g. Granick, 1975, pp. 282-8); the consequences that had been feared (shortages and disorganisation) did not materialise.

However, the implementation of the NEM did give rise to various disappointments.

Firstly, there was an excessive increase in the stocks held by enterprises, which had already been high at the outset: it was as if the 'shortage reflex' inherited from the centralised model was stronger than the disincentive effect of interest rates (which reached a general short-term level of 8 per cent). It was the same for investment. It had been planned to give priority in 1968 to the completion of projects already under way, but the propensity of Hungarian enterprises to invest increased still further (as early as the middle of the year, the limit of the resources provided for decentralised investment had been reached). The investment target in the annual plan was once again exceeded, large-scale priority projects were delayed again, and the average level of prices in the construction industry, where control is particularly difficult, exceeded the planned levels by 4 to 5 per cent.

Even more worrying was the slowing down of progress in labour productivity in industry (+ 1 per cent instead of + 5.6 per cent on average between 1965 and 1967). The reduction in hours worked (from 48 to 44 hours per week) in certain sectors is not an adequate explanation, since the trend was the same in all industries. In fact, this was a distortion attributable to wage regulation: by putting a ceiling on the average wage level in an enterprise, the control of wages was an encouragement to recruit too many poorly qualified and low paid workers, with the sole aim of lowering the average wage, and thus enable the incomes of the rest of the personnel (managers in particular) to be indirectly raised. In these circumstances, the 1968 reform, far from causing unemployment, resulted in a very tight labour market: firms were poaching workers from each other, and the turnover rate of workers, habitually very high, underwent a fresh and sudden increase.

Finally, the openly inegalitarian nature of the bonus system (up to 80 per cent of basic salary for managers, 50 per cent for executives and

15 per cent for the rest of the work-force) caused a real shock in 1969, when the bonuses were first distributed. Workers everywhere were angered by the managers' bonuses, which were not necessarily higher than before the reform, but this time they were paid as a lump sum, openly and publicly, and it was necessary to return immediately to a more egalitarian system (with a limit of 25 per cent of basic salary for all categories), at least in appearance, since from now on managers would receive additional bonuses allocated directly by the ministerial authorities, in accordance with their overall assessment of the results obtained by the enterprise.

Overall, this initial phase was quite successful, but new difficulties could be foreseen as the effects of the reform were more fully felt. The 'protective measures' (no closures, no reductions in personnel, subsidies, price stability), which made the implementation of the NEM almost too easy, tended by definition to neutralise its more powerful effects. If the reform was to bear fruit, it was absolutely vital to forge ahead.

1968-73: 'golden age' of the reform?

The limits of orientation by profits

The central idea of the Hungarian reform was to replace administrative constraints by the constraints of the market. This was in no way the same thing as excluding all state intervention, but it was supposed in principle that the state would act through the fixing of financial regulators (prices, interest rates, taxes) which would apply equally to all enterprises. Profits were given a dual role, relating both to the advance of individual incomes and the expansion of enterprises; the funds necessary to investment were basically to be provided by the enterprise, and supplemented by bank loans, 'granted on the basis of anticipated future profits' (Granick, 1975, p. 243).

These were the guiding principles. There is no doubt that the abolition of centralised allocation and detailed production targets imposed on each enterprise created a very different context than that in the USSR or in East Germany for the system of incentive through profits. Nevertheless, these were necessary but not sufficient conditions for profits to be able effectively to play the role given to them. In addition, it was necessary that:

(a) managers' direct interest in profits (in the broad sense) should be sufficiently strong to motivate their behaviour;

(b) that the autonomy in decision-making given to enterprises was respected in practice;
(c) that profits, taking account of prices and other financial regulators that determine their formation, were able 'correctly' to guide an enterprise's decisions, in such a way as to correct existing distortions, yet without creating new ones.

We shall examine these three conditions in reverse order, beginning with the third, and most fundamental one.

1 The economic significance of profits in Hungary remained very variable according to sector, enterprise and product.

It is obvious that incentive through profits is meaningful only if prices accurately reflect the relative intensity of the needs to be satisfied (and this is the case, whatever role is given to the direct expression of specific social preferences, as distinct from the collective assessment of consumers in the market). Publishing provides almost a caricature, that is fortunately quite exceptional and temporary, of the distortions caused by the 1968 reform: the number of books published fell, and there was a sudden expansion in the number of catalogues, circulars and advertising brochures, which were much more profitable for the publisher than books, the price of which was strictly controlled. In general, the price reform of 1968 stopped well short of a complete rationalisation of the price system. There were great disparities in the average rate of profits from one sector to another, for various reasons (attempts were made to take into account the investment needs of the sector, and not to change the price structure in force too suddenly and drastically). Little progress was made in unifying the rate of the tax on turnover, which was, nevertheless, considered to be a fundamental task: in 1969, for example, there was merely a reduction in the number of categories on the taxation scale for leather clothes and goods from 620 to 160, which was still very high. Thus the basic discontinuity between production costs and market valuation was not reduced. Consequently, incentive through profits lost its basic justification, since it could at best bring about only marginal corrections, without eliminating the major disparities that existed at the outset.

This obstable could no doubt have been overcome if the process of freeing prices had progressed as planned. But it had to be abandoned quickly, both because of the overall risk of inflation, and for fear that large enterprises would create new distortions in the price structure by exploiting their 'monopoly power'. Since the beginning of the 1960s, Hungarian industry had reached an exceptionally high degree of horizontal concentration. In 1970, the number of state industrial enterprises was little more than 800, each of which had an average of seven factories; those with more than 1,000 workers accounted for 45 per cent of total employment. In certain sub-sectors there was only one enterprise; where several enterprises existed side by side, they made specialisation agreements among themselves which reduced the amount of overlapping. Inquiries among managers confirmed that many of them felt sheltered from any competition; the proportion who said that competition posed a serious threat to them was minimal (and yet only a small degree of competition was necessary for managers used to the conditions of the old model to feel exposed to competition!).[1] In 1973, I. Friss acknowledged the very serious disappointment felt in this respect by those responsible for the reform: 'We expected sellers to compete with each other in the market, and that competition would limit price increases, or even bring about reductions. But in fact, competition developed only in a few, generally unimportant areas' (Friss, 1973, in *Acta Oeconomica*, vol. 10, p. 313).

2 Whereas the lack of competition and the persistence of a 'sellers' market' made it impossible to lift controls, the high degree of concentration, conversely, made it easier to maintain or re-establish supervision of enterprises by the sector ministries, in a discreet but effective way. In the striking words of D. Granick, it was sufficient to contact 291 people by telephone in order to influence immediately three-quarters of industrial production.

In Hungary as in the other socialist countries, a distinction was often made between 'recommendations' and directives. Thus enterprises had only a limited amount of real autonomy as far as investment was concerned: even excluding the large-scale projects which were the direct responsibility of the central authorities, projects financed by enterprises did not escape supervision by the ministerial authorities; the distribution of bank loans among sectors was decided at the highest level, and the distribution among enterprises often gave rise to interventions by the administration. Decisions on imports and exports were in principle the responsibility of the enterprises but the licensing system enabled the authorities once again to exercise control. There was no question of allowing an enterprise to disrupt supplies to the domestic market (or fail of its own accord to fulfil the international commitments arising from agreements made within Comecon) in order to seize a more profitable export opportunity. Similarly, managers of enterprises would not even try to improve productivity by dismissing workers: job security was tacitly acknowledged as a priority target; at best, they would try to achieve a similar result, by relying on the large number of people leaving voluntarily to create gaps that were left unfilled. Finally, the formation of the 'free prices' was itself subject to very strict rules, and the confiscation of 'illicit' profits was always possible; enterprises were sometimes dissuaded from improving the quality of a product by the difficulties they would have in obtaining a price increase that was, in fact, justified.

However, the new mechanism usually functioned in a flexible way. Enterprises were involved in permanent negotiations with their supervisory ministry on very varied questions (prices, the conditions for financing investment, subsidies or tax exemptions, the allocation of more or less advantageous export markets, and dispensations of all kinds), and a sort of overall balance tended to be established. The hierarchical nature of these relationships had obviously not disappeared: as owner of the enterprises, the state was entitled to determine their sphere of activity, to merge them, to split them up, or to create new ones; similarly, the nomination of managers, their career and even their annual bonuses continued to depend directly on the assessment of the supervisory authorites.

3 In these circumstances, it was to be expected that profits would not be a great motivating factor.

The first problem was the amount of money involved. The proportion of profits earmarked for bonuses and fringe benefits for employees was of the same order of magnitude as in the USSR. Profit-sharing was particularly low 'at the margin': in about 1972-3, if a typical enterprise made 100,000 forints additional profits, payments to its profit-sharing fund increased on average by only 6,000 forints.[2] End of year bonuses (of the order of one week's to one month's wages for all personnel) did not seem to be any higher relatively than before the reform. It is true that the higher one rose in the hierarchy, the higher the proportion of bonuses in relation to basic wages tended to be (about 50 per cent for managers), but also the looser the link with profit levels, which actually does not seem necessarily to contradict the spirit of the reform: an aggregate assessment based on all the important aspects of management from the long-term point of view is better than the mechanical application of a 'formula' giving greater weight to any one short-term indicator.

The level of profits, however, took on a new importance with the changes introduced in 1971 to the system of regulation: from now on, it was to determine, together with the increase in labour productivity, the evolution of basic wages, and no longer only bonuses. The complexity of the formula and its very restrictive application (if the average wage increased by more than 0.3 per cent for each 1 per cent increase in productivity, tax deductions quickly created disincentives) seriously reduced its efficacy. And it is perhaps particularly paradoxical that, in a model which refused to acknowledge self-management and left all decision-making powers within the enterprise to the manager, the evolution of profits influenced the remuneration of the work-force as a whole more than that of the manager himself: this contradiction was to contribute indirectly to the questioning of the reform in the 1970s.

The results of the first years of the reform

1 On the credit side, the Hungarian economy undeniably made progress for six or seven years. However, the real question is to what extent this progress can be attributed to the reform of 1968.

There was an immediate, very marked and lasting recovery in agriculture, where intervention by the administration was reduced to a minimum. The growth rate of gross agricultural production (calculated according to the five year averages) rose from 1.4 per cent in 1961-5 to 2.8 per cent in 1966-70 and 3.5 per cent in 1971-5. At the same time, Hungary's agricultural growth rate went from last to second place among the European socialist countries (immediately behind Rumania which still lagged considerably behind in absolute terms). Contrary to certain precedents, the peasants themselves were the first to benefit from the agricultural recovery: in 1968, the average *per capita* income of peasant families in the co-operatives equalled and then exceeded that of workers' families; even the serious floods of 1970 did not prevent a more rapid increase that year than that in the average income of wage earners. In a few years Hungary again became a major exporter of agricultural products (meat, *foie gras*, wine, fruit, vegetables), particularly to Western Europe: this result can be largely explained by the disappearance of the obstacles to more rational specialisation. The dynamism of the agricultural co-operatives, benefiting from new and more favourable legal arrangements and less strict controls than in the state sector, led them to launch themselves into complementary activities (food processing, construction): at least on a local basis, this was one of the few competitive elements within the Hungarian economy.

The effort to improve service industries, another sector which was lagging behind, which began with the 1971-5 FYP, was indirectly linked to the development of the reform: the stabilisation of the numbers employed in industry at the beginning of the 1970s finally enabled there to be more rapid growth in tertiary employment. But it was above all the facilities granted to private tradesmen and the common, and largely tolerated habit of taking a second job outside normal working hours which made up for the deficiencies of the state sector. Similarly, the private construction industry, sometimes in the guise of 'co-operatives' with very flexible statutes, helps to explain the rapid increase in the number of houses built, after a long period of stagnation.

Table 7.1 *Number of units of housing built (annual average, in thousands)*

1961–3	58.4	1969–70	71.0
1964–8	58.7	1971–3	83.5

Source: *Etudes sur la situation économique de l'Europe.*

Table 7.2 *A comparison of the new housing stock in GDR and Hungary (1961–73)*

	GDR	Hungary
Percentage difference in the average number of housing units built per year between 1961–63 and 1971–73	−4.5	+42.9
Number of units built between 1966 and 1971, as % of existing stock in 1966	7.8	13.8
Number of units built per year per 100,000 inhabitants (average 1971–2)	394	807
Average size (in m^2) of units built in 1972	57.1	63.4

Comparison with East Germany at the beginning of the 1970s is favourable to Hungary all the way along the line.

The evolution of industry is much more difficult to define. As we have seen, the effects of the reform were blunted by the continued existence of informal controls. There was no question of any spontaneous restructuring arising from decisions made by enterprises on the basis of purely financial criteria; investments of a certain size were always systematically examined at sector level; nor was there anywhere any sudden change in day-to-day production as a result of the 1968 reform; the abolition of centralised allocation did not cause any disruption because most of the pre-existing links were simply renewed, and adjustments, when there were any, took place only at the margin. Yet it would be wrong not to go beyond this initial impression of rigidity. On the one hand, the restructuring policy launched before the reform was indeed pursued; on the other hand, the effects on economic efficiency of the scope given to enterprises to make minor decisions were by no means always negligible.

While bankruptcies remained out of the question, there were nevertheless about twenty mergers and reorganisations within a few years, the most important of which, concerning the Budapest tractor firm Voros Csillag, brought about a change of management, twinning with a provincial firm and the retraining of 2,500 workers. Subcontracting relationships among state industrial enterprises and co-operatives with a more flexible system of management began to appear. Here and there, appreciable economies were made possible by the choice of cheaper raw materials, the earlier replacement of outdated equipment and the relaxation of the import system; in certain cases, the opportunity of buying a machine, a spare part, or an intermediate product on the Western market without excessive formalities was enough to make possible an immediate increase in production without costly investment.

The fundamental problem of the Soviet-type economies, as we have defined it in the first two parts, is the problem of the mass of resources constantly reabsorbed in the production process with minimal results in terms of final output. In this respect, the fact that net industrial production increased more rapidly than gross production in Hungary after the reform can be interpreted as a very favourable sign.

Table 7.3 *Comparisons of growth rates in net and gross production, in final and intermediate sales and in industrial exports and total sales in Hungary (1961–70)*

Relative growth rate*	1961–5	1966–70
of *net* production in comparison with *gross* production	0.88	1.19
	1968–70	1971–3
of *final* sales in comparison with intermediate sales	1.75	1.79
of industrial exports in comparison with total industrial sales	1.22	1.82

*Quotient of average annual growth rates. Calculations made from *Etudes sur la situation économique de l'Europe.*

It should be pointed out, by way of comparison, that in East Germany net industrial production increased less quickly than gross production both before and after the introduction of the New Economic System (1961–5: 0.80; 1966–70: 0.88); in Czechoslovakia, final sales increased more quickly than intermediate sales in 1968–9, and again less quickly from 1970 onwards (corresponding to the dismantling of the reform).

After a temporary fall in 1968, labour productivity in Hungarian industry began undeniably to recover (+ 6.2 per cent per year on average from 1971 to 1975, compared with 4.3 per cent from 1951 to 1965, and 3.8 per cent from 1966 to 1970). The acceleration in productivity increases was particularly marked in industrial co-operatives where the spirit of the reform was most respected.

Industrial development in Hungary during this period was largely orientated towards the consumer goods sector: for the first time in a socialist economy, the growth rate of sector B industries exceeded that of sector A industries on a long-term basis. The contrast with the other socialist countries, which was becoming clear even before the reform, was confirmed after 1968.

Table 7.4 *Ratio of sector B growth rate to sector A growth rate, Hungary and GDR (1966-75)*

	Hungary	GDR
1966-8	1.03	0.84
1971-5	1.05	0.87

The rapid expansion of sector B, in which the food industries were the most dynamic element, was based both on the agricultural recovery, and on a gradual but continuous adjustment of the structure of industrial investment.

Table 7.5 *Distribution by sector of investment in Hungarian industry (1961-72)*

	Energy	Iron and steel and engineering	Light industry and food processing
1961-5	33.7	24.5	18.4
1966-70	28.1	29.5	19.3
1971-2	24.0	25.4	22.7

This industrial orientation was inseparable from the increasing integration of the Hungarian economy into Comecon, accompanied by an even more rapid expansion of trade with the West. The Hungarian economy was the most open of the socialist economies: by the middle of the 1960s, Hungary's foreign trade accounted for about 40 per cent of GNP, and the proportion tended to rise continuously. The most remarkable expansion in the period following the reform was in imports of manufactured consumer goods, in contrast to the usual trend in Soviet-type economies. By about 1970, imported consumer goods already accounted for a sixth of the turnover of the retail trade; the share of

Western consumer goods, which was still quite low (6.1 per cent in 1971), had nevertheless doubled in three years. The government had no hesitation in using the weapon of competitive imports to force domestic producers to improve quality and hold prices. Conversely, Hungarian exports of food products and manufactured consumer goods performed satisfactorily in both Eastern and Western markets. But this strategy of openness helped to emphasise the vulnerability of the Hungarian economy, even before 1973-5, when it was hit by the full force of the consequences of the world crisis.

2 The rapid growth of the Hungarian economy from 1968 to 1973 was strongly cyclical in character, notably in the parallel evolution of foreign trade and investment.

Table 7.6 *Indicators of cyclical variations in Hungary (1968-73)*

	1968	1969	1970	1971	1972	1973
Imports	1.5	6.9	30.0	19.3	−2.9	9.0
Exports	5.2	16.5	11.2	7.9	21.2	18.0
Investment	2	8.2	16.8	11.1	−2.2	0.7
Imports of capital goods	–	8.1	40.1	40.6	−9.1	−5.0

Source: *Etudes sur la situation économique de l'Europe*; *Economic Bulletin for Europe.*

The years 1968-71 have all the characteristics of an 'overheating' phase: a growing trade deficit (particularly with the West) and repeated over-shooting of investment targets.

The stabilisation of 1972-3 showed, however, that even with the NEM the government retained vigorous means of action. The recovery of exports (in 1973, the proportion of imports from the West covered by exports had risen to 97 per cent) meant that the brake on imports could be limited in intensity and duration. But, in order to achieve this result, Hungary had to use all the means at its disposal and export all it could: the search for advantageous specialisations and the 'efficiency' of exports were relegated to the background; the improvement in the terms of trade with the West that followed the reform (+ 6.4 per cent between 1967 and 1970) stopped at the beginning of the 1970s, before giving way, in 1973-4, to a serious deterioration. Nevertheless, at this price, it was possible to maintain the openness of the Hungarian economy and more or less direct access for enterprises to foreign trade. Similarly, as far as investment was concerned, the political decision to take a part of the necessary reductions from large-scale centralised investment meant that, in contrast to many precedents, complete recentralisation of all major or minor investment could be avoided. The decree of November 1972, which placed fifty very large enterprises accounting for about half of total industrial production under special control, must be interpreted as acknowledgment of an existing state of affairs rather than a retrograde measure. Finally, it must be stressed that inflationary pressures remained moderate. The rise in retail prices increased gradually to reach 3.5 per cent in 1973, but this was largely the result of planned adjustments (the increase of the price of milk in 1973), the necessity of which had been acknowledged for a long time.

Nevertheless, the imbalances of this period were serious for the indication they gave of the functioning of the NEM: strategies at all levels of the hierarchy were all directed towards a quantitative increase in production. Enterprises sought to benefit directly from the 'potential for growth' made available by the reform, rather than to increase their efficiency. According to an enquiry carried out in December 1970, their anticipated growth for 1971-5 exceeded the growth target in the FYP by 50 per cent, but this also involved an increase in industrial employment (+ 3 per cent per annum) and in fixed capital (+ 9.3 per cent per annum) that was incompatible with adherence to planned balances. Far from bringing about a change from 'extensive' to 'intensive' growth, the reform seemed to have had the opposite effect. All the financial regulators on which factor costs depended (wages and the wages tax, the tax on interest-bearing funds, interest rates) were fixed at a level that was too low to offer any real incentive to use production factors more economically. There was thus a double trend in the Hungarian economy towards overemployment (enterprises were poaching each other's workforce) and, as we have seen, over-investment. The leaders were as reluctant to raise the level of wages (for fear of inflation) as they were to increase the cost of capital to enterprises (for fear of putting a brake on technological progress). Thus the problem of low labour productivity was usually put in terms of 'the excessive cost of capital' in comparison with 'the cheapness of labour', without it being realised that if the cost of capital were reduced still further, far from hastening the modernisation of the Hungarian economy, the only result would be to aggravate the imbalances linked to excessive investment.

Thus the implementation of the Hungarian reform of 1968 was distorted in many respects, since it proved impossible 'to resist the temptation to capitalise on the results of the NEM too quickly in the form of an acceleration of growth' (Zielinski, 1978, p. 26). This is the reason for the interventions by the administration in the distribution of investment, the continued existence of a 'sellers' market' for the majority of products and the abnormally high turnover rate for the workforce. This was also the reason for the absence, from 1969-70 onwards, of significant progress in the development of the reform (whether it was a question, for example, of autonomy for enterprises, the freeing of prices or the extension of the role of credit). The NEM was thus far from having solved 'old problems which proved to be much more intractable than expected',[3] at the very moment when the Hungarian economy was suddenly confronted, in 1973-4, with the consequences of worldwide inflation.

The NEM on trial

The reform called into question

1 The Hungarian economy is both one of the most open of the socialist economies and one of the most dependent for its supplies of raw materials and energy. Consequently, it could not fail to be severely hit by the relative price increase in raw materials and by the acceleration in worldwide inflation from 1973 onwards. The first result for Hungary was a sudden deterioration in the terms of trade with the West, which was all the more noticeable because the restriction on supplies of raw materials by its Comecon partners (particularly the USSR) had forced Hungary to turn to the Western market in order to obtain the rest of its supplies; various aggravating factors (additional restrictions applied by the Common Market to Hungarian exports of animal products; the lack of adjustment by Hungarian enterprises to conditions of worldwide inflation) helped to increase the fall in the terms of trade with the West, which reached 23 per cent in total between 1972 and 1977. The fall in the terms of trade with respect to Comecon (17 per cent between 1972 and 1977) was not quite so great, and was more delayed and spread out; the prices applied within Comecon were, however, raised as early as 1975, without even waiting, contrary to tradition, for the first year of the next five-year period.

Faced with this new problem, the Hungarian government, in a difficult political situation, first of all tried to play for time, by allowing the foreign deficit to increase (in 1975, the total deficit corresponded more or less to the direct impact of the deterioration of the terms of trade, 5 to 6 per cent of GNP), without, for the meantime, cutting back on investment or consumption. The effect of the increase in the price of imported inputs was largely neutralised, particularly in 1974, by a massive increase in subsidies. In other words, the authorities temporarily abandoned the idea of reflecting the evolution of production costs in the price structure: never since 1968 had the Hungarian price system seemed less able to orientate decentralised decisions effectively – which made new encroachments on the autonomy of enterprises inevitable, in accordance with a process that we have already had occasion to mention several times.

2 The processes of gradual recentralisation had admittedly begun much earlier. But the fate of the reform was becoming increasingly dependent on a political struggle of which the social and political implications were closely linked. The rather undramatic nature of this struggle – of which Kadar remained the undisputed referee – makes it difficult accurately to pinpoint the basic turning points. It is clear, however, that the fundamental underlying problem was discontent among the workforce. The absence of unemployment since 1968 had not been enough to dispel fears for the future. The increase in real wages had accelerated since the reform (+ 3.2 per cent per annum from 1968 to 1973, as against 2.1 per cent from 1961 to 1967), but it did not satisfy workers' aspirations, and was very close to the point at which, according to enquiries carried out in Hungary in 1970, the improvement in the standard of living completely ceased to be perceptible. This disappointing evolution was due above all to the fact that the distribution of GNP was still changing in favour of investment, i.e. to the detriment of consumption, but it was also true that the workers had benefited less from the 1968 reform than all the other categories (peasants, managers and even pensioners). The widening of wage differentials (openly advocated until about 1971, in fact quite moderate overall, but sometimes very blatant) and the new opportunities for making money, which were more or less legal and more or less linked to the reform – or rather to its weaknesses – had the effect of exacerbating social tensions.

In these conditions, the economic disequilibria and difficulties (over-investment in 1971, and the worsening of the terms of trade in 1974) were decisive in swinging the balance towards those in the party who supported the most conservative positions, who then had the advantage of being able to claim to be defenders of the workers' interests against those responsible for the reform. The decisions of the plenum of November 1972 linked the beginning of the recentralisation process with an exceptional and uniform wage increase of 8 per cent for manual workers, financed directly by the state – followed a little later by a decree suppressing 'illicit profits'. In 1974-5, R. Nyers, the politician mainly responsible for the economic reform, was removed from the Politburo, and J. Fock quit the post of prime minister that he had held since April 1967. By allowing investment to increase again suddenly (+ 26 per cent in two years from 1974 to 1975), together with a rapid growth in nominal wages (8.2 per cent per annum on average from 1973 to 1975), in a much less favourable international context, the government created the least favourable conditions possible for the smooth functioning of the NEM. At the end of 1975, the number of incomplete investment projects reached a level unprecedented either before or after the 1968 reform. In accordance with a recurrent cyclical mechanism, the increase in demand aggravated shortages, and the shortages in turn increased the opportunities for direct interventions by the authorities.

However, there is little similarity between the piecemeal recentralisation of the Hungarian economy in the middle of the 1970s and the dismantling of the East German reform in 1971. It arose from a state of affairs that already existed, rather than from a conscious decision. Allocation of the means of production by the administration was partially re-established in various forms (quotas for energy and chemical products). The sector ministries considered themselves once again directly responsible for maintaining equilibria, with all the ensuing rights of intervention. But it was above all the excessive increase in subsidies that jeopardised all the automatic mechanisms provided for in the reform: in 1974-5, subsidies of all kinds (subsidies to production, exports, imports and consumption) reached the enormous proportion of 35 per cent of government spending; conversely, 'taxes on production', justified by 'exceptional advantages', deprived certain sectors or enterprises of profits deemed to be excessive. The process of putting some order back into industrial prices was begun in 1975 and continued in 1976, but hardly reduced their arbitrariness in the short term, since the rise in the price of imported inputs was passed on in very variable ways, according to the 'desirable' level of profits in the sector. What significance can be attributed to financial results that arise from purely contractual obligations, being determined above all by decisions taken by the administration itself? The process of differentiating wages according to the efficiency of enterprises, introduced in 1971 and immediately badly received by workers, consequently no longer had any objective basis, and the administration was constantly intervening in order to correct or neutralise the planned mechanisms: instead of profitability determining the evolution of wages, the system of regulation was manipulated in each case in order to guarantee enterprises sufficient profits, and thus enable them to increase wages as planned. In particular, an enterprise which had embarked on excessive or excessively costly investment (often, it is true, under pressure from the supervisory authorities, or at least with their complicity) had the best chance of not having to bear the financial consequences. On the other hand, enterprises had no recourse against interference by the administration in their management.

3 In this difficult context, the adjustments carried out in 1976 on the eve of the fifth FYP reflect a series of compromises, the general significance of which is not easy to discern. The semi-official presentation given, for example, by O. Gado certainly sounds very different from what was being heard in 1968 (Gado, 1976). Not only had the illusion that the NEM could lead to a rapid and automatic solution of all the chronic problems of socialist economies completely disappeared, but the author was at pains to justify direct intervention by the administration in every case in which the desired result could not be achieved simply by manipulating the economic regulators. Yet he was no less vigorous in his protests against attempts to compare the adjustments of 1976 to a return to the pre-1968 system: 'The strengthening of centralised management must not be confused with an extension of the decision-making powers of the central authorities to questions that fall within the scope of the enterprise. It must involve more consistent and more systematic regulation of macro-economic processes' (Gado, 1976, p. 23), which was fully in accordance with the logic of the NEM. Was this a purely formal protest, or did it reflect an unstable balance between conflicting principles? A conclusion can be reached only by examining in detail the contents of the measures adopted.

Care must still be taken to avoid a methodological error which may well distort the diagnosis completely. If a direct comparison is made between the plan for 1976–80 and the initial outline of the reform, the conclusion will be known in advance: this will inevitably be seen as another example of recentralisation. But the only real significant term of reference is the actual functioning of the NEM in the preceding five-year period, and this second approach leads to a much more subtle conclusion. For example, as far as the regulation of wages is concerned, the measures taken in 1976 seem at first sight to be a rejection of the policies introduced in 1968, since they tended to disconnect wage increases from the financial results of enterprises, to increase the role of the national wages policy and to limit inter-enterprise wage differentiation. But was this really a retrograde step? Wherever the evolution of profits is only remotely linked with the efforts or merits of enterprises, any mechanical wage differentiation formula can only create injustices, and indirectly give rise to a proliferation of exceptions and to infringements of the 'rules of the game'. On the other hand, in those sectors where there was a minimum of competition and significant opportunities for economising on manpower, there was no hesitation in forging ahead: regulation of the average wage was replaced by regulation of the total wages fund; an enterprise which cut back on its workforce was thus able, within certain limits, to increase the wages of the remaining workers more quickly, which must have been an appreciable incentive to gains in productivity, at the same time as eliminating a significant source of distortions (p. 202).

The changes to the formation of the enterprise's funds were no less complex. The most obvious one was the increase in the 'centralised' share (i.e. deducted by various taxes) of 'net income', in comparison with the amount of profit retained by the enterprise and the widening of the category of centralised investment. However, at the same time, enterprises for the first time were given the right – which they had been refused in 1968 – to decide themselves how pre-tax profits should be distributed between their profit-sharing fund and their investment fund. Although this measure was of little practical significance in the short term, because of the draconian progressive taxation of profits thus distributed, it was a symbolic expression of the wish to continue to develop the responsibilities of enterprises.

The most significant developments took place in the area of foreign relations. The basic principle remained the same: in 1976, just as in 1968, the authorities stated that Hungarian enterprises were not to be isolated from changes in the world economy. For the time being, however, it seems as impossible totally to *protect* the Hungarian economy as it is to impose genuine *adaptation* on it. The revaluation of the forint against the dollar from December 1972 onwards, but particularly from 1976 onwards, as part of an 'active' and 'flexible' exchange rate policy, tended to compensate for the rise in world prices, but it was not enough to eliminate inflationary pressures.[4] On the other hand, even after the price adjustments of 1975-6, the rise in world prices was hardly reflected in Hungarian domestic prices. Consequently, the declared intention of reducing import subsidies was not carried out. Similarly, export subsidies remained essential in order to limit the foreign deficit; the main beneficiaries were, by definition, the least efficient exporters. On the other hand, the system of *loans for the promotion of exports* turned out to be an original innovation: enterprises had access to credit in convertible currencies for the purchase of capital goods, on the condition that they put forward a project that was sufficiently profitable to enable them to repay the loan quickly (within three years) with the currency earned from exports. This is a rather rare example of a policy that is both *selective* and *competitive*, from which the agro-food and engineering industries (buses, lorries, machine-tools) benefited particularly.

It is thus wrong to interpret the adjustments of 1976 as recentralisation pure and simple: in certain respects they foreshadow the relaunching of the reform in 1980–1. What was lacking was a strong political desire to counter the disequilibria with a return to the logic of the NEM.

The chances for a fresh start to the reform (1980–1)

1 In 1959, J. Montias concluded from an analysis of the evolution of the Yugoslavian economy in the previous decade that:

> decentralisation carried out as the result of governmental decision is not the re-establishment of a natural order, which would lead spontaneously to the elimination of all artificial distortions. It is rather a fragile state of equilibrium, perpetually challenged by bureaucratic interference, and always threatened by a fresh swing towards the opposite pole of hypercentralisation.[5]

The fate of the Hungarian reform, which seemed to have started very confidently, has from the 1970s onwards fully confirmed the precariousness of decentralising reforms. And yet the example of Yugoslavia, where the change to decentralised socialism was not really completed until after the reform of 1965, seventeen years after the first break with the Soviet model, provides some encouragement for the belief that the vicissitudes of the Hungarian reform should not be confused with its final abandonment. And, in the final analysis, the NEM has not held up so badly in particularly unfavourable circumstances: 'The fundamental success of the reforms [in Hungary],' stated R. Portes in 1977, 'is proved by their resistance to a powerful combination of factors, each of which by itself could have brought about the re-establishment of centralised allocation, compulsory planned targets . . . and the whole traditional system of planning by decree' (Portes, in JEC, 1977, p. 788).

The Hungarian reform would undoubtedly not have withstood the test if the social repercussions since 1968 had not on the whole remained moderate. In this respect, comparison with Yugoslavia is significant. Full employment has always been guaranteed in Hungary, whereas in Yugoslavia, the number of unemployed rose from 290,000 in 1971 to 540,000 in 1975 (despite emigration). The annual rate of increase in retail prices in Hungary reached a maximum of 5 per cent in 1976 (compared with 24 per cent in Yugoslavia in 1975), before going down slightly in 1977–8. It was possible to put into effect the planned increase in the price of some widely consumed products (milk, and then meat) without causing any social explosion like those experienced by Poland in 1970, 1976 and 1980, thanks to a system of monetary compensation aimed at protecting the purchasing power of low incomes; moreover, the increases were modulated in such a way as to reflect more clearly than in the past specific social preferences (in 1973, the taxes on alcohol and tobacco and on cars and motorcycles were increased). The state maintained sufficient control over the evolution of income to raise wages in the 'unproductive' sectors, to develop a family policy (a sort of wage for mothers was introduced and family allowances increased) and to solve the most serious faults in the pensions system: the influence granted in theory to the market within the framework of the NEM did not thus prevent the pursuit of broad social objectives which had in fact been very neglected before the 1968 reform. The FYPs were also on the whole more successfully implemented than they had been in the past with the old system of planning by decree, despite the vicissitudes of the 1970s. In any case, the economic reform never seemed a threat to the authority of the party: experience of the NEM very largely belied the mistrust that those in charge of the system might have felt beforehand.

However, the lack of serious disruption caused by the reforms is due largely to the fact that it was only very partially implemented. And at the same time, the fundamental problems that it was supposed to solve remain unsolved. There has been no real progress in the restructuring of the Hungarian economy since 1968. In industry, some enterprises still have a very real shortage of labour while others have a surplus ('hoarding' of manpower). The lack of 'mobility of capital' is even more obvious; the preponderance of self-financing over financing by bank loan in fact means, taking account of the conditons in which an enterprise's profits are made, that direct intervention by the central authorities has a decisive influence in investment decisions. Finally, the immediate necessity to limit the foreign deficit and the rigidity of the procedures applied within Comecon have hardly enabled Hungary to restructure its exports, by gradually abandoning the least profitable of them. In all these respects, the 'programme' of the 1968 reform has still to be fulfilled.

By about 1977 the basic elements of the problem could be schematised thus: on the one hand, the reasons which had given rise ten years earlier to the decision in favour of a radical reform had lost none of their urgency, while, on the other hand, the way in which the NEM came through the disruptions of the years from 1973 to 1977 maintained the chances of a subsequent reactivation of the reform: nothing irremediable took place.

2 The resolution adopted in October 1977 by the central committee of the Hungarian Communist Party marked the starting point of a new stage of the reform: according to J. Bognar,[6] it was a political decision 'comparable in importance to the decision taken by the Party in 1966 which inaugurated the economic reform of 1968'. The Hungarian leaders declared themselves unequivocally in favour of a growth strategy based on foreign trade and involving the alignment of the Hungarian prices structure with world prices, complete restructuring of the system of taxes and subsidies, and priority for the development of exports to the West. The direct cause of this decision was the worsening of the foreign deficit, and more particularly the deficit with the West (the 'non-socialist countries' supplied Hungary with 47 per cent of its imports in 1977, and received only 38 per cent of its exports). The most urgent requirement was thus to maintain foreign indebtedness within tolerable limits. But the Hungarian authorities realised in 1977 that merely putting a temporary restriction on imports – which was in any case detrimental to economic growth – was not a solution: the Hungarian economy would only overcome its disequilibria by adapting to the requirements of the world market, whatever the cost.

In order to assess the real importance of this decision, it must firstly be pointed out that the Hungarian economy was by 1977 one of the most open in Europe,[7] with the total of exports and imports exceeding 80 per cent of GNP. The economy had already been opened up to foreign trade by the reform of 1968. It is true that Hungary was not the first socialist country either to adhere to GATT or to increase the opportunities for industrial co-operation with Western firms, since Poland and Rumania had been the first to follow this path (for these two countries, expansion of trade with the West was a sort of substitute for economic reform). But it was Hungary that turned out to be the country with the highest debt; both in *per capita* terms and as a percentage of GNP, its foreign currency debts were far in excess of those of Poland. To go further along the same path, to continue to import plant and machinery on credit, in the hope of subsequently increasing foreign currency revenue from exports, was an extremely risky gamble: the catastrophic economic situation in Poland at the end of the 1970s clearly showed how much the failure of such a gamble could cost. On the other hand, relationships within Comecon benefited from greater stability (more staggered increase in the price of raw materials, guaranteed sales outlets); as we have seen, the relatively steady growth of the East German economy is a clear illustration of the short-term advantages to be gained from these relationships in a period of world crisis. And indeed, Hungary remained deeply committed to co-operation with its socialist partners.[8] But in 1977, the leaders of the Hungarian Socialist Workers Party rejected any 'withdrawal into Comecon', since the effect would be to prevent the adaptations that were essential in the long term.

The policy direction outlined in October 1977 was put into practice by a readjustment of all the regulators in 1980–1. This gap of a little over two years is at first sight reminiscent of the preparation for the 1968 reform. This time, however, the transition was much more chaotic. Until the beginning of 1979, the authorities tried to counter the imbalances in the economy with direct administrative measures (pressure on enterprises to reduce their consumption of energy and of imported raw materials, their stocks and their investment). But the bargaining process between the large enterprises and their supervisory ministries had the opposite effect: in 1978, there was a further increase in investment; there was an enormous increase in stocks (a precautionary reflex action against the prospect of price increases); the foreign deficit exceeded the record 1975 level, reaching a level in 1978 of 9.1 per cent of GNP, while the rate at which foreign currency imports were covered by exports fell to 72 per cent (loans for the promotion of exports continued to increase, which led in turn to an increase in imports, without the system having had time to bear fruit). Thus in 1978, the semi-administrative, semi-decentralised Hungarian economy was threatening to run completely out of control. This serious deterioration in the situation undoubtedly played a decisive role in tipping the scales in favour of a full-blooded relaunching of the decentralising reforms; the authorities recognised that, even if the challenges were external in origin, 'a response to these challenges limited only to the external sector . . . would be incomplete'.[9]

3 The '1980-1 reform', like that of 1968, was made up of several interdependent elements: immediate measures against the imbalance in foreign trade; a price reform and the readjustment of all the regulators (exchange rate and tax system); institutional changes involving the various decision-making levels, from central planning to private initiative. It is certainly too early to make any final judgment on this complex reform. But it must be stressed that the differing interpretations of it do not relate to the *general direction* of the measures taken in 1980: the aim was obviously to link openness in foreign trade and increases in efficiency, to strengthen the autonomy of enterprises and the competitive mechanisms of the 'socialist market', and to re-establish the automatic link between personal incomes and the financial results of enterprises, in full accordance[10] with the NEM of 1968. The differences in interpretation relate only to the *scope* of this new reform, that is, to its ability to overcome once and for all the obstacles that the 1968 reform had come up against. The same resistance to reform existed at the beginning of the 1980s, but it was more clearly recognised and better understood by the Hungarian leaders.

For the people, the first impact of the 1980 reform was a rigorous austerity programme. It was prefaced in July 1979 by a series of increases in retail prices, particularly in basic foodstuffs and public services. The 1968 reform had also been preceded by an adjustment of prices in 1966-7. But this time the increase was both more sudden (it was announced for the first time only two days in advance), more intense and more prolonged: with the new series of increases on 1 January 1980, the official index of prices to consumers went up by a total of 20 per cent in 1979-80; there was a slight absolute reduction in the average real wage. The usual system of lump-sum compensations lessened the impact on the lower paid. But the overall stagnation meant in reality that an appreciable section of the Hungarian people saw its standard of living appreciably reduced during the five-year period 1976-80, and the same will be true of the current five-year period: the austerity programme is to be maintained until 1985, with a planned growth rate for the average real wage of 1.3 per cent per annum.

Decreased consumption has been accompanied as usual by decreased investment. But, for the first time, in addition to this cyclical slowing down, plans have been made to tackle the fundamental imbalance caused by overinvestment and to stabilise the volume of investment for the whole of the five-year period 1981-5 (in such a way that the share of consumption in absorption – 'utilised national income' – is to rise to

82 per cent, having fallen continuously for twenty years). Consequently, with a reduction in the resources available for investment, increased production will necessarily have to depend on the increased efficiency of investment.

The general aim of the policy of austerity is, of course, to maintain the growth of the 'national income produced', while at the same time preventing any growth in 'national income utilised', in such a way as to re-establish the external balance (from 1981 to 1985, exports are to increase twice as fast as the 'national income produced' and imports).[11] But no austerity programme can by itself guarantee that foreign currency trade will automatically recover. Only for a few products – foodstuffs, for example – does the decrease in domestic consumption make available a directly exportable surplus. Specific measures, such as the loans for the promotion of exports, can make this adaptation easier. But the decisive role must be played by the adjustment of *all the regulators*, which has two indissociable aims: to ensure that the future growth is export-orientated, and to encourage enterprises to use fewer resources more efficiently.[12]

Price reform is at the heart of the plan. The reform is based on two (apparently) simple principles: firstly, that there should be a direct link between world prices and domestic production prices, and secondly, that there should be a direct link between production prices and prices to consumers, the latter to be achieved by making the tax on turnover uniform. These principles are relatively easily applied for the main primary products (energy and raw materials) that are either totally or partially imported from the West: their price is fixed on the basis of their cost in foreign currency – representing the marginal cost for the Hungarian economy – multiplied by the exchange rate; the surplus over the lower purchase price within Comecon is collected by the state. For Hungarian manufactured products, on the other hand, 'price-fixing on the basis of world prices' is a much more doubtful process; it applies only to products considered to be exportable (70 per cent of manufactured production), and in reality means that enterprises have to prove from their accounts that their rate of profit on sales to the domestic market does not exceed the rate of profit obtained from exports. Thus even for the 'competitive' sector,[13] the whole system remains distinctly administrative in character. The same is true, *a fortiori*, for the 'sheltered' sector (services and construction materials), where prices are still fixed by the administration. Agriculture, though largely orientated towards exports, has also been excluded from the price reform: whereas the price of meat would have decreased by 10 per cent if the world price had been applied, the adjustments of 1980 in fact increased the price of animal products, in order to stimulate production, even if it meant exporting at a loss. A more general problem is the central one posed by subsidies (the basic elements of which have not changed since 1968): to maintain existing subsidies, notably for imports and exports, would be to nullify the price reform; to abolish them at one stroke is unthinkable, since it would be necessary to bring a large number of enterprises to a halt; thus the only solution is to reduce them in stages, which presupposes a political will to do so and constant pressure on enterprises running at a loss. Finally, it must be stressed that all the automatic mechanisms that the 1980 reform sought to introduce operate through the intermediary of the exchange rate: by means of an 'active' and 'flexible' exchange rate policy, the authorities have a very direct influence on the level and structure of Hungarian prices, independently even of their specific interventions. In the meantime, the main decision has been *not to devalue the forint against the dollar*[14] (a decision that is justified by the low price elasticity of Hungarian exports), but *to revalue the forint against the transferable rouble*, in such a way as to make exports to Comecon countries relatively less advantageous.

The significance of this price reform can be assessed from two angles: that of the initial readjustment, and that of the price-fixing mechanism. From the first point of view, the measures taken in 1979–80 have appreciably altered the structure of Hungarian prices. The main aim of the reform – to submit the Hungarian economy to world economic conditions – was reflected in 1980 in a 15 per cent rise in the price of raw materials, and a 39 per cent rise in the price of energy (the effort in this direction has, moreover, been continued in fresh series of price rises, for example on 1 January 1982). At the same time, the average level of production prices was *reduced* by 8 per cent for manufactured goods, and *raised* by 10 per cent for agricultural products. As for wholesale prices, not only has the rise in the price of energy been passed on in full, but their average level has risen considerably since 1979 in comparison with that of wholesale prices. Thus a considerable step has been taken towards putting some order into the prices system. In all those sectors in which a 'normal' positive difference has been established between production prices and prices to consumers, there has been an opportunity to progress towards a standardised rate of tax, at least for groups of products (in place of an anarchic system of subsidies), and also partially to replace export subsidies by a system of tax refunds, which is more acceptable to GATT. On the other hand, the effect of the reform on the way in which prices are fixed is much more questionable. We should not be deceived by the official presentation, according to which the proportion of 'free prices' has risen from 57 per cent of the production of manufactured goods in 1978 to 67 per cent in 1980, since the notion of a 'free price' involves only limited flexibility. It is possible, under the supervision of the Prices Office, to regulate variations in the price of various articles around an average, but the approach is still of the 'cost plus' type. The new prices have been 'constructed' (calculated) by adding to the estimated cost a profit margin, the rate of which was, moreover, reduced at a stroke from 15 to 6 per cent (in order to lower the level of production prices). The only automatic mechanisms provided for concern the passing on of variations in world prices, and even in this case, administrative intervention remains necessary in the most important cases.

The handling of the tax regulators brings to light other discontinuities, that are characteristic of this 'indirect regulation' by the administration. In order to offset the increase in the cost of inputs and the decrease in the profit margin, the tax on the assets of enterprises – the introduction of which in 1964 had been hailed as a major step forward – was purely and simply abolished. This was a curious decision at a time when it was more vital than ever to restrict the tendency of enterprises to over-invest. Similarly, the tax on wages, the rate of which had been increased from 25 to 35 per cent in 1976, was reduced to 24 per cent in 1980 (and increased again in 1982). It is as if the price of the factors of production were, in the eyes of the Hungarian authorities, only one regulator among others, and could be subject to discretionary adjustments (and compensations). The same empiricism prevailed with regard to the taxation of profits. The basic tax on profits went up from 25 to 35 per cent. But a special statute was introduced for supplementary profits arising from cuts in the workforce or economies in the use of raw materials, and in this case wage increases under 'privileged' tax conditions became possible.[15] The authors of the 1980 reform clearly had no intention of establishing a fully consistent system of regulators: they attended to the most urgent matters.

In short, the whole reform is based on the *gamble* that the price distortions and the basic inequalities between enterprises of different sectors had already been alleviated enough for the new regulators to be able in future to operate *uniformly*. Subsidies that are granted *a posteriori* to enterprises running at a loss, exceptional wage increases that become necessary, as part of a 'catching-up' process for the workforce of these enterprises are not to be tolerated any longer. As a symbolic gesture, even the guaranteed annual increase of 1.5 per cent in nominal wages, which in any case far from compensated for inflation, has been abolished: henceforth, any increase in nominal wages is to be subject to the financial results of the enterprise. As for 'bad' managers, those acknowledged to be responsible for their enterprise's deficit, they are entitled to only 75 per cent of their basic salary, and this punishment does not exclude the possibility of more severe sanctions being taken (e.g. downgrading). This is in keeping with the most important objective of the new reform, and the one that conforms most closely to the spirit of the NEM of 1968: the desire to develop the autonomy, the initiative and the responsibility of the enterprise, and at the same time to strengthen the pressure of competition.

The 1968 reform was orientated towards a 'model' of a competitive socialist economy. In fact, for reasons that have already been analysed, competition appeared only on the *periphery* of the Hungarian economy. Firstly, it appeared in the area of relations with the West, where there were both particular incentives (the exporting enterprise retained a proportion of its foreign currency earnings, notably in order to import Western plant and equipment) and a real constraint of competitiveness, and secondly in the sphere of legal, semi-legal or illegal private activity: the increasing share of the 'second' or 'parallel' economy in house building and services of all sorts was one of the most visible phenomena in the Hungary of the 1970s. But it was hardly unique to Hungary, since Poland was experiencing similar developments, independently of any economic reform. Within the socialist sector, only the co-operatives showed signs of any significant competitive dynamism: the agricultural co-operatives, in particular, set up subsidiary enterprises which launched themselves into a wide range of activities (building, engineering, repairs, small-scale industry) within the confines of the 'second economy', and sometimes even went so far as to hire specialised labour to large state enterprises. These large enterprises, particularly those producing for the domestic market and Comecon, had hardly changed their behaviour since 1968: a very high degree of concentration,[16] a sellers' market for most products, the re-establishment of detailed supervision by the ministries and permanent bargaining procedures were the main causes of rigidity.

In 1980–1, an attempt was made to remedy this situation by means of a whole series of measures.

The most significant institutional change was the abolition of three sector ministries responsible respectively for heavy industry, the engineering industry and light industry, and their replacement by a single ministry of industry, which was no longer to intervene in day-to-day management. Approximately half of the personnel of these three ministries was transferred to enterprises or to functional organisations (prices and materials office, national bank), and these latter inherited some of the responsibilities of the former ministries. The specialised departments of the central committee of the Hungarian Communist Party, whose task it was to supervise the management of the various sectors, were also abolished.[17] Finally, in order to emphasise the indicative nature of planning, the FYP for 1981-5 no longer includes detailed quantitative targets. All these measures are clearly in keeping with the 1968 reform in their attempt to reduce intervention by the administration.

Other 'positive' measures are aimed at expanding the ways in which competition can penetrate the Hungarian economy.

The first of these is openness to foreign trade, which is the central idea of the reform. The idea is given reality by the right of direct access to foreign markets granted to an increasing number of Hungarian enterprises, by the incentives to co-operate with Western firms, by an import licence policy that is as unrestrictive as possible in a period of austerity, by the development of the system of loans for the promotion of exports, and finally by the pivotal role given to the rate of profit obtained from exports to Western markets.

The second is the expansion of private initiative. This is the most spectacular innovation: from January 1981 onwards, the state put more than 1,000 restaurants and wholesale shops under management by tenant; the only obligation of the tenants is to pay a rent, determined by competitive tender and awarded to the highest bidder. This measure contributed more than any other to the 'brand image' of the Hungarian reform, but it would be wrong to see it simply as a concession to the 'logic of private profits'. It is rather a symbol of the authorities' desire to integrate the second economy (which prospers particularly when semi-legal activities exploit the deficiencies of the official economy). In reality, competitive tendering seems to have had the effect of strictly limiting the opportunities for making profits, while at the same time reducing – in theory – the risks of corruption.

From 1981-2 onwards, Hungary also committed itself to an even more ambitious programme of industrial restructuring. The aim is both to find a solution for the excesses of centralisation, by breaking up certain large enterprises and dissolving certain trusts, and also to recreate a network of small and medium enterprises, by encouraging the setting up of municipal enterprises or autonomous branches of enterprises already in existence and the development of industrial co-operatives. The importance of this element of flexibility, which is totally foreign to the logic of administrative planning, is thus much better recognised than in 1968.

Finally, the pressure of competition is to make itself felt in the labour market: the leaders have proposed in principle that *the right to a job* should no longer mean the *right to a specific job*, and that workers will from now on have to accept a certain degree of mobility. The example is given of those enterprises which, like the large engineering enterprise Gyor, have succeeded in increasing productivity by reducing their workforce. This new interpretation of full employment, which does not exclude dismissals, is made more acceptable by the favourable outlook for re-employment, due to the development of services and small industrial enterprises.

4 The 1980 reform has not given rise, either in Hungary or in the West, to the same illusions as that of 1968. The reason is obvious: the permanent limits to any reform, even the most 'radical', are now well known. The most fundamental is linked to the existence of particularly inefficient enterprises and of loss-making activities, which are incapable of standing up to competition, but whose closure is excluded for the time being. Stable employment and a continuous reduction in wage differences (despite all the official declarations of the past twenty years announcing a return 'tomorrow' to 'fair differentiation') are the main gains from socialism in the eyes of the workers: no competitive logic can make them accept that inequalities among enterprises should suddenly be reflected in a corresponding differentiation in wages, or, *a fortiori*, in massive redundancies. In any case, the international position of the Hungarian economy means there is no question of a sudden change. By reason of its membership of Comecon, Hungary is trapped in a network of close relationships with economies which are still functioning according to the principles of centralised, micro-economic command planning. Trade between Hungary and its socialist partners thus remains organised, as it does for all the Comecon countries, within the framework of a bilateral package deal. Such relationships have both advantages (preferential supplies of raw materials) and constraints (rigid long-term specialisations) for the Hungarian economy. The enterprises concerned have similar constraints (externally imposed conditions

of trade) and advantages (guaranteed sales outlets). There is here a whole series of contradictions with the competitive model that the regime cannot allow itself to ignore, but which it can influence at best only very marginally.

Thus for the foreseeable future, the Hungarian economy will remain, in the words of J. Kornai, a 'mixed socialist economy'.[18] The expression does not refer to the common distinction between the 'private sector' and the 'socialist sector': the example of the co-operatives shows that flexibility and a sense of initiative are not exclusive to private enterprise. The aim of the 1980 reform is precisely to narrow the gap between the official economy and the 'second economy', and to allow the influence of market mechanisms to penetrate the socialist sector. But, paradoxically, the success of this programme depends above all on the action of the central authorities: the gradual elimination of subsidies and the reorganisation or conversion of loss-making enterprises require decisions to be taken in each individual case, and there is no point in gambling on the commitment of Hungarian managers to their enterprises (or, on the other hand, in deploring their 'bureaucratic behaviour') if a minimum level of equal opportunity is not created at the outset. Moreover, certain sectors escape competition by their very nature, or because of the smallness of the Hungarian economy, or because of their orientation towards Comecon: it is thus inevitable that direct controls, this time permanent ones, will be maintained. It can hardly, therefore, be a surprise to learn that the institutional changes of 1980 have allowed the traditional networks of influence and bargaining processes to remain. In a sense, all the existing market economies are mixed economies, and it would be somewhat of an exaggeration to describe the Hungarian economy as 'schizophrenic'[19] for that reason.

Are the chances of success for the 1980 reform, with aims that are comparable to those of the 1968 reform, better than for the earlier reform? The prognosis depends directly on the criteria used. If the criterion is the appearance of radical changes in the relationships of power and the institutional structure,[20] or in the behaviour of the leaders, then the answer is clear: the 1980 reform is no more a radical reform than its predecessor. If the desire for the reform is assessed according to the number of dismissals or the widening of wage differentials, it is easy to show the disparity between reality and the declarations of principle that accompanied the reform. And then, taking one step forward, one can console oneself by predicting the failure of this new partial reform, and that this will lead finally to a 'truly radical' reform: 'Eventually economic performance will deteriorate so far', writes E. A. Hewett,[21] 'that there will be no alternative to true reform'. Another approach is to judge the 1980 reform by its own objective: the gradual reintroduction of competition, through a combination of openness to foreign trade, putting some order into the system of regulators and the remodelling of industrial structures. This is in fact the main innovation in comparison with the NEM of 1968: the contradiction between the model of the socialist market and excessively concentrated structures is now clearly perceived. The reduction in the level of subsidies, the reorganisation of large loss-making enterprises and the re-establishment of an industrial network of small and medium enterprises thus appear to be the best tests of the progress of the reform. But that is a long-drawn-out task.

The 1980 reform has two favourable factors to its advantage: an attitude of benevolent neutrality on the part of the USSR, and the absence of any structured opposition within the Hungarian Socialist Workers' Party that might be capable of putting forward an alternative programme. But, in contrast to the 1968 reform, it is being implemented in a context of rigorous and prolonged austerity; even to maintain the standard of living is an ambitious aim. It is clear that the reform is unlikely to inspire any great enthusiasm among the populace; the best that can be hoped for is some understanding. The more the effect of the competitive mechanisms is felt, the more pressure there will be to neutralise the consequences of the reform for certain disadvantaged categories – which is the usual starting point for the processes of re-centralisation. The foreign deficit is an even more immediate threat: it severely limits the recourse to competitive imports, compromises the only really popular aim of the reform – the openness to foreign trade – and tempts the authorities to intervene directly at any given moment in the activity of enterprises in order to spread the shortages more evenly.

5 It will be five or ten years before it is possible to make a proper assessment of the new Hungarian reform. But it is clear that the most immediate task is to re-establish the external balance, and on this depends the fate of the whole reform. There has been a very clear short-term recovery since 1979: for trade in strong currencies, the rate at which imports are covered by exports went up from 80.5 per cent in 1978 to 103.5 per cent in 1980, and the balance of payments is also in surplus for the first time. There are numerous factors in this recovery, the first of which is, of course, the temporary slowing down in the level of imports. The most significant factor, however, is the dynamism of exports, notably of agricultural and food products, manufactured consumer

goods and capital goods, the last of which reached a level in 1981 of 12.1 per cent of the total value in foreign currencies of exports. The export credit system has no doubt played a directly supportive role. But the recovery is also part of a longer-term development: since 1968, a growing number of Hungarian enterprises have gradually developed a more flexible approach to exports, and, since the middle of the 1970s, as a recent econometric study shows (Murrel, 1981), the structure of Hungarian exports has diverged significantly from that of Soviet-type economies and drawn closer to that of market economies. Two other factors have contributed to the rebalancing of trade in foreign currencies: there has been a drive to reorientate Hungarian exports towards the West, and in 1980–1 the terms of trade with the 'foreign currency zone' developed favourably (for both exogenous and endogenous reasons), which is rarely the case when a country has to push its exports to the maximum. However, a precise distinction must be made between trade with *the non-socialist countries* and trade *in convertible currencies* (the 'non-rouble zone'), as Hungarian statistics do, bearing in mind a not insignificant new trend: the development of trade *within Comecon paid for in dollars*. This trade is in products for which there is a very high demand (imported energy, exported meat, etc.) over and above the minimum stipulated by the medium-term trade agreements.

Table 7.7 *Hungarian foreign trade in convertible currency (1976–81)*

	1976	1977	1978	1979	1980	1981
Share (%) in total exports						
Non-socialist countries	40	38	39	42	45	42
Non-rouble zone	51	50	50	55	57	56
Share (%) of total imports						
Non-socialist countries	46	47	48	47	49	48
Non-rouble zone	52	54	55	53	55	54
Evolution of the terms of trade						
(Annual percentage difference)						
Rouble zone	−2.1	−3.0	−2.3	−1.8	−1.1	−3.9
Non-rouble zone	+6.5	−3.8	−0.8	−1.2	+1.6	+2.2

Source: *L'U.R.S.S. et l'Europe de l'Est en 1981–1982*, Documentation Française, pp. 133 and 136.

Table 7.7 clearly shows that there has been no dramatic switch in Hungarian foreign trade towards the West,[22] despite the recent much more favourable evolution of the terms of trade with the dollar zone than with the rouble zone. But it must be noted that Hungary obtains an appreciable surplus from its trade in strong currencies with Comecon countries (which amounted to 14 per cent of total exports and 6 per cent of total imports in 1981), which practically offsets its deficit with the West.[23] The Hungarian economy also benefits directly from its particular position between the East and the West. Such an advantage cannot, however, be without its negative aspect, and it certainly excludes the possibility of any real withdrawal from Comecon. Neither the admission of Hungary to the IMF in 1982, nor – as P. Marer (P. Hare, H. Radice and N. Swain (eds), 1981; JEC, East European Economic Assessment, 2 vols, 1980–1) shows quite clearly – the prospects for the convertibility of the forint can be interpreted as decisive changes. The real gains seem rather to be the maintenance of a regular flow of imports (without which Hungary would have experienced as acute a crisis as Poland), opportunities for access to foreign markets that are as non-discriminatory as possible (which is equivalent for Hungarian importers to *de facto* convertibility for the forint) and finally, increasing opportunities for Hungarians to visit Western countries as tourists, which symbolises the country's openness.

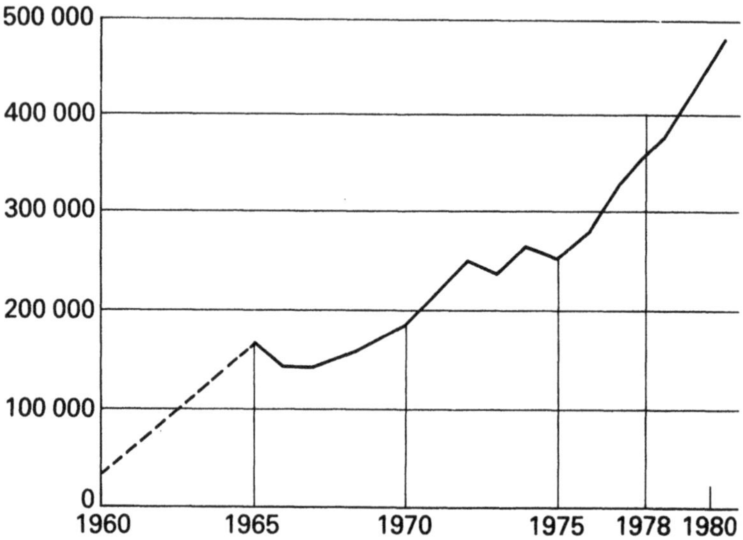

Figure 7.1 Number of Hungarians travelling to non-socialist countries
Source: Annual Statistics.

If the growth of the Hungarian economy has not been strangled by the external constraint, it has nevertheless been severely affected by the limitation of all productive resources.

The consumption of energy has continued to increase until 1978 at an excessive rate (5.4 per cent per annum between 1975 and 1978); it stabilised suddenly in 1979–80 under the combined effect of direct interventions and the rise in prices. Energy investment is now more than a quarter of total industrial investment, and the low growth in available energy planned for 1981–5 is to come almost entirely from domestic production.

The volume of productive investment has been reduced successively in 1979, 1980 and 1981 (−14 per cent in total in three years, which far exceeds the usual range of the investment cycle). Thus most of the slowing down in the rate of absorption has been at the expense of investment, which has at the same time made a significant contribution to the reduction in imports.

Growth, however, must more than ever depend on increases in productivity. Total industrial employment has decreased regularly since 1976, and particularly since 1979 (−2.6 per cent per annum between 1979 and 1981), often even in excess of the planned targets. In general, there has been no need for redundancies in order to achieve this result: in an economy with a high degree of spontaneous mobility between enterprises and in which transfers can be affected without any problem, all enterprises have to do is not to replace workers who leave. In these conditions, and despite the slowing down of industrial growth, labour productivity has continued to increase at a steady rate. Apart from a drop in 1980 (just as in 1968), the increases in productivity have reached or exceeded 4.5 per cent each year, which puts Hungary in a very favourable position in comparison with the other Comecon countries, including East Germany. The constantly renewed criticisms of the

Table 7.8 *Average annual growth rate of labour productivity in Hungarian industry (1963–81)*

1963–7	1968–70	1971–5	1976–80	1981
3.8	2.6	6.2	4.6	4.5

Sources: 1963–1970: Hare, Radice and Swain (eds), 1981, p. 70.
1971–1981: *Etudes sur la situation économique de l'Europe.*

damage caused by guaranteed employment or of the inadequacy of the incentive system should not be allowed to conceal a *relatively* honourable performance in this respect: the failure of the 'transition to intensive growth' is no longer as obvious for Hungary as for the other socialist countries.

On the other hand, all the indicators of the standard of living have deteriorated in recent years. The government decided that Hungary could not continue to live 'beyond its means', and price rises reduced the average real wage in 1979 (−1.2 per cent) and in 1980 (−0.5 per cent to −2.6 per cent, according to different estimates). Over and above any temporary slowing down, comparison with East Germany, which was favourable to Hungary until the middle of the 1970s, was reversed in favour of East Germany during the last five-year period.

Table 7.9 *Evolution of real income* per capita, *Hungary and GDR (1976-81)*

	1976-80 plan	1976-80	1981	1981-5 plan
Hungary	3.4-3.7	1.6	2.2	1.1-1.4
East Germany	3.9-4.2	4.3	4.0	3.9-4.2

Admittedly, such a comparison must be treated with a certain amount of scepticism, since the stability of the official East German prices index (the 'recognised' increase has not exceeded 0.1 per cent per annum since 1976) conceals a certain amount of hidden inflation, at least for luxury products sold in special shops. Nevertheless, the whole range of indirect[24] or partial indicators – from *per capita* consumption of meat[25] to the number of cars per 1,000 inhabitants – certainly confirm the reversal of the trend in favour of East Germany. If Hungary retains an advantage, it lies in more flexible adaptation to demand and in the regularity of its supply system: this is the real gain from the NEM (and more particularly from the agricultural reform), but it is very difficult to quantify. On the other hand, in an area as essential as house-building, the worsening of the position, both absolutely and relatively, of Hungary is absolutely obvious and undeniable.

The austerity policy is imposed on Hungary above all by its foreign deficit. The need to re-establish equilibrium at any price is for the time being the overriding consideration, and excludes the fundamental option for a strategy of 'open growth'. The contrast with East Germany, where the problem of accumulated deficits is less acute, is again revealing.

Thus it would no doubt be fairer to compare the performance of Hungary with that of the other socialist countries (Yugoslavia, Rumania and Poland), which opened themselves up to the West from the end of the 1960s or the beginning of the 1970s, using credit to finance their

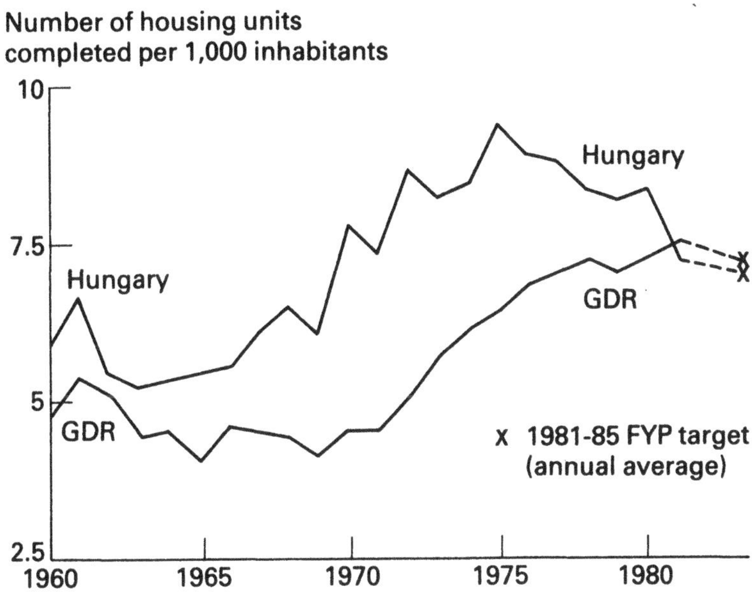

Figure 7.2 Number of housing units completed per 1,000 inhabitants – Hungary and GDR
Source: J. Boncoeur (University of Paris I) from the COMECON Statistical Yearbooks and the *Bulletin annuel de statistiques du logement et de la construction pour l'Europe.*

Table 7.10 *Evolution of foreign trade, Hungary and GDR (1976–80)*

	1976–80	1981–5 plan
Hungary		
Exports	7.0	6.5–6.8
Imports	3.9	3.4–3.5
East Germany		
Exports	5.8	6.3
Imports	5.2	6.3

imports. Yugoslavia, for example, to say nothing of Poland, has had to implement an even harsher austerity programme, which cut real wages by 13 per cent in 1979–80, at a time of severe inflation. Even if the situation is under better control, the new Hungarian reform will not bear fruit in the foreseeable future.

Conclusion: decentralised socialism, profits and competition

She: Would two hundred kilometers in ten days be an achievement, with twelve dogs harnessed to the car?
He: And I should also point out that I have had the handbrake full on since we set off.
She: Are you not erring on the side of caution, my friend?
He: Man was born to proceed at this speed.
She: Can you see all those people watching us go past?
He: They envy us.
She: They look more astonished to me.
He: Because they realise that we are capable of realising the boldest dreams of humanity.

(I. Orkeny, 'Our boldest dreams', *Minimyths* (translated from the French translation by T. Tardos))

Conceived at the outset by those responsible as a 'once and for all' change to a new economic model, that of the 'regulated socialist market', the Hungarian reform has turned out in reality to be a very long process, marked by interruptions and partial retreats. The obstacles encountered *en route* were of various kinds: circumstancial factors, basically of an international kind, over which Hungary had no control; the stamp left by the Stalinist past on all the economic structures, which was much stronger than had been thought in 1968; the permanent constraints linked to membership of Comecon; the potential conflict between the unfurling of a competititve logic and certain social exigencies (job security, and the rejection of blatant economic inequalities) common to all the socialist countries. Despite its many specific characteristics and its incompleteness, the experience of the Hungarian reform provides the basis for some more general reflections on the possibility of a decentralised socialist model, essentially different from the Soviet model yet distinct from Yugoslavian self-management.

Material incentive in the Soviet-type economies is not an innovation introduced in the reforms of the 1960s: it has always had an important place in the workings of the planned economy. Although differentiation of basic wages was supposed to involve the principle of 'to each according to his labour', it was above all the bonus which was to vary in accordance with the merits of the individual, assessed on the basis of individual results, or in the case of management personnel, according to the overall results of the enterprise. The underlying claim to be able to evaluate (in the proper sense of the word) the merits of each worker raises, in itself, breathtaking problems that the traditional practice of Soviet-type economies helped to conceal, by adopting an implicit principle that is at first sight very simple: the fulfilment and exceeding of planned targets (or of the norms fixed for each job) are used as a standard in the assessment of each individual contribution. It is difficult to see how this approach could be considered consistent, even on the assumption that the planning apparatus could be omniscient, since if the potential of each worker was perfectly well known, why not stick to instructions pure and simple? Be that as it may, the incentive system as conceived in this way causes a whole series of distortions, the seriousness of which is not disputed by anyone.

This long-standing awareness might have led to the questioning of the very principle of material incentive through bonuses based on short-term results, a veritable 'Trojan horse' within the system of centralised planning. Yet all the Soviet-type economies – except for Rumania – started off in the opposite direction with the reforms of the 1960s, by seeking to increase the influence of material incentives. But this process was indissociable from a complete reorientation. The various economic reforms, despite their differing options, all originally had in common the crucial importance attached to profits as the pivot of the incentive system. There was no longer any dispute that the efficacy of the incentive system depended first of all on the simplicity of the criterion of success, on its uniformity and on the corresponding confidence of everyone in the stability of the rules of the game. To the extent that they answered these various requirements, profits seemed to offer a guarantee against the arbitrariness of the incentive system in force before the reforms, which was a complex, individualised and unstable system. Among all the indicators of success, profits also commended themselves through their ability to reflect in an aggregate manner all aspects of an enterprise's performance: not only increases in production, but also reductions in costs and adjustment to demand. Finally, profits, as the result of the common efforts of the whole workforce, reasserted the value of the collective dimension of incentives.

This whole argument thus led to the expectation that the choice of profits as the main indicator of success – a major victory over ideological prejudices – would be an important step towards rationalisation of the Soviet-type economies. Rarely have the facts so clearly contradicted expectations. After a few years, the disparity between the initial plan of the reforms of 1963-8 and their implementation was obvious everywhere. Not that the influence of profits on bonuses was always negligible, but it operated only indirectly and partially; the intention of radically simplifying the incentive system by giving it an objective basis had never been realised and the earlier distortions persisted. Even in Hungary, the only country where the payment of bonuses was no longer indexed to the fulfilment of detailed compulsory targets sent to each enterprise, profits only very partially played the role of regulator given to them by the reform of 1968, and this failure was in itself synonymous with the halting of the reform: 'What we are lacking,' acknowledged T. Nagy, 'is the automatic mechanism which . . . through differences in profitability, would guarantee the introduction of new products and the adjustment of production to the structure of demand and the requirements of purchasers' (in *Régulation et division* . . . 1978, p. 161).

The conclusions of the various national experiments thus appear so far to concur. And unless all the disappointments can be explained by the resistance of vested interests and the conservatism of the bureaucracies, the following question cannot be evaded: do we not have to see in recent developments the final confirmation of a fundamental incompatibility between socialism and the 'profit economy'? 'Profits,' said Marie Lavigne, 'cannot be a real incentive in a socialist economy'; in societies where managers of enterprises are not responsible (in all the senses of the word) for decisions on investment, where they have hardly any incentive to increase their money wages because of the lack of really attractive opportunities to spend them, but where, on the other hand, they have an overwhelming interest in not risking the loss of their job and their social status, 'profits are not the means by which they might be encouraged to act in the general interest. . . . Socialist societies are not money orientated, and that is where their strength lies. Any attempt to develop the role of profits is an attempt to change this strength into weakness' (Lavigne in Fallenbuchl (ed.), 1975, pp. 60-1).

It cannot be denied that the system of incentive by profits is now in jeopardy. However, it is less obvious that this state of affairs is necessarily unavoidable in a socialist economy: in any case, it arises from a combination of very diverse factors whose link with the 'socialist ethic' is often, to say the least, indirect.

The specific objections that can be made against incentive by profits must first of all be distinguished from more general, and older problems raised by the very principle of material incentives, particularly in the form of additional cash payments, in a socialist economy. Let us just point out in this respect that the shortage of attractive goods available on the consumer goods market is not necessarily a permanent factor, inherent to every socialist society. Moreover, the risks that the managers of Soviet enterprises were prepared to take as early as the Stalinist period in order to gain more bonuses, or the now frequent practice in several countries of Eastern Europe of the 'second job' or 'moonlighting', would seem to show quite clearly that monetary gain is not always an unimportant motive in a socialist economy.

The small part played by profits in those countries which opted for a limited reform, of the Soviet or East German type, does not require much explanation. The initial illusion of being able to recast the system of material incentive, while at the same time challenging the very principle of regulation by market mechanisms, simply proves that those responsible for these reforms, just like those responsible for the Polish reform of 1957, had underestimated the inherent stability of the traditional system, and its ability to neutralise, completely alter or reject as and when necessary innovations introduced (cf. Zielinski, 1978, pp. 6–7). As long as the centralised model inherited from the Stalinist period is not replaced by a consistent set of organisational principles that are the product of a different model, 'micro-economic' interventions by the administration will remain indispensable to the regular functioning of the economy, and the essential task for enterprises will be to carry out orders: it is therefore understandable that they will be rewarded according to this criterion. This does not prevent the annual increase in profits, for example, in the same way as the reduction in costs, from keeping its place in the battery of indicators of success used to express the efficiency of an enterprise.

However, the internal consistency of the reforms is not the only thing at stake. Their implementation has brought to light an additional limitation: the absence of any corresponding reorientation of economic policies (except at times in East Germany). It is true that the improvement of the standard of living always figures among the main aims of development. But the authorities refuse to admit the existence of a conflict between an increase in consumption and the speed of growth (a conflict which, for the reasons analysed in this book, goes well beyond a mere temporary sacrifice of consumption), and this refusal invariably results in the priority given to the quantitative increase of production potential being maintained. Tight planning thus persists, and the imbalances that it causes help directly to trigger off the recentralising mechanisms.

Hungary is no exception in this respect: the 'extensive' nature of growth was even emphasised after 1968. Nevertheless, Hungary deserves special attention, since the Hungarian reform was the only one, apart from the Czech reform that was abandoned in 1968-9, that originated in an unequivocal decision to transform the whole 'economic mechanism'. Those who believe in the insurmountable antagonism between Soviet-type societies and the logic of the market are justified in putting particular emphasis on developments in Hungary: does the gap which separates the 1968 plan from the realities of the Hungarian NEM not prove that the organisation of economic mechanisms is indissociable from the rest of the social structures, and that the consistency of the 'model' for the reform has turned out to be an illusion?

Yet most Hungarian economists today consider that the fundamental principles of the 1968 reforms were neither incorrect, nor inapplicable, but that more time was required for them to be implemented completely. Considering what is at stake in this debate, one should not allow oneself to be influenced by the superficial changes in Western opinion: there was a sudden vogue in the middle of the 1960s for the reintroduction of market mechanisms into the socialist planning system; the present trend that considers the whole question of the relationships between planning and the market 'out-dated' is no sounder. On the other hand, it is certain that the lessons of the Hungarian experiment must now be incorporated into this question, which arose from Oskar Lange's theoretical studies of more than forty years ago, since they bring out in a more concrete way the major difficulties that have still not been solved.

It would seem that several important lessons can be drawn from the experience of recent years.

1 The Hungarian reform of 1968, like those of the other socialist countries, gave profits made by enterprises a central role in the incentive system, without any systematic thought having been given beforehand to the economic significance of differences in profitability and the suitability of profits as a regulator for micro-economic decisions. The functioning of the NEM very soon highlighted the seriousness of this

initial mistake, and gave rise at the same time to more subtle analyses. 'After long and searching discussions,' wrote I. Friss in 1973, 'those responsible for the economic reform have come to the following conclusion: profits are the aggregate indicator which, under normal conditions, i.e. when market conditions and prices do not deviate too far from an equilibrium situation, correctly expresses the overall results of an enterprise's activity' (Friss, 1973, *Acta Oeconomica*, vol. 10, p. 305). The reference to 'normal conditions' is not merely a standard formula: the whole problem is that these 'normal conditions' do not always in fact exist. Differences in profitability, as T. Nagy, for example, acknowledged in 1978 (*Régulation et division* . . . , 1978, p. 150), very often 'do not reflect real differences in economic efficiency, but are the results of deficiencies in the state regulation of prices'. The gradual freeing of prices would not solve this problem, since in the present conditions of disequilibrium, 'market forces' tend of their own accord to re-establish the superiority of the seller; combined with the 'monopoly power' of the large enterprises (another essential factor in view of the small size of the Hungarian economy), they could only cause new distortions. In these circumstances, it is hardly surprising that incentive by profits is largely held in check and that the increase in payments, including the bonus element, generally remains automatic and uniform. It is thus impossible for profits to retain the place in the incentive system given to them by the reform unless they first of all fulfil correctly their regulatory function.

2 Even if the problems mentioned under (1) above were solved, the orientation of investment could not be determined exclusively by decisions taken by enterprises according to criteria of profitability. The need to take into account interdependencies ('external economies'), and the direct expression of long-term social preferences are justifications for intervention by the central authorities; thus Lange's model, for example, provided for decisions on investment to be taken at the level of the sector and not of the enterprise. This point would hardly be worth noting, if there had not been at the outset a certain misunderstanding of the implications of the Hungarian reform, and if the 'attacks on the autonomy of enterprises' were not invariably cited as additional proof of the 'incomplete' or 'unfinished' nature of the Hungarian reform. In fact, the division of responsibilities between the enterprise and the superior decision-making levels, according to the amount and impact of the projected investment, is an integral part of the 'model' adopted by the Hungarian reform.

3 The link between individual earnings and profits (even on the assumption that profits accurately reflect the efficiency of production) raises much more formidable problems. Not that profit-sharing necessarily implies a widening of hierarchical differentials (between the earnings of directors, managers and workers): comparisons over time (between 'before' and 'after' the reforms) and in space (between Hungary and the other socialist countries) show that many other factors come into play, and that any possible inegalitarian effect of bonuses can be offset, in accordance with a political decision, by greater levelling of basic wages. On the other hand, profit-sharing calls into question even more fundamental options which concern the very nature of earnings in a socialist economy. Maximum incentive can, in theory, be sought in two very different directions: the first approach, directly transposed from capitalism, limits profit-sharing to managers who are thus encouraged to cut back on all production costs, including the wages bill; the second approach, which corresponds to the Yugoslavian self-management model, is to distribute the 'gross income' of the enterprise among the whole personnel. This implies marked earnings differentials, for the same qualification, in accordance with the profitability of the enterprise. As F. Renversez clearly shows in *Régulation et division . . .*, 1978, neither of these two 'fundamental models' was an acceptable choice for Hungary (even if there was initially some ambiguity). The first reason for this was that job security was considered overwhelmingly important, both socially and politically. On the other hand, the lack of self-management removed the main justification for earnings differentials according to enterprise: it was practically inconceivable to make all the workers bear the financial consequences of decisions to which they were not party; this reason alone (that is, once again, quite apart from the problems discussed under (1)), would be sufficient to explain why developments in this direction which had begun in 1971 came to a rapid halt. As for the system introduced in 1968, which caused very great variations in profit-sharing according to position in the enterprise's hierarchy, this proved right from the start to be socially intolerable, because it created a real gulf between directors, managers and ordinary workers. More awareness of the management of large Western firms (also entrusted to salaried directors) might have put those responsible for the 1968 reform on their guard against a certain oversimplification in their conception of profits. For about ten years, the Hungarian experience has simply confirmed that the activity of those in charge of enterprises cannot be limited to the maximising of short-term profits,

that their 'performance' must be the subject of an aggregate assessment, which is very difficult to contain within a rigid formula (with the evolution of profits operating as only one element among others in the assessment), and finally that career prospects are normally a more powerful motivation than annual bonuses.

If the current contradictions and blockages in the Hungarian reform could be overcome, the result might be an original and coherent model of competitive socialism. This model represents only one of the possible 'horizons' for the Hungarian reform, but it could be defined, taking account of the main lessons of the past ten years, by the following characteristics:

1 The functioning of enterprises is subject to regulation by profits. This basic principle has nothing to do with individual behaviour guided by runaway accumulation, and all the associated images. It means that any normally functioning enterprise must function without deficit; on the other hand, any activity which functions at a loss (i.e. where the value of the output does not cover production costs) must be reorganised or reconverted. The elimination of inefficient processes is not only an initial source of static gains in efficiency (i.e. liable to be achieved only once). It is above all a permanent source of dynamic gains in efficiency: in a competitive situation, where the profits of the most efficient producers correspond to the difference between their own production costs and those of the 'marginal' enterprises (who are only just able to balance their expenditure and their income), the leading enterprises can maintain their profits only by re-establishing their lead over their competitors as the gap between them tends to narrow.

2 The economic significance of profits depends on the existence of market relationships. Profits then acquire a social significance that they do not have in centralised economies, being only an accounting difference betweeen two assessments by the authorities (concerning respectively output and resources used in the production process). They play their full role as a regulator when any impetus from demand is automatically passed on to producers, and when the pressure of competition is sufficient to eliminate relatively inefficient production processes.

3 However, it is not possible to take the competitive nature of economic relationships for granted, any more than it is in a capitalist economy. To create (and maintain) competitive conditions is a major task of planned management in a 'decentralised' socialist economy. The splitting up of large enterprises in sectors in which there is room for several producers, an orientation policy for growth and investment aimed

at preventing the imbalances which put the purchaser at the mercy of the seller, and systematic recourse to competitive imports are economic strategies whose use by the central authorities is an integral part of the logic of the model.

4 Yet whatever effort is exerted 'upstream', it would be illusory to seek to solve all problems by relying purely and simply on automatic competitive mechanisms; this is even more true of a small economy (such as Hungary), where technical indivisibilities leave room in many sectors for only a very small number of enterprises. At least this concentration makes it easier to a certain extent to control prices and production costs. In any case, the juxtaposition of a (more or less) competitive sector and a (more directly) controlled sector is inevitable; but their co-existence may be viable if the authorities make every effort to ease the disparities between their respective operating conditions.

5 Competition between all sectors of the economy for the utilisation of various types of resources ('living labour' with various qualifications, material means of production, credit) seems to be even more fundamental. The competitive nature of the economy is not altered if the central authorities fix the price of the main resources at a level which is the same for all and which corresponds to their social opportunity cost and ensures equilibrium in the market. The same is true for all the centrally fixed regulators (taxes, interest rate) provided that they are applied on an equal basis to all the enterprises concerned.

6 The 'cost of capital' in particular ought in principle to be the same for all enterprises. A difference in level between the rate of the tax on an enterprise's own capital and the (basic) rate of interest on borrowed capital cannot be justified, since socialist enterprises are never the 'owners' of their capital, and both tax and interest fulfil one and the same function: to express a minimum requirement for the efficiency of capital, which is in principle valid for all its possible utilisations. In any logic of competition, it should be credit – and not self-financing – that is the normal method of financing investment in a decentralised socialist economy. There is no *a priori* reason why the distribution of gross profits (by sector, etc.) should correspond to future investment needs: only credit can ensure the mobility of capital throughout the whole of the economy. Finally, it has the dual advantage of putting all enterprises on an equal footing as far as possible, while at the same time allowing suitably motivated government preferences as regards sectoral or regional equilibrium to prevail in a flexible way through the modulation of lending conditions (rate of interest and terms of repayment).

7 In the same way as the interest rate for credit requests, the cost of labour (for each type of qualification) must play the role of a 'minimum efficiency norm', discouraging enterprises from retaining surplus staff. It is essential that it is the same for all enterprises, so that the less efficient are forced to reorganise or move over to a new type of production, rather than allowing them to survive by paying abnormally low wages. This solution also contributes to the increased mobility of the labour force; it could involve accepting frictional unemployment with full compensation for loss of earnings. However, it leaves room for an active labour policy, particularly from a regional point of view: the granting of subsidies, preferably temporary, for the employment of unqualified workers in an overpopulated area does not amount to an infringement of the competitive logic, if there is no discrimination among enterprises in the same region. Similarly, making enterprises pay (in the form of wages + taxes) the economic cost of labour does not mean that an active wages policy has to be abandoned, implementing fundamental social policy decisions. The existence of the tax, the rate of which is not necessarily uniform (if necessary, the rate could be negative, i.e. a subsidy), means that the cost to the enterprise and the wage drawn by the worker can to a certain extent be dissociated. Thus a temporary shortage of qualified specialists in a particular field does not necessarily mean that their wages must be raised by socially unacceptable amounts: it would be possible to prevent enterprises from poaching qualified workers from each other by means of higher wage increases through the imposition of a surtax on the higher wages. Conversely, subsidising the employment of unqualified labour may be a way of paying decent wages without causing unemployment.

8 This concept of interest and wages as an expression of the economic cost of the 'factors of production' would inevitably have the effect – with respect to the current situation in Hungary and no doubt everywhere else – of lowering the general level of profits: a good number of enterprises would function normally without making any significant 'pure profit' (i.e. after payment of taxes and interest charges). This would not, however, exclude all incentive through profits. The first obvious reason is that the incentive effect depends not on the total amount of profits, but on the share paid into the enterprise's fund (more accurately, on the proportion 'at the margin'). On the other hand, investment would be financed by credit, and regular sound management (the regulatory role of profits) would keep all its importance as a criterion for the allocation of credit. Finally, profit-sharing by the individual

must not be confused with the regular payment of a proportion of profits: experience shows that all 'institutionalised' bonuses tend to become automatic, to become integrated into the basic wage, with a consequent weakening of the incentive effect; on the other hand, the occasional payment of substantial bonuses (even just the equivalent of a month's wages) when an enterprise achieves particularly good results, for example after a successful innovation, can be a significant incentive. Such bonuses, comparable in that respect to the exceptional bonuses granted within enterprises to the initiator of an innovation, would be much more socially acceptable than permanent differentials in average wages for the same qualification from enterprise to enterprise. Having said that, it is obvious that profit-sharing cannot possibly be the only form of incentive. For managers in particular, the attraction of a post in keeping with their abilities is of paramount importance, and there is no reason why their opportunities for promotion should be limited to the enterprise where they started their careers: 'mobility of managers' could thus increase considerably, and a competitive socialist economy would thus succeed in making the best use of the 'scarce resource' of management ability.

9 Such a model would link the systematic use of competition, wherever it can operate, as a regulator and incentive to innovation, with a system of central planning that is sufficiently well equipped to control its social consequences. Thus it is practically impossible for an inefficient enterprise to be reorganised without any loss for its workforce and managers, but it is possible to reduce this loss as much as possible (by taking into account, should the case arise, the various responsibilities). Similarly, the recourse to material incentive involves the acceptance of inequalities in income, that it is often dangerous to correct retrospectively by arbitrary manipulation of prices to consumers (even in favour of basic consumption), but whose evolution can and must be socially controlled. When an enterprise, for example, enjoys a permanent advantage relative to its competitors, guaranteeing high profits irrespective of the efforts of its workforce, the bulk of the profits should be deducted by means of an *ad hoc* tax system. The development of competition is itself capable of correcting certain types of inequalities that are directly linked to the failures of the market (abnormally high earnings for certain types of 'moonlighting', and corruption among those controlling access to services and goods in short supply). Thus the most fundamental inequalities in Soviet-type societies are inequalities that lie outside of the market. The increase in competition and the reduction of inequalities could, therefore, go hand in hand, each consolidating the other.

It is still too early to predict whether or not the Hungarian economy will draw nearer to this model of competitive socialism. Some of the developments that we have analysed certainly point in this direction, sometimes consciously, sometimes spontaneously, so to speak; on the other hand, in other respects, the dominant ideas – particularly as regards the economic function of profits, of interest and of the tax on assets (which is now abolished) – remain extremely ambiguous. However that may be, current developments, for example towards the reintroduction of a minimum level of competition in the product markets, have hardly begun. Nor is it possible to ignore the reaction of the threatened bureaucracies (even if Hungary, as W. Brus stresses, is today the classic example of a 'relative liberalisation which does not question the foundations of the political system'), the ability of vested interests to put a brake on change and their ability to use public discontent and anxiety to prevent change.

The model of competitive socialism broadly outlined above is thus only one of the possible aims of the Hungarian reform. Moreover, it does not exclude the introduction at a later date of elements of self-management into the functioning of enterprises. But it certainly corresponds better than the Yugoslav model to the fundamental options of the communist regimes. It retains the effective primacy of the plan for the fulfilment of social and economic targets defined at the national level, with the central authorities retaining in particular the means to prevent unemployment and the development of cumulative inequalities. The mobility of all 'factors of production' (particularly the mobility of capital and of managers) tends to maintain equality of earnings for equal qualifications and work, in contrast to the most fundamental implications of the Yugoslav model. The crucial role of credit, finally, reflects directly the requirement of a society in which from now on, in the words of J. Vanek, 'it is the workers who hire capital', and no longer the other way round.

Yet on one single point prediction is much easier. The influence of the 'Hungarian model' – although those responsible for it are careful not to use the term 'model' – will remain limited for the foreseeable future, and its chances of spreading to other socialist countries, except perhaps Poland, are nil. Whatever permanent sacrifices may be made by consumers, only a sharply deteriorating economic situation could force radical changes; and the margin for possible rationalisation within the framework of the centralised model remains considerable.

Notes

Introduction

1 Yugoslavia has not been included in the present work basically because its early repudiation of the Soviet model (from 1948 onwards) created different conditions in all respects.
2 The seven countries under consideration all implemented a system of planned management of the national economy, based on the collective appropriation of the principal means of production. For this reason, they define themselves as socialist countries. We shall use the term socialist countries to describe them, without any implication of a value judgment on our part (we shall also avoid the implicit value judgment contained in the systematic use of quotation marks when writing 'socialist' countries).
3 Notably in *Ogolne problemy funkcjonowania gospodarski socialistycznei*, Warsaw, PWN, 1961; see Brus, 1970.
4 Paradoxically, it is only the permanence of the centralised model that enables certain reversals of economic policy to be understood. Thus the agricultural problems that were put to one side at the time of forced collectivisation eventually re-emerged and remain acute. Having been obliged to contribute enormous amounts of money to the industrialisation process throughout the Stalinist period, agriculture has benefited since 1953 from an increasing amount of resources from other sectors for its own modernisation programme, although even this aid has not been sufficient to bring about a real solution within the framework of the centralised model.
5 Hungarian authors, following J. Kornai and G. Peter, commonly speak of 'economic mechanism' rather than 'model'; but these two terms, which arose from parallel and contemporaneous discussions, are synonymous in meaning.
6 That we shall avoid identifying *a priori* with the 'decentralised model' of Brus. In any case, for the authors of the most radical reforms, decentralisation of day-to-day decision making was to go hand in hand with increasing the efficiency of central planning.

1 The fundamental elements of the centralised model

1 *Ekonomika promyshlennosti SSSR*, Moscow, 1956, p. 393; See Nove, 1968, p. 41.
2 The main originators of this concept are the Polish economists J. Zielinski and A. Wakar.

2 From the requirements of the model to the realities of socialist countries

1 G. Duchêne speaks of 'despecialisation', and stresses the various aspects of the 'autonomisation of the ministries'; see Duchêne, 1975, pp. 402 *et seq*.

2 That is, the additional production likely to be obtained in another part of the national economy as a result of the resources made available.

3 Cf. A. Katsenelinboigen, 'Coloured markets in the Soviet Union', *Soviet Studies*, 29 (1), January 1977.

4 Exceptional circumstances sometimes lead the Soviet leaders themselves implicitly to acknowledge this: whereas for Western countries, a war economy is synonymous with centralisation, the need for immediate efficiency in the USSR from 1941 onwards made limited but significant concessions to the principle of the market necessary (state enterprises were authorised to resell surplus materials without prior authorisation from their ministry).

5 Particularly if the cost price during the first year of manufacture is taken as a base; the producer will benefit from the subsequent reduction in the cost of production, which is often very appreciable after the 'assimilation' period for the new product.

6 The extent of the distortions in all directions (non-systematic distortions) makes the central problem of the theoreticians, that of finding an underlying 'basis for prices' (e.g. by the use of such price formulae as (i) prices proportional to value, or (ii) prices based on average production costs), seem relatively unimportant.

7 One example is the shortage of children's shoes in Hungary in the 1950s caused by fixing the price of this article at only half that of a pair of adult shoes.

8 Whatever efforts are made to impose a centralised wages scale, enterprises quite easily manage to alter the amount of wages actually paid (e.g. by exaggerating the qualifications of their personnel).

9 In contrast, particularly, to housing.

10 In the USSR, the price of meat was raised by 15 per cent in 1956 and by 30 per cent in 1962, and in Poland by 25 to 28 per cent in 1959, and each subsequent attempt to raise the price (in 1970, 1976 and 1980) triggered off a major political crisis.

11 By this we understand as complete a satisfaction as possible of individual needs, taking into account the resources allocated to the priority objectives of the state (national defence, accumulation and collective consumption).

12 Cf. J. Zielinski 'The consumption model and means of its implementations' in *On Political Economy and Econometrics. Essays in honour of Oskar Lange*, Warsaw, PWN, 1965, p. 629.

13 In assuming that the tax indicates total net production, we are disregarding, for simplification, the profits of production enterprises and commercial margins.

3 Quasi-cyclical changes

1 J. Marczewski (in Marczewski, 1955 and 1956, pp. 271–4) provides a survey of the official statements that marked the turning point of 1953; the quotations are taken from this source.
2 Z. Vas, 'Szabad Nep', 27 October 1954, quoted in *Etude sur la situation économique de l'Europe en 1954*, p. 50, note 6.
3 All the more so since the equipment required by the *kolkhozy* (lorries, tractors) was not always available, in view of the low priority given to agriculture after 1958.
4 This problem was not so serious in the more newly industrialised East European countries.
5 The Council for Mutual Economic Aid (Comecon) was set up in 1949, but did not actually function until after the death of Stalin. At the beginning of the 1960s, the member countries included the USSR, Czechoslovakia, Poland, Hungary, Bulgaria, Rumania and East Germany, as well as Mongolia, which became a full special member in 1962.
6 Literally: national economic councils.
7 The average population per *sovnarkhoz* was barely equal to that of the French regional action areas.
8 Quoted by L. Smolinski and P. Wiles (1963).
9 Cf. Kende, 1964, p. 44.
10 Cf. the series of five articles published by W. Brus in issues 1 to 5 of *Zycie Gospodarcze*, 1957: 'The Yugoslav model examined more closely'.
11 Analysed by J. Montias in Bornstein (ed.), 1973, p. 273, which gives a remarkable overall view of the Polish debates of the end of the 1950s.
12 Cf. A. Nove in Nove, 1961, French translation, pp. 365 *et seq*.
13 The evolution of the Hungarian economy was significantly less uneven, both because the 1957 reform in Hungary had been particularly cautious and limited, and because of a more moderate investment policy than in Poland and Czechoslovakia (in 1961, the government had been able in time to put the brake on the expansion of investment).
14 Translated in *Economie et politique*, October 1968, p. 13.

4 The basic trends

1 Speech by W. Ulbricht to the 5th party conference (*Neues Deutschland*, 11 July 1958).
2 Report to the plenum of March 1962 (quoted by N. Nimitz, 'The lean years', *Problems of Communism*, May 1965).
3 Quoted in Smolinski and Wiles (1963). The authors also mention the calculations made by A. Dorodnitsyn, according to which the work involved in the planning of the Soviet economy would have become by the beginning of the 1960s '1,600 times more complex' than in 1928; one mathematical economist, Glushkov, ventured to predict that by 1980 the volume of planning work would have increased 36 times, by which time it would employ the whole of the working population (Smolinski and Wiles, 1963). These rash extrapolations above all reveal a sudden awareness of the problem.

4 In 1967, *per capita* consumption of cereals in East Germany exceeded that in West Germany by 36.4 per cent, and of potatoes by 42.3 per cent, but *per capita* consumption of meat was 12.6 per cent lower in East Germany, and 63.7 per cent lower for fresh fruit (according to E. M. Snell and M. Harper, in JEC, 1972, p. 591).

5 The Czech economist I. Strup ('Comparison between the standard of living and the overall efficiency of production in Czechoslovakia and France', *Politicka Ekonomie*, 2, 1968, translated in *Eastern European Economics*, Summer 1968) reaches the fantastic conclusion that the 'standard of living' in Czechoslovakia in 1964 was only 30 per cent of that in France, by making various deductions in order to take account of the higher 'rate of activity' (loss of leisure time, considered to be equivalent to a 10 per cent reduction in the standard of living), of the poor quality of services, of queues in the retail shops and of the waiting periods for the delivery of certain durable goods.

6 The capital goods sector grows indefinitely 'for its own sake'; this term is borrowed from P. Wiles, who talks of a 'solipsistic enclave', which is quite distinct from an 'autarchic' enclave, since its growth is constantly fuelled by new resources taken from the rest of the economy.

7 In an article published in *Izvestia* on the 2 October, 1964, Khrushchev – by chance repeating almost word for word an article by Malenkov also published in *Izvestia* on the 3 October, 1954 – wrote: 'Now that our industry is strong and the country properly defended, the party is proposing much more rapid development for the consumer goods sectors' (Quoted in Felker, 1966, pp. 41 and 36 respectively).

8 Estimation by M. Boretsky, in JEC, 1962, pp. 90 *et seq*.

9 Quoted in J. P. Hardt, in JEC, 1960, pp. 133-4.

10 Speech televised in the summer of 1968 and quoted by E. M. Snell in JEC, 1972, p. 245.

11 This contrast is commonly described as a contrast between 'hard products' and 'soft products' (rather as currencies are described as 'hard' or 'soft').

12 According to a study by the Czech economists J. Klacek and J. Pleva (*Politicka Ekonomie*, July 1967), quoted by E. M. Snell in JEC, 1972, p. 256. As early as 1960, a similar study in East Germany had led to the same conclusions.

13 Calculations carried out according to JEC, 1972, pp. 50, 59, 564 and JEC, 1970, p. 184.

14 The share of light industries and the food industries in total industrial investment: 1956-60: 15.6 per cent; 1961-5 plan: 16.7 per cent; 1961-4: 18 per cent. Source: *Bulletin économique pour l'Europe*.

5 Limited or fundamental reform?

1 This manichean contrast dominates Gamarnikow, 1968.

2 Cf. W. Ulbricht ('Marx's "Capital" and the socialist system developed in the GDR', *Economie et Politique*, March 1968, pp. 175-84): 'Co-operation [between enterprises] cannot be achieved completely through the administration alone . . . but must logically be based on real economic relationships within industry.'

3 Cf. Liberman ('The Soviet Economic Reform', *Foreign Affairs*, October, 1967, pp.58-9): 'Producers know their own potentialities better than anyone, and they must be able to examine and get to know the needs of their customers.' The three quotations relating to East Germany, Poland, and the USSR respectively have been chosen deliberately: there was at the outset a clear intention to reduce the methods of centralised management even in those countries which did not opt for radical reform.

4 Intervention by G. Peter, in Bognar, 1969, p. 80. Similarly, in the text adopted on the 27 January 1965 by the central committee of the Czech communist party, the first of the 'guiding principles of the new system' was: 'the development and better utilisation of centralised management'. There is a multiplicity of similar quotations.

5 Guidelines for the New Economic System for the planning and management of the national economy in the GDR, document adopted by the Council of Ministers of the GDR on 11 July, 1963, translated in *Recherches internationales à la lumière du marxisme*, 47, 1965.

6 'Le Capital de Marx et le système socialiste développé en RDA', *Economie et Politique*, March 1968, p. 175.

7 'The new phase of the prices policy requires great flexibility in the determination of industrial prices. It is necessary systematically to adjust prices to values and to take into consideration the evolution of market conditions and requirements' (speech by W. Ulbricht in December 1965 to the plenum of the central committee of the SED).

8 Cf. J. Zielinski, 'Centralization and decentralization in decision-making', *Economics of Planning*, 3, 1963, and 'Economics and politics of economic reforms in Eastern Europe,' *ibid.*, 3, 1969.

9 'Hospodarske Noviny', 1 April 1966, quoted by M. Gamarnikow in Gamarnikow, 1968.

10 Geographical proximity contributed to this: the headquarters of the VVB was generally situated in the region in which most of the enterprises were located.

11 Even better was the attempt in Poland to implement the initial phase of an economic reform while at the same time postponing all price reforms.

12 The slide was particularly marked in Czechoslovakia and Poland: the result was a much greater increase than planned in the average level of prices in certain sectors and a corresponding increase in the profits of enterprises which had pleaded their cause only too well.

6 The USSR and East Germany: the remains of the reforms

1 Employment in the supply and distribution agencies increased from 340,000 in 1960 to 343,000 in 1965, then to 396,000 in 1969, excluding the central apparatus of Gossnab and the ministries (source: Schroeder, 1972, p. 103).

2 N. Drogichinsky, quoted in Nove, 1977, p. 43.

3 *Ekonomicheskaia Gazeta*, 6, 1968, quoted in Nove, 1977, p. 179.

4 Cf. M. Haendcke-Hoppe, 'Structures et systèmes', *Documents*, March 1973, p. 98.

5 As some of them admitted to D. Granick (Granick, 1975, pp. 195–6).
6 Cf. J. Naor, 'How dead is the GDR New Economic System?', *Soviet Studies*, October 1973.
7 As in the case of the Takraf combine (heavy machinery) or the wool and silk combine.
8 G. Mittag, *Neues Deutschland*, 26 August 1978, quoted by M. Melzer, 'Combine Formation and the Role of the Enterprise in East German Industry', in I. Jeffries (ed.), 1981.
9 According to M. Melzer, 'Combine formation in the GDR', *Soviet Studies*, January 1981.
10 Cf. M. Melzer in I. Jeffries (ed.), 1981, p. 108.
11 Quoted by A. Smolar, 'La planification comme processus d'apprentissage', *Revue d'études comparatives Est-Ouest*, September 1978.
12 According to I. Edwards, M. Hughes and J. Noren, 'US and USSR: Comparisons of GNP', JEC, *Soviet Economy in a Time of Change*, 2 vols, 1979. It is impossible to make a direct comparison with the East German distribution given in Table 6.3, since it is presented according to Marxist concepts.
13 The assessments of military and space programme expenditure are even more debatable; their share in Soviet GNP is about three times their share in American GNP.
14 Comparison of planned targets (P) and results (R) during the five-year period 1976–80 (expressed as annual percentage difference).

	Fixed investment			*Net material product*		
	P	*R*	*Difference*	*P*	*R*	*Difference*
USSR	3.2	3.9	+0.7	4.7	4.2	−0.5
GDR	4.2	5.3	+1.1	5.0	4.1	−0.9

15 The official statistics again 'admit' to a complete standstill in *per capita* consumption of meat in the last five-year period (57 kg. per annum in 1980 just as in 1975).
16 According to G. Schroeder and B. Severin, 'Soviet Consumption and Incomes Policies in Perspective', JEC, *Soviet Economy in a New Perspective*, 1976.
17 Cf. below, p. 235 (comparison with Hungary).

7 Hungary: the reform that survived

1 Cf. B. Balassa, 'The firm in the New Economic Mechanism', in Bornstein (ed.), 1973, p. 357.
2 A simple order of magnitude. According to T. Bacskai, 'New developments in state enterprise taxation', in *Acta Oeconomica*, 1971, vol. 6, p. 119, and S. Balazsy, 'Financial regulating system and technical development', in *Acta Oeconomica*, 1973, vol. 10, p. 333.
3 B. Csikos-Nagy, 'Tenth anniversary of the Hungarian economic reform', translated under the title 'Le nouveau méchanisme économique hongrois', in *Régulation et division . . .*, 1978, pp. 3–12.
4 The forint was revalued by a total of 30 per cent against the dollar between

1970 and 1976, while the increase in the price of imports in dollars between these two dates was 138.4 per cent (according to P. Marer in JEC, *East European Economic Assessment*, vol. 1, 1980–1).

5 'Economic reform and retreat in Yugoslavia', *Foreign Affairs*, January 1959.

6 'Les options nouvelles de la politique économique extérieure de la Hongrie', in Renversez and Lavigne, 1979, p. 15.

7 Cf. S. Pasztor, 'How open is the Hungarian economy?', *Acta Oeconomica*, vol. 25 (1980), nos. 1-2. The openness of the Hungarian economy (defined, for example, as the ratio of exports to DGP) is immediately behind Belgium, the Republic of Ireland and Holland, but exceeds that of Switzerland and the Scandinavian countries, as well as that of all the other socialist countries; it is double that of Poland.

8 W. Andreff (1981, p. 21) suggests that the investment boom in 1977 – a factor in the worsening of the foreign deficit – was a result of Hungary's commitments to Comecon.

9 B. Kadar, 'Adjustment problems and experiences of the Hungarian economy', *La Spettatore Internazionale*, April 1981, pp. 189-90.

10 Cf. E. Hewett, 'The Hungarian economy: lessons of the 1970s and prospects for the 1980s', in JEC, *East European Economic Assessment*, vol. 1, 1980–1, and P. Hare, H. Radice and N. Swain, 1981, pp. 15 *et seq.*; H. Radice, 'The state enterprise in Hungary', in I. Jeffries (ed.), 1981, pp. 131 *et seq.*; X. Richet, 'Réforme dans la réforme? La nouvelle politique économique hongroise au seuil des années 80', *Revue d'Etudes Comparatives Est-Ouest*, September 1981; A. Tiraspolsky, 'La Hongrie en 1981: une année difficile', *Courrier des Pays de l'Est*, June 1982.

11 The hierarchy of growth rates fixed as targets in the 1981–5 FYP is revealing: (a) exports 6.5 to 6.8 per cent; (b) imports 3.3 to 3.5 per cent; (c) net material product 2.7 to 3.4 per cent; (d) total household consumption 1.4 to 1.7 per cent; (e) 'utilised' national income 0.

12 The five-year period 1981–5 is characterised by a severe limitation on *all* resources: imports, investment and labour. The reduction in imports alone may well cause growth to be halted and a vicious circle of the Polish kind, unless there are significant increases in efficiency.

13 Cf. particularly E. Hewett and W. Andreff.

14 More precisely, Hungary changed over from a dual exchange rate (a 'commercial' exchange rate for exports and imports of goods, and a 'non-commercial' exchange rate for Western tourists that was twice as favourable) to a single exchange rate. The unification of the two systems, which was carried out in stages, was completed on 1 October 1981 under the following conditions: (i) the 'non-commercial' rate rejoined the 'commercial' rate, which implied – with respect to tourists, for example – a large devaluation of the forint; (ii) as far as the 'commercial' exchange rate itself was concerned, the revaluation policy came to an end in 1979 and was replaced by a very slight depreciation. It appears that a much larger devaluation was considered, but rejected.

15 A progressive surtax limited to 'only' 50–100 per cent (instead of 100 to 300 per cent in the case of 'ordinary' profits).

16 After a pause for a few years around 1968, the process of concentration

began again (812 state enterprises in 1970, 702 in 1980). Enterprises with more than 1,000 employees represented in Hungary a record proportion of total employment: 73 per cent compared with 43 per cent in East Germany and 39 per cent in West Germany (cf. Hare, Radice and Swain (eds), 1981).

17 According to X. Richet, 1981.

18 Intervention at the Bloomington (Indiana) symposium on the Hungarian economic reform, March 1982.

19 This is the expression used by W. Andreff (1981), about, more specifically, the 'Comecon effect' on the management of enterprises.

20 Cf. P. G. Hare, in Hare, Radice and Swain (eds), 1981.

21 JEC, 1980–1. This approach raises several questions. Are the threat of dismissal and the widening of wage differentials necessary and sufficient conditions for the achievement of 'capitalist efficiency'? Can low labour productivity be attributed mainly to lack of individual effort by workers? And finally, is it possible to rely on a seriously deteriorated economic situation in order to impose a 'real' reform? The Polish example would seem to indicate that this is not the case.

22 From 1970 to 1981, the value (in dollars) of Hungarian trade with the Western industrial countries increased fivefold, as did that of East Germany, whereas that of the USSR increased tenfold.

23 In 1981, the rate at which imports in foreign currencies were covered by exports exceeded 98 per cent (whereas it was only 82 per cent for imports from the West).

24 During the five-year period 1976–80, the structure of household expenditure changed as would be expected in a period of increase in the standard of living (steady decrease in the share of expenditure on food and an increase in the share of items with a high income elasticity, such as consumer durables) in the case of East Germany, but not in Hungary, where there was a reversal of the tendency. The explanation certainly lies partly in the freezing of food prices in East Germany and the large increases in Hungary. This did not prevent these increases from having very real effects in Hungary (cf. note 25).

25 There was sustained increase in East Germany, and a large decrease in Hungary in comparison with 1971–5. *Per capita* consumption of meat in Hungary reached 88 per cent of that in East Germany in 1975, but was only 79 per cent of the East German total in 1980.

Bibliography

Acta Oeconomica, quarterly, Hungarian Academy of Sciences, Budapest.

Adam, J. (1979), *Wage Control and Inflation in the Soviet Bloc Countries*, London, Macmillan.

Andreff, W. (1981), 'Redéploiement ou renouveau de l'économie hongroise?', *Revue d'Etudes Comparatives Est-Ouest*, December.

Balassa, B. (1973), 'The firm in the new economic mechanism', in Bornstein (ed.) (1973).

Bergson, A. (ed.) (1953), *Soviet Economic Growth*, Evanston, Row, Peterson & Co.

Bergson, A. (1961), *The Real National Income of Soviet Russia since 1928*, Cambridge, Mass., Harvard University Press.

Bergson, A. and Kuznets, S. (eds) (1963), *Economic Trends in the Soviet Union*, Cambridge, Mass., Harvard University Press.

Berliner, J. (1957), *Factory and Manager in the USSR*, Cambridge, Mass., Harvard University Press.

Berliner, J. (1976), *The Innovation Decision in Soviet Industry*, Cambridge, Mass., MIT Press.

Bobrowski, C. (1968), *Formation du système soviétique de planification*, Paris, La Haye, Mouton.

Bognar, J. (1969), *Les nouveaux mécanismes de l'économie socialiste en Hongrie*, Paris, Editions du Pavillon.

Bornstein, M. (ed.) (1969), *Comparative Economic Systems*, Homewood, R. D. Irwin.

Bornstein, M. (ed.) (1973), *Plan and Market. Economic reform in Eastern Europe*, New Haven, Conn., Yale University Press.

Bornstein, M. and Fusfeld, D. (eds) (1974), *The Soviet Economy*, Homewood, R. D. Irwin.

Brus, W. (1970), *Problèmes généraux du fonctionnement de l'économie socialiste*, Paris, Maspéro (1st edn, Warsaw, 1961).

Brus, W. (1975), *Socialist Ownership and Political Systems*, London, Routledge & Kegan Paul.

Bulletin économique pour l'Europe, United Nations, Economic Commission for Europe, Geneva.

Cave, M., McAuley, A. and Thornton, J. (1982), *New Trends in Soviet Economics*, New York, London, Sharpe.

Chavance, B. (1983), *Système économique soviétique*, Paris, le Sycomore.

Clarke, R. (1968), 'Soviet agricultural reforms since Khrushchev', *Soviet Studies*, October.

Collette, J.-M. (1965), *Politique des investissements et calcul économique*, Paris, Cujas.
Denis, H. and Lavigne, M. (1965), *Le problème des prix en Union Soviétique*, Paris, Cujas.
Dobb, M. (1966), *Soviet Economic Development since 1917*, London, Routledge & Kegan Paul.
Duchêne, G. (1975), 'Essai sur la logique de l'économie planifiée soviétique', thesis, Paris I, 1975.
Durgin, F. (1964), 'Monetization and policy in Soviet agriculture since 1952', *Soviet Studies*, April.
Eastern European Economics, quarterly.
Economic Reforms in Eastern Europe and Prospects for the 1980s, NATO Colloquium, Brussels, 1980, Oxford, Pergamon Press, 1980.
'L'Economie hongroise entre l'Est et l'Ouest' (1981), special number of *Courrier des Pays de l'Est*, September.
'Economie officielle et économies parallèles' (1981), special number of *Revue d'Etudes Comparatives Est-Ouest*, June.
Ellman, M. (1979), *Socialist Planning*, Cambridge University Press.
Engels, F. (1971), *Anti-Dühring*, Paris, Editions Sociales, 3rd edn.
Ernst, M, 'Postwar economic growth in Eastern Europe', in JEC (1966), reproduced in Feiwel (ed.) (1969), pp. 75–111.
Etude sur la situation économique de l'Europe en . . ., annual, United Nations, Economic Commission for Europe, Geneva.
Fallenbuchl, Z. (ed.) (1975), *Economic Development in the Soviet Union and Eastern Europe*, New York, Praeger.
Feiwel, G. (ed.) (1969), *New Currents in Soviet-Type Economies*, Scranton, International Textbook Co., 2nd edn.
Felker, J. (1966), *Soviet Economic Controversies*, Cambridge, Mass., MIT Press.
Friss, I. (ed.) (1969), *Reform of the Economic Mechanism in Hungary*, Budapest, Akadémiai kiadó.
Gado, O. (1972), *Reform of the Economic Mechanism in Hungary, Development 1968-71*, Budapest, Akadémiai kiadó.
Gado, O. (1976), *The Economic Mechanism in Hungary. How it Works in 1976*, Budapest, Akadémiai kiadó.
Gamarnikow, M. (1968), *Economic Reforms in Eastern Europe*, Detroit, Wayne State University Press.
Granick, D. (1975), *Enterprise Guidance in Eastern Europe*, Princeton University Press.
Grossman, G. (ed.) (1968), *Money and Plan*, Berkeley and Los Angeles, University of California Press.
Haase, H. (1980), *Development Trends in the GDR during the 1980s: A Prognosis of its Problems*, Berlin, Berichte des Osteuropa – Instituts an der Fraien Universität.
Hare, P., Radice, H. and Swain, N. (eds) (1981), *Hungary: a Decade of Economic Reform*, London, George Allen & Unwin.
Hare, P. and Wanless, T. (1981), 'Polish and Hungarian reforms – A comparison', *Soviet Studies*, October.
Hohmann, H., Kaser, M. and Thalheim, K. (eds) (1975), *The New Economic*

Systems of Eastern Europe, London, C. Hurst, Berkeley and Los Angeles, University of California Press.
Jasny, N. (1949), *The Socialized Agriculture of the USSR*, Stanford University Press.
Jasny, N. (1961), *Soviet Industrialization 1928-1952*, Chicago University Press.
Joint Economic Committee, Congress of the United States (hereafter JEC) (1960), *Comparisons of the United States and Soviet Economies*, Washington, US Government Printing Office.
JEC (1962), *Dimensions of Soviet Power*.
JEC (1964), *Annual Economic Indicators for the USSR*.
JEC (1966), *New Directions in the Soviet Economy*.
JEC (1968), *Soviet Economic Performance 1966-1967*.
JEC (1970), *Economic Performance and the Military Burden*.
JEC (1972), *Economic Development in Countries of Eastern Europe*.
JEC (1973), *Soviet Economic Prospects for the Seventies*.
JEC (1974), *Reorientation and Commercial Relations of the Economies of Eastern Europe*.
JEC (1976), *Soviet Economy in a New Perspective*.
JEC (1977), *Eastern European Economies Post-Helsinki*.
JEC (1979), *Soviet Economy in a Time of Change*, 2 vols.
JEC (1980-1), *East European Economic Assessment*, 2 vols.
Jeffries, I. (ed.) (1981), *The Industrial Enterprise in Eastern Europe*, New York, Praeger.
Karcz, F. (ed.) (1967), *Soviet and East Europe Agriculture*, Berkeley, University of California Press.
Katsenelinboigen, A. (1978), *Studies in Soviet Economic Planning*, New York, Sharpe.
Kende, P. (1964), *Logique de l'économie centralisée. Un exemple: la Hongrie*, Paris, SEDES.
Kerblay, B. (1968), *Les marchés paysans en URSS*, Paris, Mouton.
Kerblay, B. (1977). *La société soviétique contemporaine*, Paris, A. Colin.
Keren, M. (1973a), 'Concentration amid devolution in East Germany's reforms', in Bornstein (ed.) (1973).
Keren, M. (1973b), 'The new economic system in the GDR – an obituary', *Soviet Studies*, April.
Kornai, J. (1959), *Overcentralization in Economic Administration*, Oxford University Press.
Kornai, J. (1971), *Anti-equilibrium*. Amsterdam, London, North Holland.
Kornai, J. (1980), *Economics of Shortage*, Amsterdam, New York, Oxford, North Holland.
Kornai, J. and Martos, B. (eds) (1981), *Non-price Control*, Amsterdam, New York, Oxford, North Holland.
Krejci, J. (1976), *Social Structure in Divided Germany*, London, Croom Helm.
Krejci, J. (1982), *National Income and Outlay in Czechoslovakia, Poland and Yugoslavia*, London, Macmillan.
Laky, T. (1980), 'The Hidden Mechanisms of Recentralization in Hungary', in *Acta Oeconomica*, vol. 24, no. 1-2.
Lange, O. (1936 and 1937), 'On the economic theory of socialism', *Review of Economic Studies*, October 1936 and February 1937, in *On the Economic*

Theory of Socialism, B. Lippincott (ed.), New York, A. M. Kelley, 1970 (first edition, 1939).
Lavigne, M. (1975), 'Economic reforms in Eastern Europe: ten years after', in Fallenbuchl (ed.) (1975).
Lavigne, M. (1977), 'L'oligopole dans la planification socialiste', *Economies et sociétés*, Serie G, no. 34.
Lavigne, M. (ed.) (1978), *Economie politique de la planification en système socialiste*, Paris, Economica.
Lavigne, M. (1979), *Les économies socialistes soviétiques et européennes*, Paris; A. Collin, (first edition, 1970).
Lavigne, M. (ed.) (1981), *Travail et monnaie en système socialiste*, Paris, Economica.
Leptin, G. and Melzer, M. (1978), *Economic Reform in East German Industry*, Oxford University Press.
McAuley, A. (1979), *Economic Welfare in the Soviet Union*, Hemel Hempstead, George Allen & Unwin.
Marczewski, J. (1955 and 1956), *Planification et croissance des démocraties populaires*, Paris, PUF, 2 vols.
Marczewski, J. (1972), *Crise de la planification socialiste?* Paris, PUF.
Marer, P. and Montias, J. (eds) (1980), *East European Integration and East-West Trade*, Bloomington, Indiana University Press.
Marx, K. (1965), *Le Capital*, edited by M. Rubel, *Oeuvres*, 2 vols, Paris, Gallimard, 1965 and 1968 (La Pléiade).
Melzer, M. (1981), 'Combine Formation in the GDR', *Soviet Studies*, January.
Montias, J. (1962), *Central Planning in Poland*, New Haven and London, Yale University Press.
Montias, J. (1973), 'The Czechoslovak economic reforms in perspective', in Bornstein (ed.) (1973).
Murrel, P. (1981), 'An Evaluation of the Success of the Hungarian Economic Reform', *Journal of Comparative Economics*, December.
Nimitz, N. 'Soviet agricultural prices and costs', in JEC (1966b).
Nove, A. (1961), *The Soviet Economy. An introduction*, London, George Allen & Unwin, 3rd edition, 1968 (first edition, 1961; French translation, Paris, Plon, 1963).
Nove, A. (1961), *The Soviet Economy. An introduction*, London, George Allen
Nove, A. (1979), *Political Economy and Soviet Socialism*, London, Boston, George Allen & Unwin.
Nove, A. (1982), *An Economic History of the USSR*, Harmondsworth, Penguin.
On Political Economy and Econometrics. Essays in the Honour of Oskar Lange, Warsaw, 1965.
Pécsi, K. (1981), *The Future of Socialist Economic Integration*, Avmorok, New York, Sharpe.
Portes, R. 'Hungary, economic performance, policy and prospects', in JEC (1977).
Problems of Economics, monthly.
Pryor, F. (1963), *The Communist Foreign Trade System*, London, G. Allen & Unwin.
Pryor, F. (1968), *Public Expenditures in Communist and Capitalist Nations*, London, G. Allen & Unwin.

Pryor, F. (1973), *Property and Industrial Organization in Communist and Capitalist Nations*, Bloomington, Indiana University Press.

Régulation et division internationale de travail, Franco-Hungarian conference, Nanterre, February 1978, F. Renversez and M. Lavigne (eds), Paris, Economica, 1979.

Les revenus dans l'Europe d'après-guerre, 2nd part of *l'Etude sur la situation économique de l'Europe en 1965*, United Nations, Economic Commission for Europe, Geneva, 1969.

Richet, X. (1981), 'Réforme dans la réforme? La nouvelle politique économique hongroise au seuil des années 80', *Revue d'Etudes Comparatives Est-Ouest*, December.

Robinson, W. (1972), *The Pattern of Reform in Hungary*, New York, Praeger.

Schnitzer, M. (1972), *East and West Germany: a comparative economic analysis*, New York, Praeger.

Schroeder, G. (1968), 'The Soviet economic reforms – a study in contradictions', *Soviet Studies*, July.

Schroeder, G. (1969), 'The 1966-1967 Soviet industrial price reform – a study in complications', *Soviet Studies*, April.

Schroeder, G. (1972), 'The "reform" of the supply system in Soviet industry', *Soviet Studies*, July.

Schumpeter, J. (1950), *Capitalism, Socialism and Democracy*, New York, Harper (1st edn, 1942), (French translation by G. Fain, Paris, Payot, 1954).

Seurot, F. (1983), *Inflation et emploi dans les pays socialistes*, Paris, PUF.

Shaffer, H. (ed.) (1977), *Soviet Agriculture: an assessment of its contribution to economic development*, New York, Praeger.

Sik, O. (1967), *Plan and Market under Socialism*, White Plains, IASP.

Sik, O. (1978), *Pour une troisième voie*, Paris, PUF.

Smolar, A. (1978), 'La planification comme processus d'apprentissage', *Revue d'Etudes Comparatives Est-Ouest*, September.

Smolinski, L. and Wiles, P. (1963), 'The Soviet Planning Pendulum', *Problems of Communism*, November.

Spulber, N. (1979), *Organizational Alternatives in Soviet-type Economies*, London, Cambridge University Press.

Szamuely, L. (1974), *First Models of the Socialist Economic Systems. Principles and Theories*, Budapest, Akadémiai Kiádó.

Tendances et perspectives structurelles de l'économie européenne, 1st part of *l'Etude sur la situation économique de l'Europe en 1969*, United Nations Economic Commission for Europe, Geneva, 1970.

Treml, V. and Hardt, J. (eds) (1972), *Soviet Economic Statistics*, Durham, Duke University Press.

Van Brabant, J. (1980), *Socialist Economic Integration*, Cambridge University Press.

Wadekin, K. (1977), 'The place of agriculture in the European communist economies', *Soviet Studies*, April.

Wellisz, S. (1968), *Initiation aux économies socialistes*, Paris, Editions Ouvrières.

Wilczynski, J. (1982), *The Economics of Socialism*, London, George Allen & Unwin.

Wiles, P. (1962), *The Political Economy of Communism*, Oxford, Blackwell.

Wiles, P. (1968), *Communist International Economics*, Oxford, Blackwell.
Wiles, P. (1977), *Economic Institutions Compared*, Oxford, Blackwell.
Zaleski, E. (1962), *Planification de la croissance et fluctuations économiques en URSS*, Paris, SEDES.
Zaleski, E. (1980), *Stalinist Planning for Economic Growth, 1933-1952*, Chapel Hill, The University of North Carolina Press.
Zauberman, A. (1975), *The Mathematical Revolution in Soviet Economics*, London, Oxford University Press.
Zielinski, J. (1963), 'Centralization and decentralization in decision making', *Economics of Planning*, vol. 3.
Zielinski, J. (1969), 'Economics and politics of economic reforms in Eastern Europe', *Economics of Planning*, vol. 3.
Zielinski, J. (1973), *Economic Reforms of Polish Industry*, Oxford University Press.
Zielinski, J. (1978), 'On system remodelling in Poland', *Soviet Studies*, January.

Index

Figures in italics refer to tables.

For Product Safety Concerns and Information please contact our EU representative GPSR@taylorandfrancis.com
Taylor & Francis Verlag GmbH, Kaufingerstraße 24, 80331 München, Germany

www.ingramcontent.com/pod-product-compliance
Ingram Content Group UK Ltd.
Pitfield, Milton Keynes, MK11 3LW, UK
UKHW022111190926
475702UK00013B/1372
9780415866460